Rise of the Fighter Aircraft 1914-1918

Richard P. Hallion

Foreword by
Brig. Gen. Jay W. Hubbard, USMC (Ret.)

The Nautical & Aviation Publishing
Company of America, Inc.
Baltimore, Maryland

Library of Congress Cataloging in Publication Data

Hallion, Richard.
  Rise of the fighter aircraft, 1914-18.

  Bibliography: p.
  Includes index.
  1. Airplanes, Military—History. 2. World War, 1914-1918—
Aerial operations. I. Title.
UG1240.H35 1984   358.4'3'09   83-26947
ISBN 0-933852-42-8

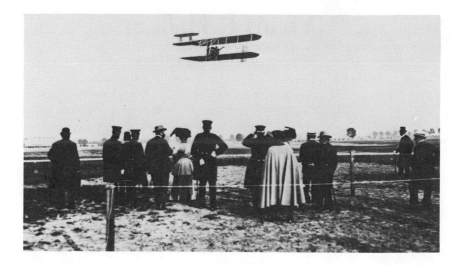

Second printing, 1988

Library of Congress Catalog Card Number: 83-26947

ISBN: 0-933852-42-8

Printed in the United States of America

Acknowledgments

I have dedicated this essay to the memory of three remarkable historians: Professors Adrienne Koch, Gordon Prange, and Walter Rundell, Jr., all of the Department of History at the University of Maryland. There are many others who have been of assistance, and I wish to note their contributions with grateful appreciation.

In Great Britain: Helene Montgomery-Moore (whose husband Cecil flew Sopwith Dolphins with 19 Squadron); Group Captain Paddy O'Sullivan, RAF, Ret. (who flew night-fighters against the Gothas); Derek Dempster; the late Chris Wren (who, with his sketches and doodles, made dining at the RAF Club such a pleasure); Philip Jarrett of *Flight;* John Fozard and Graham Weller of British Aerospace; the late Charles Gibbs-Smith of the Science Museum; Joe Michie and the many other pleasant members of the London chapter, Cross & Cockade of Great Britain; and James S. Lucas of the Imperial War Museum.

In the United States: Lt. Col. William "Flaps" Flanagan, USAF, who offered valuable insights and comments on the issue of single vs. two-place fighters and the development of aerial weapons; Professor Robin Higham of Kansas State University; Professor John F. Guilmartin of Rice University; Professor John H. Morrow of the University of Tennessee; Professor Howard G. Fisher of the University of California at San Diego; Professor Roger E. Bilstein of the University of Houston; Walt Kraus, Command Historian, Air Force Systems Command (who deserves a special note of thanks); Pat Harahan and Bill Heimdahl of the Office of Air Force History; Peter Grosz, who furnished an important von Richthofen letter from his extensive archive; Colonel Richard Uppstrom and the research staff of the United States Air Force Museum; present and former staff members of the National Air and Space Museum, Smithsonian Institution, especially Deputy Director Don Lopez, Tom Crouch, Paul Garber, Dom Pisano, Jay Spenser, Alexis "Dusty" Doster, Frank Winter, Bob Mikesh, Phil Edwards, Pete Sutherd, Liz Hand, Joyce Goulet, and the late Brig. Gen. Ben Kelsey, USAF, Ret.; Doug Pirius and Jacqueline Sweaza of the American Aviation Historical Society; Lonnie Raidor of the Society of World War I Aero Historians; Jan Adkins and Mike Long of the National Geographic Society; Maj. Gen. Philip Conley, USAF, Ret.; Maj. Gen. Leigh Wade, USAF, Ret.; and Brig. Gen. Harold Harris, USAF, Ret.; Dr. Jim Young and Lucille Zaccardi of the History Office, Air Force Flight Test Center; Ken Baas, with special appreciation for his excellent drawings; Joe Guthrie and Clyde Good of the Society of Experimental Test Pilots; Harvey Victor of the Western Thunderbolt Pilots; Barrett Tillman of the Champlin Fighter Museum; Bill Bettis, Maurine Corn and Tom Miller, who, together with Brig. Gen. Jay Hubbard, USMC, Ret., made evenings at *Nieuport 17* informative as well as enjoyable; and Jeanne and Richard "Mr. B" Blalock. I have profited from discussions with and comments from a number of serving and former fighter pilots and personnel of the Air Force Flight Test Center, Edwards AFB, especially the following: Colonels Kenneth Brotnov, Cal Jewett, Pete Knight, Jim McFeeters, Dave Milam, Ben Nowland, Bob Taylor, John Taylor, Jim Thomas, and Ray Young; Lieutenant Colonels Jim Bettcher, Billy Brooks, Marty Bushnell, John Hoffman, Ray Houle, Doug Joyce, Paul Nafziger, Charles Saxer, Mike Sexton, Gerry Sherrill, Dave Spencer, and Ed Thomas; Majors Ron Schena, and Don Underwood (USA); Captains Rick Caniglia (USA), Bill Daniels, Jim Hudson, Jay Jabour, Roger "Flash" Keith, Mark Rogers, Jim Shawler, and Jim Smolka; Lieutenant Deborah Warneking; and Senior Master Sergeant Reinhold Koszczewski.

Finally, a very special salute to two friends who've made their last flights: NASA research pilot Dick Gray of the Dryden Flight Research Facility, and Major Cecil Snyder, Air Force Flight Test Center.

Richard P. Hallion
Lancaster, California

Contents

Foreword

The study of military history offers both the hope and the challenge of incorporating lessons from past experience into one's present problem-solving efforts.

The First World War, with its clash of established military doctrines with new technologies such as the airplane, the tank, and the submarine could serve as an example to many military planners of the Western alliance today, especially as they confront the forces of Soviet expansionism in Europe.

It is good, then, to have this book, which is an exercise in discerning and uncovering historical precedents: precedents that are vital to better understanding and comprehending today's airpower needs. The author, a distinguished aerospace historian, clearly demonstrates his central thesis—namely, that the evolution of the fighter in the First World War necessarily caused the tactical theories of air superiority, interdiction, and close air support to emerge as new military doctrines which we still follow today. His research redresses a misinterpretation that has joined the folklore of conventional wisdom: a misinterpretation that Brig. Gen. Noel F. Parrish, USAF (ret.) has dubbed "The Myth of Ineffective Airpower in World War I." The importance of air power in battle has never abated since its introduction and it is still determinitive in NATO's battle problem now.

As a former Marine infantry "grunt" turned fighter-attack pilot in 1946, I was struck by the fresh confirmation this book offers of how many too-often fatal lessons of those first four years of incorporating the "aeroplane" into what had heretofore been a two-dimensional battle arena had to be relearned at great cost in the Second World War, Korea, Vietnam, and the Middle East. It is disturbing because, as the author himself notes, "conflicts today do not offer combatants the grace and promise of time to catch up with their adversaries."

For example, a multiplicity of requirements of aircraft capabilities, then as well as later, has too often resulted in compromised designs that addressed few real operational needs. Moreover, airplanes which were compromised by putting too much on them were then ordered in too few numbers to contribute substantially to combat. Even worse, the rapid changes necessary to adapt to the combat environment would render the best design obsolete. Yet today planners procure fighter and attack aircraft designed to have service lives of twenty to twenty-five years.

It is also surprising—but should not be—how well thought-out the basic tactics and rules of survival in air combat were in World War I, and how applicable many of these are today. As the author shows, there is a basic continuity here that runs from the era of Boelcke and Mannock to the present. That great fighter tactician (and close personal friend) Frederick C. "Boots" Blesse, could just as easily have been writing of the "fighting scouts" of the Western Front when he penned his own rules of engagement fresh from a combat tour in Korea where he became a double jet ace over the Yalu. His "No Guts, No Glory" was the "bible" for Air Force, Navy, and Marine fighter squadrons—especially ones I commanded—and it is good to see portions of it reprinted here in a proper and appreciative historical context.

Finally, from a personal and admittedly parochial viewpoint, it was pleasing to find in the experience of the First World War the proof of what has been a consistent Marine Corps doctrine with respect to the procurement of tactical aircraft: namely, that these exciting, beautiful, impressive, and increasingly expensive birds can only be justified to the extent that they directly ease the combat burden of the most precious weapon system of all: the infantryman, closing the enemy on the ground.

Rise of the Fighter will take its place alongside the author's other fine works as a standard reference and essential historical analysis of what is significant to military aviation today from the awful lessons of the Great War.

Jay W. Hubbard
Brigadier General
U. S. Marine Corps (Retired)

26 January 1984

Preface

The air war of 1914-1918 has been the subject of numerous books, including a number of excellent aircrew memoirs, reliable official histories, and a virtual flood of articles and popular works. Indeed, there is a society of historians of the first war in the air, who publish their own journal. Why then another book?

In part, it is because, as Major W. E. de B. Whittaker of Great Britain's General Staff wrote in 1918, "It is a matter of high interest to follow throughout the war the progress of aerial fighting from the days when contests were few and were almost in every case accidental to the last phase when it had become an exact science and was a deliberate and vital part of war."[1] With the passage of time, however, the structure of the air war over Europe and the lessons learned (or unlearned) from that first aerial conflict have, it seems, become increasingly more obscure. Most accounts of the first air war, unlike the many fine historical accounts of the war at sea or on land, picture brightly painted Fokkers cavorting with drab Sopwith Camels or Spads as if they are locked in some timeless moment of Wagnerian combat. Then there is the air war as slapstick comedy: pilots and observers heaving bricks at each other, blazing away with revolvers and carbines, Snoopy vs. the Red Baron of comic-strip fame. Both views miss the essential characteristic of the air war, which was its intensely technological nature. To a far greater degree than the war at sea or on land, the air war demanded continuous striving for technological supremacy; there was a challenge and response drive innate in the air war that operated quite apart from the mindless artillery barrages and futile "pushes" across no man's land that characterized that hell called the Western Front. Aircraft entered service, and either proved useful and adaptable, or quickly disappeared. Even successful designs were forced into an early obsolescence by the pace of technological development: the average fighter design retired from operational service in a little over a year following its introduction to combat. The most successful designs tended to produce "families" of aircraft, such as the various Nieuports or Albatros's, the Sopwith Pup, Camel, and Snipe, and Spad fighters, as well as inspiring outright copies. Though occasionally revolutionary, more often than not the design process was extrapolative and evolutionary — as it has been in later times. Like other conflicts both before and since, the First World War furnished lessons in the uses of new technologies and the inter-relationship between technology and tactical and strategic doctrine. Many aspects of the continuing debate over desirable attributes of fighter aircraft were first explored in the crucible of air combat over the Western Front.

Yet, too often, the more romantic or "glamorous" events of that horrid conflict have obscured the underlying struggle of early air leaders and combat aircrews to acquire ever more capable machines with which to face their foes. The aerospace arms race began in the skies over the Western Front, and has continued, unabated, to this day. The tactical roles and missions of airpower — especially those of air superiority, interdiction, and close air support — currently incorporated in the strategies of the world's leading nations were first promulgated and exercised "Over There." Little of this is appreciated, however, and as a result, the "lessons learned" in the skies over Verdun and the Somme all too often became "lessons relearned" in other skies from the time of the Spanish Civil War, the Second World War, and the Korean War to the wars in Vietnam and the Middle East. It is well to re-examine those lessons, lest they continue to be lost, for conflicts today do not offer combatants the grace and promise of time to catch up with their adversaries.

Rise of the Fighter Aircraft 1914-1918

WESTERN FRONT: The Arena of Combat, 1914-1918

I.
The Birth of the Fighter

Historians and students of military affairs have long recognized that the First World War constituted a watershed in the historical evolution of warfare and weaponry. It was a conflict characterized by bitter ironies: a war none wanted but virtually all embraced, marked by savage mercilessness and isolated chivalry, a war fought to preserve a European system that the war itself eventually destroyed, a war in which nineteenth-century tactics confronted emerging twentieth-century technology and science. Out of the First World War came weapons that would profoundly alter subsequent conflicts, notably the submarine, the tank, and the airplane.

The airplane offers the best example of how wartime exigency forced an immature technology into a deadly adulthood. In 1914, airplanes were short-ranged, underpowered, and virtually impotent as weapons. By 1919, aviation technology had so advanced that production aircraft were being built that could span oceans. Indeed, 1919 witnessed no less than three crossings of the Atlantic, one by a seaplane, another by a modified bomber, and a third by a rigid airship, which also made a return flight. Yet before the general European war that all nations feared was coming actually erupted, only a few military thinkers foresaw an important role for the airplane. Those who did look to the skies as well as the land and the sea placed greater faith in hydrogen-filled airships, whose lifting power could transport a sizable bomb load. Yet by war's end, the destructive airship was revealed to be an overrated chimera, while the airplane emerged an essential weapon in a nation's military arsenal.

A few far-sighted staff officers in prewar Europe and America believed that the noisy, field-hopping airplanes of the day might possibly fly reconnaissance sorties above enemy lines, or spot for artillery fire, or act as message carriers. In 1910, one of these individuals, Lieutenant Fred Humphreys of the U.S. Army Corps of Engineers — and one of the first two American military aviators — wrote perceptively,

> From a military standpoint, the first and probably the greatest use will be found in reconnaissance. A flyer carrying two men can rise in the air out of range of the enemy, and, passing over his head out of effective range, can make a complete reconnaissance and return, bringing more valuable information than could possibly be secured by a reconnaissance in force. This method would endanger the lives of two men; the other would detach several thousand men for a length of time and endanger the lives of all.[1]

It would not be long before his ideas were put into practice, for in 1911 the airplane made its combat debut amid the sun and sand of North Africa. Engaged in a war with Turkey over possession of Tripoli, Italy decided to employ her fledgling army air service in the struggle. On October 23, Captain Carlos Piazza flew a reconnaissance mission from Tripoli to Aziza in a French-built Blériot XI monoplane. Just over a week later, Second Lieutenant Giulio Gavotti of the *Squadriglia di Tripoli* dropped four small bombs from a German-built Etrich *Taube* on the towns of Taguira and Ain Zara, though, as one historian has reported, "Any effect that the bombs did have in Tripoli was due to the fact that the inhabitants were not used to airplanes."[2] While it was only a small imperialist brushfire conflict, the Tripoli campaign presaged the subsequent employment of airplanes in the First World War; Piazza, for example, experimented with aerial cameras for photographic reconnaissance. Bombing sorties became commonplace, so impressing one war correspondent that he penned, "This war has clearly shown that air navigation provides a terrible means of destruction. These new weapons are destined to revolutionize modern strategy and tactics."[3] That same year, Captain Bertram Dickson, Britain's first flying military officer, predicted that armies of the future would be dependent upon aerial reconnaissance, and that the struggle to prevent one's enemy from obtaining reconnaissance information would lead to fighting between armed airplanes.[4]

What were these new vehicles that would so rapidly take their place in the arsenals of the European nations? To understand what the technology of 1914 aviation was like, it is necessary to understand the progress of aviation in the previous eleven years. In 1903 the Wright brothers flew the first successful airplane. By 1905, they had made it a practical flying machine; three years later, in public displays in America and Europe, they clearly demonstrated that the age of heavier-than-air flight had arrived. European aviation, dormant since the glider accident of Otto Lilienthal in 1896, received a great stimulus from the two Wright trips to the Continent in 1908 and 1909. Thereafter, spurred to rapid experimentation on the right track of development thanks to the technological approach of the Wrights, European aviation quickly matched and then surpassed that of the United States—a situation that would persist until the mid-1920s. The awkward prewar open-framework biplane soon gave way to the enclosed-fuselage tractor biplane or monoplane. By 1914, the average European airplane was a tractor airplane (i.e., having its engine in front) with a wooden framework covered by doped fabric, and externally braced wings and tail surfaces. Retractable landing gear and such high-lift devices as flaps and slats were things of the future, as were the enclosed cockpit, the controllable-pitch propeller, the supercharged engine, and all-metal, internally-braced contruction. There were few reliable powerplants; one notable engine that had a profound influence upon European aeronautics was the trim-looking Gnôme rotary designed by France's Séguin brothers. Airplanes flew between 60 and 80 miles per hour, though speeds slower than this were not uncommon. Some had ailerons for roll control, but most utilized Wright-inspired wing-warping. Pilots and observers flew out in the open, often with gouts of castor oil engine lubricant blowing back in their faces—with predictable physiological results. Engines were prone to fail, and, contrary to popular belief, prewar and wartime aircraft often had vicious handling characteristics—with power off, the high drag of these heavily braced configurations gave them alarming sinkrates. A forced landing required fine piloting if disaster was to be averted.[5]

To be sure, there were some glimmers of improvement. In Russia, Igor Sikorsky had already created a revolutionary four-engine transport known as *Le Grand*, the forerunner of all multiengine aircraft. Eugene Ruchonnet and Louis Bechereau had experimented with so-called *"monocoque"* or shell construction, building up a smooth external fuselage shape from bonded plywood layers. The product of Bechereau's work, the 1912 Deperdussin Monocoque Racer, became the first airplane to fly faster than 100 miles per hour. In Germany, a young expatriate Dutch aircraft manufacturer, Anthony Fokker, was experimenting with steel-tube structures, aided by the inventive genius of Reinhold Platz. Europe already had a strong scientific tradition in aeronautical research, with such individuals as Ludwig Prandtl and his tempestuous pupil Theodore von Kármán drawing upon classical fluid mechanics to understand what happened to an airplane as it passed through the air. All this boded well for the future of aviation.[6]

Despite some prewar agitation from air-minded staff officers like Italy's Giulio Douhet and Germany's Count Helmuth von Möltke (the latter Germany's chief of the general staff), the air arms of the European nations were inextricably bound up within the rigid framework of the existing armies and navies. At the outbreak of the war, France and Germany possessed the largest aviation forces. Germany had about 230 aircraft serving usually in parcels of six with thirty-three field flying detachments (*Feldfliegerabteilungen*, abbreviated *FFA*), and approximately four aircraft apiece serving with.eight detachments assigned to German fortresses on the frontier (*Festungfliegerabteilungen*). No less than thirty of the *FFAs* were stationed on the Western Front, to guard against French and British forces. France's own *Aviation militaire* had a total of 138 aircraft spread among twenty-one army squadrons (*escadrilles*), averaging six aircraft apiece and two cavalry squadrons with five aircraft each. The nascent British Royal Flying Corps (RFC) quickly dispatched four squadrons averaging twelve aircraft each—essentially all the serviceable aircraft that could make the trip—from England to France to assist the British Expeditionary Force. The first three British units, Nos. 2 and 3 Squadrons, plus A and B Flights of No. 4 Squadron, took off from Dover for Amiens on August 13, 1914. This gaggle of mixed British and French designs successfully traversed the Channel—no small feat, for Louis Blériot had made his pioneer cross-Channel flight only five years earlier, on July 25, 1909.[7]

For all of its shortcomings, the airplane gave ample proof of its usefulness during the opening weeks of the war in its predicted role as an aerial observer, essentially an extension of that traditional reconnaissance branch, the cavalry. For example, British airplanes detected a German troop build-up in time to prevent a possibly disastrous attack upon Allied forces as German units swept through France in the opening weeks of the war. Then, at the Marne, French and British reconnaissance patrols enabled the Allied high command to position forces that inflicted the strategic defeat Germany suffered at the gates to the City of Lights, ending the war of motion and beginning the war of stalemate that would last until the armistice. Further east, at Tannenberg, aerial reconnaissance kept von Hindenburg accurately informed as to the strength and location of Russian units, enabling the German army to bring the unexpectedly rapid Russian advance through East Prussia to a sudden and calamitous halt. By the fall of 1914, then, the reconnaissance plane had proven its worth. On the ground, troop commanders found themselves pondering yet one more problem: how to shield their units from the prying eyes of enemy airmen.

The answer, of course, lay in developing armed aircraft that could shoot down enemy reconnaissance airplanes. Early in the war, aircraft from opposing sides frequently passed one another while going about their duties. At first the observers and pilots—most of whom had flown in the same European air meets as flying enthusiasts—were inclined to wave at each other and be on their way. But gradually, more realistic attitudes replaced this touching but naive notion of kinship. As the value of reconnaissance to military planners became more and more apparent, the camaraderie of the airmen soon dissolved. Pilots and observers began carrying pistols, rifles, carbines—even hand grenades, grappling hooks, and arrow-like *fléchettes*—to bring down an enemy. Now when enemy planes passed,

WESTERN FRONT: Line of Greatest Advance 8 Sept. 1914

each might be greeted by the sharp crack of a rifle or carbine instead of a salutatory wave.

Before machine guns became standard aircraft armament, rifle and carbine fire brought down a surprisingly large number of aircraft; if conditions were favorable, enemy aircraft could often be forced down without gunfire. On August 25, 1914, for example, Lieutenant H. D. Harvey-Kelly, the first RFC pilot to land in France, managed to force down a German *Taube* (Dove) over the front. Harvey-Kelly and two other British airmen had spotted the *Taube,* and he maneuvered himself so that he was directly behind the German plane, his propeller spinning ominously and perilously close to the *Taube*'s fragile tail surfaces. Harvey-Kelly's two companions boxed the *Taube* in, and the three British planes—sedate B.E. 2 two-seater reconnaissance craft—herded the elegant *Taube* down to earth. The German crew escaped through a forest, but Harvey-Kelly landed, burned the abandoned *Taube,* and collected some souvenirs of the action to take back to base. That same day, another German craft was forced down by British airmen near Le Quesnoy.[8]

While rifles and carbines could not be passed off as lightly as might be expected, the most desirable weapon for an airplane was, of course, the machine gun. As on the ground, the machine gun would prove to be the master of the air, the plane mounting it assuming the role of a flying gun platform. Early military aviators were not blind to the advantages of arming aircraft with such weapons. Indeed, before the First World War, several experiments with machine-gun-equipped aircraft had been carried out, notably in the United States. But the low state of aviation technology at first prevented the successful wedding of the machine gun and the airplane: the weight of the weapons decreased the performance of the high-drag, under-powered designs of the day, and synchronizing a machine gun to fire forward through the arc of the racing propeller was obviously a problem. Nevertheless, zealous airmen tried their best. On August 22, for example, a German reconnaissance plane flew high over the Royal Flying Corps base at Mauberge. Several B.E. 2's took off to intercept it, the crews armed with various rifles and carbines, and a two-seat Henri Farman pusher biplane staggered into the air carrying a Lewis machine gun. The pilot, Lieutenant Louis Strange, had not sought permission to install the gun on the plane, and now the weight of the machine gun and his observer brought the interception to naught. The German biplane made off while Strange's Farman droned slowly over the field, and Strange imagined the German crew enjoying "a good laugh at our futile efforts." Worse was to come, for upon landing, Strange was directed by his commanding officer to remove the machine gun at once from his plane and stick with the proven rifle instead.[9]

More powerful two-seaters did not have the problems that afflicted Strange on his sortie. Provided the craft was powerful enough to haul the machine gun, its ammunition and an observer into the air, a two-seater enabled the observer to fire a machine gun either for defensive or offensive purposes, unlike a single-seat tractor monoplane, which required the pilot to fire the machine gun through the propeller, or off-set the machine gun to avoid the propeller arc (seriously degrading its accuracy). Eventually, most Allied and German two-seaters were equipped with machine guns. The dubious distinction of being the first airmen shot down by such a weapon fell to the hapless crew of a German Aviatik biplane on a recon-naissance sortie over Rheims on October 5. They took little notice of a two-seat French Voisin pusher that approached from ahead. In the Voisin, Corporal Louis Quénault readied his Hotchkiss machine gun as pilot Sergeant Joseph Frantz maneuvered the plane. As the Voisin closed the Aviatik, Quénault loosed burst after burst, and the unfortunate Aviatik erupted in flames and fell to earth.[10] Most air combat between two-seaters in the future would more closely resemble sea fights between ships of the line during the Age of Sail. Two aircraft would fly on roughly parallel courses as the observers blazed away at one another. Often such skirmishes ended inconclusively as one or the other observer ran out of ammunition and his pilot immediately broke off the combat. Occasionally, however, an observer would get in a telling burst, one that crippled the engine, wound-ed or killed the pilot, riddled or ignited the fuel tank. Then the victim would spiral earthwards, another in the growing number of casualties of aerial combat.

By the spring of 1915, an increasing number of fights were occurring in the skies over the Western Front as pilots and observers endeavored to bring down their opponents with rifles and machine guns. So far, however, units assembled expressly for air fighting had not made their appearance in any of the combatant air arms. Every *escadrille*, RFC squadron, and German field flying detachment had a few aircraft on hand for "fighting scout" duties, including escorting the unit's reconnaissance planes and at-tacking enemy reconnaissance aircraft. In France, Commandant Edouard Barès, the far-sighted and able organizer of France's *Aviation militaire*, had moved to centralize France's air fighting forces, proposing as early as October 8, 1914, that sixteen fighter *escadrilles* of three to six aircraft apiece be established, equipped with Morane-Saulnier aircraft. Eventual-ly, Barès got his wish, and he also centralized France's bomber and recon-naissance forces.[11] Sir David Henderson, Britain's commander of the Royal Flying Corps, shared Barès's belief that greater effectiveness could be achieved if fighter aircraft were organized into squadrons of their own. Henderson's notions, however, were so contrary to accepted British doctrine on the employment of aircraft that his proposal was not adopted.[12] Later, after the soundness of his beliefs became evident, the RFC did send its first fighter squadron to France. The first unit, No. 11 Squadron, arrived at the front in late July 1915, flying two-seat Vickers F.B. 5 pushers armed with Lewis machine guns and manned by an observer-gunner. This influential little biplane, dubbed the "Gunbus," was the result of an experimental prewar Vickers project to build a "fighting biplane" for Britain's Admiralty. Already under test in the summer of 1914, the Gunbus saw combat before the end of the year when one of them, on Christmas Day, engaged a German *Taube* on a scouting mission over the south of England and the Thames estuary. (Though conclusive proof is lacking, the *Taube* apparently was shot down—but by rifle fire, as the machine gun had jammed.)[13] Germany was even slower to recognize the value of specialized air fighting formations, not moving to create its first fighter groupings for tactical effectiveness until after the Battle of Verdun and the Somme debacle forced a change in operational doctrine.

Historical events are often associated with a specific catalyst—a bright spark that sets off a train of development leading to a major historical watershed. So it is with the evolution of the fighter aircraft, for the inauguration of the era of the fighter plane came in April 1915, when a spark was ignited by an innovative and daring French pilot, Roland Garros.

Garros was one of the best-known of Grance's prewar galaxy of aviators. The son of a prosperous lawyer, Garros had been born on the island of Reunion, in the Indian Ocean, in 1888. Sent to France to study music, young Garros found the romantic aerial exploits of Alberto Santos-Dumont, Brazil's expatriate sportsman-pilot, more interesting. Santos-Dumont, then the toast of Parisian society, taught young Garros to fly, and the eager Garros soon excelled in the air. In 1912 Garros joined a fledgling French aviation firm established the year before by Raymond Saulnier, Leon Morane, and Gabriel Borel; Borel had dropped out, and the firm, Morane-Saulnier, soon became known for its elegant yet high-performance monoplanes. In 1913, Garros became the first pilot to cross the Mediterranean Sea by flying 456 miles from St. Raphaël to Bizerte. Caught in Berlin at the outbreak of the war, Garros managed to avoid internment and flew back to France via Switzerland in his Morane. He volunteered for military duty and was assigned to a French squadron, *Escadrille* M.S. 23, flying Moranes.[14]

Garros has often been hailed as the inventor of the synchronized machine gun but the true situation was more complex. Before the First World War, a number of leading European technologists had begun work on synchronizer mechanisms that would permit a pilot to fire a machine gun through a propeller without hitting the blades of the prop. Franz Schneider, a Swiss-born engineer working with Germany's *Luft-Verkehr Gesellschaft,* patented such a device before the war, as did France's Robert Esnault-Pelterie. In April 1914, working alone and without knowledge of the other work in the field, Saulnier developed his own design, which performed quite well during firing trials at the Hotchkiss firing range, validating its basic principle. Unfortunately, individual machine gun rounds were not uniform, and some rounds took longer to fire than others. Hence, even though the synchronizer worked perfectly well, occasionally the gun fired late, and a bullet drilled through the frail propeller. Saulnier experimented with installing armored metal bullet deflectors on the blades. In December 1914 Garros was passing through Paris and visited Saulnier, who explained to him about the firing trials. Garros, meantime, had become exasperated at the difficulties of trying to maneuver a plane so that his observer could shoot at a German adversary with a rifle, carbine, or shotgun. Garros volunteered to test Saulnier's device in flight, and appealed for permission from French authorities. Most held that such a thing was impossible; a pilot could not maneuver an airplane precisely enough to aim the whole plane at an enemy machine, and fire the gun. But Commandant Barès thought otherwise, and Garros soon received the necessary permission. Garros and his skilled mechanic Jules Hue examined Saulnier's deflectors and rejected them as too weak—a fact dramatically demonstrated when, following a flight, the engine of the test plane was restarted on the ground and a deflector separated itself from the prop (the resulting vibration shook the plane to pieces!). Hue designed stronger deflectors attached to both the prop and its shaft, and fitted the armored propeller and machine gun to a standard Morane-Saulnier Type L Parasol—a slab-sided monoplane having its wing perched above the fuselage on short struts, hence the name. A gale reduced the plane to matchwood before Garros could fly it in combat, but Hue salvaged the gun and propeller and installed them on another Type L in early 1915.[15]

Poor flying weather during the early months of 1915 prevented Garros from trying his novel weapon in combat, but he took advantage of the delay by having a bomb rack capable of carrying two small 155-millimeter bombs installed on the plane. Thus equipped, Garros took off from Dunkerque—which would gain its own measure of fame a quarter-century later, in another war—on April 1, 1915. He planned to bomb a German rail station, but as fate would have it, he spotted a German reconnaissance biplane (described variously as an Aviatik or an Albatros two-seater). He approached the unsuspecting plane in a gradual curve that placed his Morane behind and within firing range, a maneuver subsequently christened the "pursuit curve," for it placed a fighter at its enemy's

WESTERN FRONT: December 1914

vulnerable "six-o'clock" position. The German crew looked on curiously, then in horror as the Morane's Hotchkiss sputtered to life. Twice Garros had to change ammunition magazines as the Albatros dove and desperately strove to escape. Finally, his bullets riddled the doomed craft and its crew, and it fell off in a flaming dive to earth. The machine gun had proven itself.

Two weeks later, another German plane fell before his sights, and an Albatros went down under his fire on the morning of April 18. Later that day, Garros escorted another plane on a mission to bomb a rail station at Courtrai. They approached the target at about 6,500 feet. Antiaircraft fire drove one plane off; but Garros spotted a train, and descended to less than 200 feet, dropped one bomb, and circled tightly for a second attack. The guards on the train fired back; Garros dropped his second bomb and was climbing away when his engine quit; bullets had severed a fuel line. His decision to make a second pass had been fatal. Landing safely near Ingelmunster, he hurredly tried to burn the plane, but without success. Garros headed for the Dutch border just forty miles away, but within a few hours he stumbled into the midst of a party of German infantry foraging for wood. They promptly hauled him into captivity, an imprisonment he would escape in early 1918, though not long survive. His partially burned airplane, together with its armored airscrew and machine gun, was shipped to Iseghem for technical analysis.[16]

What happened next has been the subject of several widely differing historical accounts, including two contradictory ones by German aircraft manufacturer Anthony Fokker, the central figure in the story. What is known is that German military authorities studied the relationship between the gun and the propeller, and, despite Franz Schneider's prewar patent (which had been published in the German aviation magazine *Flugsport* two months after the outbreak of war) they decided to copy the armored propeller. But firing tests did not go well; German machine guns had a high muzzle velocity, and the impact of their high-strength steel-jacketed bullets tore the test copies apart; ricocheting bullets and wreckage narrowly missed test observers. At this point, the authorities turned to Fokker.

Like Garros, Fokker had been born outside Europe; he lived in Java following his birth in 1890, until his parents decided that he and his sister should be educated in Holland. The family settled down in Haarlem, and the precocious child soon proved he was adept with tools. Fascinated by flight, he schemed his way into the field. Sent to the *Technicum* at Bingen, Germany, young Fokker quickly transferred to a school for automobile engineers at Zälbach that offered a beginning course in aviation; when the school's first home-built airplane crashed, the aviation course crashed with it, and Fokker was on his own. Together with a German army officer thirty years his senior, he constructed a monoplane of his own design and flew it briefly in December 1910. Shortly afterwards, his partner taxied it into a tree, completely ruining it. After rebuilding it, Fokker flew it again in 1911, passed his German aviator's examination on May 16, and on June 7 of that year received Germany's 88th aero license from the *Fédération Aéronautique Internationale.* In 1912, he established the *Fokker Aeroplanbau* at Johannisthal, and the next year the firm won a design competition for ten army aircraft, the first production order it received.[17]

Like many other early aircraft designers, Fokker was a skilled pilot; in fact, he was easily more at home in the cockpit of his airplanes than he was trying to design them. And, like other early designers, he had a talent for making up for this deficiency by attracting a skilled group of professional technologists. Fokker had several assistants, notably designer Martin Kreutzer, also a good pilot, and welder Reinhold Platz, who would receive recognition in later years as the true genius behind Fokker's finest aircraft, the Fokker D VII of 1918. There were others, too, notably Fritz Heber and Heinrich Luebbe, and it was to these two individuals that Fokker turned when asked to come up with a means of firing through a propeller.

Why was it Fokker who attracted the attention of Oberstleutnant Hermann von der Lieth-Thomsen, chief of Germany's field aviation? Fokker certainly had a good reputation, but it is inconceivable that, as he later claimed, he was unaware of Schneider's earlier patent. Indeed, it is likely that his team was already working on such a mechanism (with the knowledge of the German military), and that Garros's capture was but a happy coincidence, spurring him on in this line of research. The choice of Fokker becomes much more understandable under this interpretation than if one accepts the "chance in history" argument advanced by Fokker's defenders. (Peter Grosz has pointed out that some obscure German text references from the 1930s hint at Fokker machine-gun experiments prior to the Garros revelations. The validity of these after-the-fact claims, alas, cannot be authenticated at this point.)

War is filled with ironies, especially, it seems, aerial warfare. Fokker's engineering team successfully developed a cam-operated synchronizer mechanism. They succeeded in part because German machine guns, notably the Parabellum, could be adapted more easily for such a mechanism than the French Hotchkiss. But the irony is in Fokker's selection of the Fokker M 5 *Eindecker* (monoplane) for carrying this novel weapon.

The M 5, a shoulder-wing monoplane with broad, constant-chord wings, was essentially a German copy of the prewar Morane-Saulnier Type H! In 1913, Fokker had had the opportunity to study one stored at Johannisthal, and at the end of the year he bought a used Type H, using it to derive the basic aerodynamic configuration of the first of his own monoplanes; Fokker was not alone in doing this since even outright copying was not quite as unusual as one might think. Fokker's fellow designers at the Pfalz *Flugzeugwerke* were equally impressed with the Morane monoplanes, but they, at least, had the courtesy to purchase a license to manufacture them in Germany.[18] Fokker built two versions of the M 5; a long-wingspan version designated the M 5L (for *lang:* long), and a short-span version, the M 5K (for *kurz:* short). Though not in widespread service, the M 5Ks were used for rapid communication, powered by a generally unreliable 80-horsepower Oberursel rotary engine that was itself a copy of the prewar Gnôme. Now Fokker installed Heber and Luebbe's mechanism in a M 5K designated the M 5K/MG, and given the military serial E.1/15, the first of his fighters. At a demonstration at Doeberitz, Fokker himself tested the gun both on the ground and in the air, riddling a set of airplane wings propped up on the ground. While impressed, many onlookers contended that the only true measure of its ability would be whether it could shoot down an enemy plane. Fokker states in his memoirs that he was asked to give a final "proof of concept" demonstration by shooting down an enemy aircraft. Though protesting his neutrality, he soon found himself at the front, near Verdun. Fokker again demonstrated the weapon, this time before the German Crown Prince Wilhelm at his headquarters at Stenay. But aside from this notable demonstration, he had no opportunity to grapple with the French, and, in hopes of better hunting, went north to Douai.[19]

To prevent his being shot as a spy in the event of capture, Fokker was issued a German aviator's uniform and identification as an officer of the German air service. He flew for five days, morning and evening, without once sighting an enemy plane, returning each night to Field Flying Detachment 62, whose pilots would soon exploit the little *Eindecker* to good effect. After a week, Fokker finally spotted a likely target: a plodding Farman reconnaissance airplane droning its way ponderously across the sky. As he approached from behind, the unsuspecting crew made no effort to evade. As Fokker edged ever closer, his neutral instincts bothered him: he had no animosity towards the Farman crew; he was just out to test his invention. Finally, Fokker recounts, he decided he could not commit what to him was simple murder. He flew away, determined to leave the killing to the belligerents.[20]

The airmen at Douai understood and accepted Fokker's reluctance, but unlike the Dutchman, they harbored no neutral feelings. Before he left the front, the company had delivered eleven brand-new *Eindeckers* to the various detachments at Douai, and Leutnant Kurt Wintgens quickly demonstrated the new machine by shooting down a Morane over French lines. Two of the *Eindeckers* were assigned to Leutnants Oswald Boelcke and Max Immelmann, both soon to become household names in Germany and Great Britain. On August 1, a formation of British airplanes bombed the Douai airfield. Boelcke and Immelmann, mistaking the planes for French, clambered into their new aircraft and raced into the air.

Immelmann and Boelcke climbed above their opponents, and then dived to the attack. Boelcke opened fire, but an almost immediate jam of his gun forced him to land to clear it, taking him out of the fight. Immelmann closed to firing range on the British planes, selected one, and came so close that he nearly collided with it. He cooly noted that the pilot was flying without an observer because of the weight of the bomb load. After firing sixty rounds his machine gun jammed, but he managed to clear it and continued the attack. Twice more the gun jammed and each time, with exasperation, Immelmann had to break off the attack and use both hands to pound and manipulate the arming levers until he had cleared the gun and could return to the attack. Finally, near Arras, the combat came to a close after eight or ten minutes. Immelmann's *Eindecker* closed to point-blank range with a British plane and he fired a long burst that wounded the pilot and riddled the plane. It nosed earthwards and the wounded airman brought off a skillful forced landing. Immelmann himself landed nearby, determined to take the pilot prisoner; only then did he find that his victim was British; the plucky RFC airman, wounded in the left arm, complimented Immelmann on his shooting.[21]

Coming four months to the day after Garros revolutionized the air war, Immelmann's victory marked the beginning of a new period, a dreary phase for the Allies long remembered as the era of the "Fokker scourge." Not inappropriately, many Allied pilots and observers would soon begin regarding themselves as "Fokker fodder."

II.
The Fokker Scourge . . .

At first the Allies did not grasp the implications of Immelmann's victory, and they continued flying on both sides of the front. On August 19, Boelcke shot down his first victim, and with increasing frequency, Fokker encounters made their way into Allied pilot reports. The same day that Boelcke claimed his first aircraft, Hugh Trenchard was appointed to succeed Major General Sir David Henderson as general officer commanding the Royal Flying Corps. It was Trenchard who would have to defeat the Fokker menace, and this aggressive officer, whose commanding presence and loud, authoritative voice would earn him the nickname "Boom," was equal to the task. A veteran cavalryman, Trenchard was known for his strength of character and will. He once played a memorable and hard-fought polo match with Winston Churchill, then a young hussar. Shot through the lung and partially paralyzed in the Boer War, Trenchard returned to England to find his military career and his health both considered finished, but, phoenix-like, with the help of grueling therapy, his athletic constitution reasserted itself. He took up flying at age 39 in 1912, and won his wings. Impressed with the military potential of the airplane, Trenchard began formulating the offensive air doctrines that would win him recognition as one of the three prophets of air power, with Douhet and Mitchell.[1]

The initial lack of concern over the Fokker soon came to haunt the RFC. Maurice Baring, the gifted writer who served as Trenchard's aide, recollected that in August of 1915 the RFC "was so used to doing what it wanted in the air without serious opposition that not enough attention was paid to this menace, and the monoplane, in the hands of a pilot like Immelmann, was a serious, and for us a disastrous, factor."[2]

In September, the situation became critical. Colonel Sir W. Sefton Brancker, the newly-appointed commander of the RFC's Third Wing, ordered that reconnaissance aircraft be escorted on their sorties by Vickers Gunbus fighters, a not altogether satisfactory solution, but the only one that Brancker could offer at the time. The Gunbus had entered squadron service over the spring and summer of 1915, and equipped the RFC's first all-fighter unit, No. 11 Squadron, when it deployed to the Western Front in late July 1915. Because it was a pusher, with the engine behind the crew, the gunner-observer was free to fire his weapon forward. It shot down a number of German two-seaters, and would remain in combat service through the Somme offensive of 1916—long after it was hopelessly outclassed. Despite its slowness (its maximum speed was 70 miles per hour) the Vickers Gunbus was a surprisingly effective aircraft—in late September, a Vickers crew forced down Immelmann himself, though he returned to fly again—and such was the impression the Gunbus made on the Germans that they tended to refer to any pusher they encountered as a "Vickers" even in their postwar memoirs.[3]

Only towards the end of the Battle of Loos in October did the true magnitude of the Fokker menace become apparent. The German air service was in an excellent position to attain air superiority over the Western Front by using their new weapon. Already, Fokker was busily developing refined versions of the *Eindecker*, some with twin synchronized machine guns doubling their firepower. Emboldened by the success of their Fokker-flying brethren, German reconnaissance and army cooperation crews were venturing across the lines in increasing numbers, apparently unconcerned by British and French opposition.[4]

In truth, the Fokker *Eindecker* was an excellent example of the low-cost threat forcing a high-cost and complicated defense. As aircraft go, it was largely undistinguished. It did represent a successful marriage of a relatively advanced configuration (the monoplane) with a synchronized machine gun, but the real secret to its success lay in its synchronized gun, for which no equal existed on the Allied side. The Allies had aircraft in service that, one on one, were equal to or better than the Fokker, but none had the Fokker's synchronized gun. For example, Morane's angular Type N "Bullet" monoplane clearly outclassed the *Eindecker*, as evidenced by a mock dogfight between a Type N and a Fokker in April 1916. The Type N was in service with the French in October 1915, and with the British in March 1916, but it still relied on the outdated Garros-style deflector plates on the propeller. Another clearly superior aircraft was the Bristol Scout, a trim biplane whose lines and handling characteristics were more typical of 1917 than 1915. Had it carried a synchronized weapon, the Scout might have swept the German air service from the skies. As it was, it remains an example of a highly refined airframe and propulsion system, with well-harmonized controls and a good structure, limited by the availability of armament. Pilots did affix machine guns to the Scout, in often awkward arrangements to try to prevent hitting the propeller. In one notable case, Captain Lanoe Hawker, a daring pilot with the RFC's No. 6 Squadron, mounted a Lewis gun on the left side of a Scout's fuselage to fire slightly downward and at an angle to avoid the propeller. Almost unbelieveably, with this awkward weapon that demanded the most precise flying to hit a target, Hawker attacked three armed two-seaters, shooting one of them down in flames, while on a single mission on July 25, 1915. For this he justly won the first Victoria Cross awarded for action in the air. Hawker's example, of course, was the exception rather than the rule, and was a tribute more to his abilities as a pilot than to the practicality or potential effectiveness of his installation.[5]

Other airmen mounted a machine gun above the center section of a biplane's top wing, and such installations appeared with notable success on such later aircraft as the Nieuports, the S.E. 5, and even the Sopwith Camel. But though the bullet trajectory now passed above the propeller, aiming and reloading such a weapon was still tricky and often dangerous—especially in the midst of a swirling dogfight, when one had to keep track of opponents, retain control of the plane, change the drum of ammunition, and avoid being thrown out of the aircraft. On May 10, 1915, while flying a Martinsyde S.1 Scout equipped with a wing-mounted Lewis gun, Louis Strange fired a whole drum of ammunition at an Aviatik biplane without apparent effect. He stood up to reload the gun, tugging at the empty drum which had wedged in place. The control stick, gripped between his knees, came loose; the Martinsyde nosed up into an abrupt climb, then pitched over into an inverted spin, throwing Strange out of the cockpit, his only handhold now being the recalcitrant drum, a mechanism designed to slip smoothly off its mount! After strenuous endeavor, Strange succeeded in righting the plane, getting into the cockpit, and regaining his seat, and returned to base.[6] Presumably there were other such incidents.

The only real solution, of course, lay in the development of Allied synchronizer mechanisms, but none would appear until the summer of 1916 and the introduction of the Scarff-Dibovsky gear conceived by Lieutenant Commander V.V. Dibovsky of the Imperial Russian Navy and designed by Warrant Officer F.W. Scarff of the Royal Navy. Slightly later, a hydraulic synchronizer was developed by the Rumanian George Constantinesco and British Major G.C. Colley: the so-called "C.C. gear" proved superior in its simplicity and performance to earlier British mechanical mechanisms, and became a standard installation on British fighters. A French mechanism, the Alkan, became standard on that nation's warplanes. But until these appeared, the Allies were stuck with makeshift gun installations and deflector plates, and the pusher configuration exemplified by the Vickers

Gunbus and its similar-looking brethren, such as the De Havilland D.H. 2 and the Royal Aircraft Factory F.E. 2 series. Meanwhile, in 1915 and early 1916, tactical formations became unwieldy as the Allies were forced increasingly to furnish close escort for lumbering reconnaissance aircraft. The very characteristics that made some of these aircraft good observation and photographic platforms, their stately and extraordinary stability—especially that of the Royal Aircraft Factory's B.E. 2c, with which most British observation squadrons were equipped—made them sitting ducks for the more agile Fokker.

The Fokker pilots initiated tactics which, though often elaborated upon, have remained largely unchanged to this day. Cruising over the lines, a Fokker would wait for an enemy plane to appear. Sighting one, the German pilot would position himself between the sun and the victim to render his stalk almost invisible. (As it was, the small Fokker was difficult to spot; Lieutenant W. Sholto Douglas, a future marshal of the Royal Air Force, described the Fokker as "a tiny thin black line in the sky with a blob on the end of it.")[7] This characteristic tactic led to an RFC training saying, "Beware of the Hun in the sun." Judging the correct moment for his attack, the *Eindecker* pilot would dive from above and behind his victim, hold his fire until well within range, and then loose a devastating burst of fire. If the plane did not fall at once, the Fokker would continue its dive, zoom back to altitude using the speed gained in the dive, and repeat the attack. This was known as the "Fokker bounce." If the victim was a two-seater with a defensive machine gun, the Fokker pilots would dive behind and zoom underneath the victim, then loose a burst aimed at the underside of the target, using the masking provided by the fuselage of the target itself, as well as abrupt turns, to avoid defensive fire. Or a Fokker pilot might remain below and behind his victim, again letting the reconnaissance plane's fuselage mask his approach. Eventually, when the Allies developed their own fighter aircraft, these tactics were adopted and elaborated upon by French and British fighter pilots as well. The characteristic climbing zoom used by Immelmann after completing a firing pass was quickly dubbed the "Immelmann turn," and has been described as a half loop with a half roll at the top of the loop so that the airplane again regains an upright position. But as famed British test pilot Frank Courtney has pointed out, with the *Eindecker*'s wing-warping method of lateral (roll) control and relatively low power, such a maneuver was quite impossible for Immelmann—or anyone else—to perform. Courtney, one of the first to encounter (and survive) an attack by the great Immelmann himself, and other keen-eyed observers describe the maneuver as a climbing turn (what the French referred to as a *chandelle*); once back at altitude, the German pilot would initiate the hawk-like pursuit curve dive. The climbing turn had been seen many times in prewar European aviation meets, and thus Immelmann cannot be credited as having invented it; rather, he seems to have been the first to have used the maneuver as part of a standardized method of attack during air combat. Oddly enough, airmen who encountered the Fokkers during the fall of 1915 often commented on the Germans' apparent reluctance to make follow-up attacks if their first pass failed. Usually one pass was enough, especially if an unwary crew was caught napping. But in other cases, once the element of surprise seemed lost, the *Eindecker* would fly off, as if the entire encounter were a laboratory experiment. Courtney was witness to one of the first Fokker attacks, on a B.E. 2c several miles away: "I noticed that it was being overtaken by a smaller monoplane, which suddenly dived behind it and swooped up under its tail. The B.E. wallowed as if surprised or hit, while the smaller plane continued upward in a steep climbing turn, heading back the way it had come. . . . The B.E. had headed homeward, and the monoplane had hovered dimly in the distance, making no attempt to renew the attack."[8]

FOKKER BOUNCE

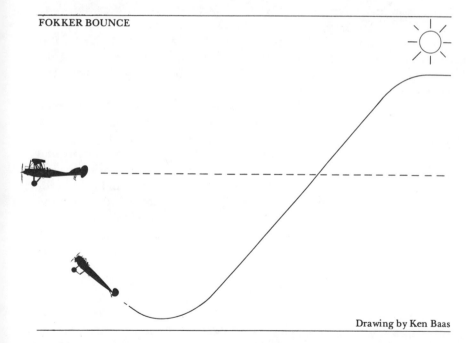

Drawing by Ken Baas

Max Immelmann's fame spread across both sides of the front by the fall of 1915; if a plane were missing or badly damaged, especially if it had been fired on around Douai, the knowing shook their heads: "Professor" Immelmann had scored again.[9] Like many other successful fighter pilots, Immelmann entered flying via the ground forces. His father, a factory owner, died of tuberculosis when young Max was seven years old. At an early age, the boy showed a pronounced mechanical aptitude and also a lively interest in sports; he decided to become an engineer. After attending a Saxon cadet school, he joined the *2. Eisenbahn-Regiment* (2. Railroad Regiment) as an officer cadet. In August 1911, he entered the military academy at Anklam to continue his studies; Anklam was the city where Otto Lilienthal, the great German gliding pioneer of the late nineteenth century, had studied the art of soaring flight. After two years at Anklam, he enrolled as a student at the *Technische Hochschule* at Dresden, equivalent of a polytechnical college. At the outbreak of war, his old regiment called him to active service. He applied for flight training and eventually his request was approved and he departed for Adlershof to train as a pilot. But at best he was only an average pilot. After completing flight training and being sent to the front, he was almost immediately posted back to Germany for additional training: his landings were sloppy, and he was breaking up too many aircraft. After diligent practice, he finally passed his third flight examination and was assigned in April 1915 to *Feldfliegerabteilung 62* at Douai. Here he piloted stately Albatros C I reconnaissance biplanes, and in time he became quite a proficient flyer. After Fokker left his first small batch of *Eindeckers* at Douai, Immelmann began flying one of the single-seaters, under the tutelage of Oswald Boelcke, with whom Immelmann developed a close friendship.[10]

While Immelmann was the most famous of the early Fokker exponents, increasing numbers of German pilots were flying the new plane as well. Many seemed (in the eyes of their RFC adversaries) to be unsure initially of their new mounts, but by the first weeks of October, their familiarity and proficiency was unquestioned. The quality of individual airmen varied, and occasionally the slow, ultrastable B.E. 2c's of the RFC and the equally vulnerable Farmans and Caudrons of the French could defy the odds and strike back. On October 22, for example, two Fokkers attacked a B.E. 2c over Cambrai, but the doughty gunner skillfully riddled one, which plunged into a forest; the second turned and fled.[11] But this, of course, was unusual, and the reconnaissance aircraft plodding about their duties fared badly at the hands of the Fokker. The majority were slow and unmaneuverable. Even those carrying an observer with a machine gun could be shot down by two or three Fokkers making simultaneous attacks or by the attack tactics previously described. Sometimes the very design of an observation plane conspired against its survivability. In the case of the British B.E. 2c, its defensive firepower was limited, the observer sat forward of the pilot, and directly under the top wing, his usefulness and field of fire severely constrained. He had to transfer his Lewis gun from one to another of four socket mountings—no easy task in the open cockpit of a maneuvering airplane generating positive and negative g forces, with Fokkers shooting at him. One observer in those trying days of the Fokker scourge was an enlisted mechanic, Ira Jones, who would later become one of the RFC's most distinguished fighter pilots. Reflecting on his experiences as a B.E. 2c observer-gunner, Jones concluded that "British squadrons were hopelessly outclassed. Debris of B.E. aircraft were scattered widespread behind the German lines. Unexampled bravery alone cannot achieve the initiative, which is the deciding factor in air warfare. Superior aircraft performance is also a vital necessity. The Fokker had that superiority over the B.E. . . . When flown by such masterly, determined pilots as Boelcke and Immelmann, it was almost invincible."[12] And the Fokkers did not plague the British alone. To René Fonck, a future French fighter pilot then flying with a Caudron reconnaissance *escadrille*, it seemed that "the Fokkers multiplied endlessly above the enemy lines."[13] Throughout the fall and winter of 1915-1916, the *Eindecker* took its toll of Allied planes, sending scores of victims spinning earthwards.

Trenchard, facing rising losses, had reason to be happy about one thing: so far the Germans were not pursuing air superiority by aggressively patrolling over British lines. Rather, they were trying to win superiority by battling over their own lines, essentially using barrier patrol tactics. Trenchard, always an advocate of offensive airpower, was convinced that the Germans were going about the struggle the wrong way. Instead of remaining over their own lines, he felt they should cross over the trenches to limit RFC operations on the Allied side of the line. Destroying the RFC over its own territory and blunting its offensive air activity, Trenchard believed, would be the best method of preventing British aircraft from penetrating German airspace. Trenchard noted with satisfaction that the Fokkers were making no effort to attack in large units or in squadron strength. Unlike Trenchard and his predecessor Sir David Henderson, or France's Commandant Barès, the German leaders did not seem to think that fighters should be organized in units rather than parceled out among reconnaissance and cooperation squadrons. Operating singly or in pairs, the *Eindeckers* could not seal off the borders of German airspace to British and French aircraft.[14]

Given his interpretation of the situation, Trenchard faced a cruel dilemma brought on by Fokker superiority. On the one hand, he wished to cut his losses. On the other, he did not want to provoke the Germans into abandoning their defensive strategy in favor of an offensive one that might include crossing the lines in numbers, perhaps with organized fighter units. He feared that a change in British tactics would force a change in German ones that could destroy the Royal Flying Corps. Trenchard decided to make only minor tactical changes, continuing offensive air operations, but ensuring that all reconnaissance aircraft crossing the lines had defensive guns, and escorts of one or two aircraft. He recognized that RFC casualties would certainly rise; but he chose to accept the risk, buying time until technologically superior Allied fighters could enter service and offset the Fokker. As expected his losses rose alarmingly: from November 1915 through January 1916, nearly fifty British airmen perished in the skies over the Western Front.[15]

While Trenchard and his airmen pondered their survival, Immelmann and Oswald Boelcke began flying together as a team, originating what is still the basic fighter formation, the wingman and leader. Both recognized that a two-man team can fight far more efficiently and safely than a lone wolf. Thus began the tradition of close tactical support that was perhaps best exemplified by the teamwork of Mustang aces Don Gentile and John Godfrey during the Second World War. A dramatic and predictable example of the Fokkers' war on British reconnaissance aircraft occurred on December 29, when Immelmann and Boelcke and four other Fokkers bounced two lumbering B.E. 2c's piloted by Sholto Douglas and Lieutenant David Glen. The two B.E.s had left their base at Marieux for an extended reconnaissance to Cambrai and St. Quentin, both deep in German-held France. They crossed the front at 6,500 feet, drawing accurate antiaircraft fire (dubbed "Archie" by the British) near Cambrai. The waiting Fokkers pounced next, and Glen's B.E., acting as an escort for Douglas's plane, went down almost at once, falling victim to Max Immelmann. At this time, a considerable debate was going on among British aircrews as to the best method of defending against a Fokker. Some, like the unfortunate Glen, believed the best defense lay in flying straight and steady, affording the observer-gunner a stable platform from which to fire at the marauding Fokker. Others, like Douglas, believed in evasive maneuvering—or at least as much maneuvering as the ultra-stable and maneuver-resistant B.E. offered—for, as Douglas subsequently phrased it, "I was convinced that in a duel between a Fokker firing through the propeller and an observer in a B.E. 2c with a rather wobbly Lewis gun shooting back over the tail, the former was far more likely to win."[16] With Glen going down, followed by two Fokkers, the remaining four *Eindeckers*, including the Boelcke-Immelmann team, turned their attention to Douglas, now maneuvering frantically to escape.

Douglas's observer quickly shot one of the four when it presented a good target, and the stricken monoplane fell off in a dive. The remaining three pressed home their attacks. Douglas spiraled tightly earthwards, determined to deny the German pilots the advantages of their diving attack. His observer's accurate fire discouraged one Fokker, which broke away from the fight, but Boelcke and Immelmann continued hovering about, waiting for an opening. The B.E. 2's maneuvers caused the observer to become air-sick, leading Boelcke to believe that he had killed the British observer. Finally, the near impossible happened. Douglas managed to run Boelcke out of ammunition. The German pilot continued feigning attacks to confuse the British pilot, but then Boelcke's engine cut out, and he had to land hurriedly, as the B.E. 2c disappeared behind some trees. (Boelcke believed the B.E. had force-landed nearby, and went to take the crew prisoner. Douglas was long gone, as Boelcke learned that night from Immelmann. Appraising Douglas's spiral and the daring low-level tactics, Boelcke wrote in his diary, "Crafty of the fellow! Not many will imitate him.")[17] Now it was Douglas vs. Immelmann. Still dodging and running for the Allied lines, Douglas saw Immelmann's plane suddenly turn away from the fight; a gun jam had forced the "Eagle of Lille" to break off the pursuit. Climbing to 800 feet, his engine sputtering falteringly, Douglas crossed the trenches and landed behind Allied lines, amid a French artillery position. The B.E. had rents and tears from more than 100 bullets. This fight, so typical of many of the engagements between British and French aircraft and the light-tan Fokkers with their white bands and black Patée crosses, came at a time when the *Eindecker* was nearing the apogee of its fighting reputation, for the Fokker successes peaked in January of the new year.[18]

Fittingly, that month both Boelcke and Immelmann were recognized for their service to the Fatherland; by January 12, each had shot down eight Allied aircraft, and they received notification that each had been awarded the *Pour le Merité*, Germany's highest award for valor, the famed "Blue Max" created by Frederick the Great in 1740.[19] But January 1916 was memorable in less pleasant ways for the Allies, for it was the month that the Fokker made its greatest impact upon operational planning.

So severe were the ravages of the Fokker upon British reconnaissance patrols that Trenchard, in order to curtail losses, was forced to release the following dramatic order on January 14 to the RFC squadrons fighting in France:

Until the Royal Flying Corps are in possession of a machine as good as or better than the German Fokker it seems that a change in the tactics employed becomes necessary. It is hoped very shortly to obtain a machine which will be able to successfully engage the Fokkers at present in use by the Germans. In the meantime, it must be laid down as a hard and fast rule that a machine proceeding on a reconnaissance must be escorted by at least three other fighting machines. These machines must fly in close formation and a reconnaissance should not be continued if any of the machines becomes detached. This should apply to both short and distant reconnaissances. Aeroplanes proceeding on photographic duty any considerable distance east of the line should be similarly escorted. From recent experience it seems that the Germans are now employing their aeroplanes in groups of three or four, and these numbers are frequently encountered by our aeroplanes. Flying in close formation must be practised by all pilots.[20]

Thus the Fokkers succeeded in forcing the RFC to provide a large number of aircraft for each reconnaissance airplane sent out, sharply limiting its operations and reducing the effectiveness of the service. While the army still required the same information on German forces, and had the same mission requirements, the number of aircraft available changed dramatically, for, as the RFC historian subsequently wrote, "many more aeroplanes had to be set aside for each job."[21] If Germany had accompanied its tactical success in introducing the Fokker to service with a change in air doctrine so that the Fokker could operate Trenchard-style across the front, the Allies might have lost air superiority over the Western Front over the fall and winter of 1915-1916. As it was, Trenchard's order clearly admitted the Fokker's supremacy, and the order led to some incredible formations. For example, a plan for a reconnaissance over German-occupied Belgium on February 7 required a B.E. 2c reconnaissance plane from No. 12 Squadron, plus *twelve* other escorting planes of no less than four different types! Though this mission was not flown, one wonders how Trenchard's desired "close formation" might have worked with thirteen planes of widely varying performance characteristics trying to fly close formation and provide mutual protection at the same time.[22]

The development of suitable protective formations and the training of pilots in formation flying soon came to occupy a major portion of the British squadrons' time and attention. Lacking radio communication, flight crews had to rely on visual hand signals. A major problem, of course, was posed by the performance characteristics of early aircraft. They simply lacked an adequate margin of engine performance to permit pilots much leeway in flying. If a plane dropped even slightly out of formation, it often took all of its pilot's effort and concentration to return it to the formation. A flight leader had to be constantly aware of the position of planes in his flight, lest a sudden and abrupt maneuver scatter the formation across the sky, increasing its vulnerability to marauding fighters. At first, like Boelcke and Immelmann, Allied tactics stressed flying in pairs. With constant practice pilots eventually were able to stick together through turns and more complex maneuvers. Ultimately, the British adopted the unit of four, and incorporated it in three basic formations: line abreast, line astern, and echelon. In line abreast, a formation flew essentially beside one another, spaced about fifty yards apart. Initially, the leader led the formation from the flank, but difficulties in following the leader during maneuvers led to a gradual change so that the leader adopted an inside position in the middle of the line, where his movements could be followed more easily. Line astern tactics with the airplane in a stepped formation (the leader lowest, and "tail-end Charlie" highest) proved easiest to follow, and ideally suited for bombers, but fighters at the rear of a line astern for-

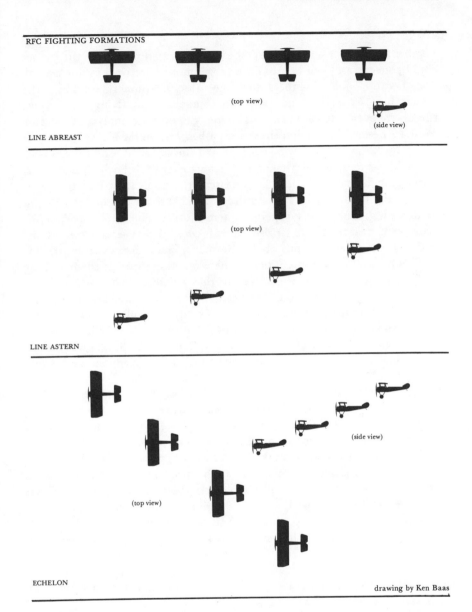

RFC FIGHTING FORMATIONS

(top view)

(side view)

LINE ABREAST

(top view)

LINE ASTERN

(side view)

(top view)

ECHELON

drawing by Ken Baas

mation, especially the last aircraft, were terribly vulnerable. Echelon flying made it easiest for a leader to communicate his wishes by hand to his
flight, but it was difficult maintaining proper spacing, and if, for some
reason, the leader suddenly turned into (across) the formation, the result
was often, at best, an undesirable scattering and, at worst, a mid-air collision. Fighter flight leaders tended to favor the line abreast formation;

bomber flight leaders favored the line astern formation because the planes could concentrate their bombs on a target more effectively in line astern, and because most bombers had an observer-gunner watching the vulnerable "six o'clock" position. To counter enemy flying formations, there were even primitive attempts to apply operations analysis. Frederick W. Lanchester, an aviation theoretician best known for his early study of vortex formation around wing tips, derived the so-called "end-square law" or, as it was most popularly known, "Lanchester's law," which essentially stated that formation leaders should attempt to apply the triangular principle of the Pythagorean Theorum $(c^2 = a^2 + b^2)$ to air combat as a means of defeating numerically superior enemy forces. Since $(5)^2 = (4)^2 + (3)^2$, Lanchester reasoned, five British aircraft could defeat seven German aircraft by first attacking four of the German planes, overwhelming them, and then turning their attentions to the remaining three. If the five flung themselves headlong against all seven, they would be defeated. This, of course, was a quantification of the old concept of "divide and conquer," and was, within limits, quite valid, but, of course, it could not take into account such imponderables as pilot alertness and ability, or the technological matching of the various opposing aircraft. Still, it was a clear indication that air combat was becoming more complex and more thoughtful.[23]

Generally speaking, as a result of Trenchard's order of January 14, 1916, a tactical formation for escorting reconnaissance aircraft over the front evolved, consisting of the reconnaissance airplane flying at the apex of the formation, with two escorts, one at each quarter position, and one directly aft. Thus, if superimposed on the face of a clock, the formation leader (the reconnaissance airplane) would be at the twelve o'clock position, with escorts at the nine, three, and six o'clock positions. The formation was staggered in height as well, with the reconnaissance airplane lowest, the two quarter escorts 500 feet higher, and the six o'clock escort a full 1,000 feet higher. Thus it was hoped the Fokker's standard pursuit dive from astern would be thwarted, and the interlocking defensive fire from observers' machine guns would afford some protection. In any case, rigid formation flying could not of itself furnish salvation; that depended on constant vigilance and awareness.[24]

By February of 1916, the supremacy of the Fokker was already waning; its time had passed, and soon, almost unbelievably soon in the minds of German airmen, it would be completely obsolete and unsuited for combat. The seeds of this dramatic reversal were planted in France and Great Britain in 1915, by the designers of new and imaginative aircraft that would establish a deadly ascendancy over the Fokker, first at Verdun in early 1916, and then in the skies over the Somme later that summer.

III.
. . . And Its Eclipse

In the predawn cold of February 21, 1916, over 850 German cannon boomed forth, sending thousands of shells whistling towards French positions around the fortress city of Verdun, signaling the beginning of Operation *Gericht*. It was the opening of a ten-month battle that would drain both the French and German armies, a battle, as Alistair Horne has perceptively written, that was "the indecisive battle in an indecisive war; the unnecessary battle in an unnecessary war; the battle that had no victors in a war that had no victors."[1] But though the ground fighting resulted in bloody stalemate, the air fighting greatly influenced both Allied and German air doctrine. The battle of Verdun (and later the Somme) gave rise to strategy and tactics that lasted for the remainder of the air war.

When the Crown Prince's divisions opened their drive on Verdun, the beleaguered French had only one fighter *escadrille* available to oppose them. But now the foresight of Barès in organizing and centralizing France's fighter resources paid off handsomely. Barès, organizational director of the French air service, quickly established his headquarters at Bar-le-Duc, and within a week, six fighter *escadrilles*, and eight of reconnaissance aircraft, were on hand. Confronting this Gallic force were 168 German aircraft, including *Eindeckers* and a number of two-seaters, fourteen battlefield observation balloons called *Drachen*, and even four Zeppelins. Commandant Jean du Peuty, responsible for French combat operations at Verdun, had to decide how he would conduct his air operations in the face of the German thrust.[2]

By nature more cautious and conservative than the aggressive Trenchard, du Peuty was not completely in accord with his British friend's unswerving faith in offensive air operations over enemy territory. At Verdun, he had to choose between an offensive policy involving deep penetration of German airspace and a defensive policy of staying over French territory and covering army cooperation aircraft with fighter escort — the latter policy was heavily favored by army commanders. Du Peuty eventually opted for the air offensive, though not without strong protests from the army. His decision was a prudent one, but he faced equipment shortages that could lose him the battle just as surely as poor strategy; he appealed to Trenchard for help. Trenchard recognized that any victory by du Peuty's airmen over the German air service would, in the long run, materially aid his own struggle in the north, and, as a consequence, he sent the French air leader as much equipment as he could spare, including Lewis guns (which were hurriedly mounted on du Peuty's Nieuports), tracer bullets, and bombsights.[3]

Commandant Tricornot de Rose, a celebrated prewar aviator, assumed control of the six fighter *escadrilles* in a single combat command, and directed that they patrol behind enemy lines in units of three to six planes (this was the first use of organized fighter sweeps over the Western Front). The *escadrilles'* mission, bluntly stated in an operational order issued on February 29, was "to seek the enemy in order to engage and destroy him."[4]

De Rose's fighter pilots were in a unique position to do so, for the *escadrilles* were now in possession of an excellent little airplane designed expressly for air fighting, the Nieuport 11. This nimble and distinctive silver biplane appeared in French service at the beginning of 1916, just in time for Verdun. It owed its origins to the earlier two-seat Nieuport 10, to which it bore a distinct family resemblance. The Nieuport 10, in turn, had been loosely based on a prewar racer designed by Gustave Delage but never built. Powered by a neatly-cowled 80-horsepower Le Rhône rotary engine, the little Nieuport 11 had a conventional upper wing, but its lower wing, though equally broad, had a small chord that gave it what is technically known as a "sesquiplane" (1½ wing) configuration. The lower wing was joined to the upper by distinctive V-shaped struts, and the entire airplane had a purposeful, streamlined, and elegant appearance that presaged later designs. With a maximum speed of 97 miles per hour, a service ceiling of up to 15,000 feet, a 2½ hour duration, and a forward-firing Lewis machine gun mounted above the wing center section — France still lacked acceptable interrupter gun synchronizers — the Nieuport 11 (dubbed "*Bébé*" by its pilots) could be a fearsome opponent. Quite simply, it outclassed the *Eindecker* in agility and speed.[5]

If this were not enough, Germany now crippled its Verdun operations by adopting a cumbersome and ineffective defensive air strategy called the *Luftsperre* (air blockade). Under this doctrine, the front was divided into small sectors patrolled by a pair of German fighters to prevent intrusions by French aircraft. However appealing it may have been in theory, the *Luftsperre* had nothing to recommend it in practice, for Germany would have had to field nearly a thousand aircraft in order to make it work. French airmen had no difficulty in penetrating German airspace, whether on reconnaissance or offensive patrols. When engaged, the highly maneuverable Nieuports held their own over the Fokkers, and swarmed all over the Albatros and L.V.G. two-seater reconnaissance machines. The ease with which French cooperation and reconnaissance aircraft evaded interception — and even did some intercepting themselves of German two-seaters — led to an obvious conclusion: the *Luftsperre* tied down a large number of aircraft in a futile effort to seal off the airspace behind German lines and greatly reduced German aerial effectiveness without diminishing the strength of the Allied air offensive.[6]

Major Wilhelm Siegert, responsible for the technical development of Germany's military aviation forces and a prewar aviator of note, summed up his feelings concerning the *Luftsperre* with characteristic directness. "The *Luftsperre*," he wrote, "as an end in itself is nothing but an admission of inherent weakness. Is there nothing better against an invasion than passive door closing? Yes! There is the indirect defense. And we have reached it with our fighter forces."[7] But, in truth, Germany had not — not yet, in any case. Germany was confronting not simply a strategic problem, but a technical one as well; the *Eindecker* was a generation behind the Nieuport in technology. Germany would not overcome this technical inferiority until the introduction of the Halberstadt and, especially, the Albatros biplane fighters in the late summer of 1916. Additionally, Germany did not have sufficient fighter forces to hinder both French and British air activities. What was needed was effective organization of the fighter aircraft into tactical units that could patrol offensively behind Allied lines and destroy Allied aircraft over their own territory. Eventually, of course, Germany did follow the Allied lead, and create specialized fighter squadrons that employed tactics first brilliantly demonstrated by Oswald Boelcke in the fall of 1916. However, the ironically defensive nature of German air operations remained a hallmark of the air war over the Western Front essentially through 1918, for even after the first German fighter units were formed, the fighters operated primarily over their own territory against Allied air incursions, and only rarely over Allied territory. Thus, though Germany quickly abandoned the *Luftsperre* and the notion of distributing fighters in small parcels equally over a front, her air strategists still pursued a defensive air doctrine.

By mid-April, de Rose's fighter pilots ruled the skies over Verdun. Known as the *Groupe des Cigognes* (Stork Group), they were a galaxy of now legendary airmen including Jean Navarre, Georges Guynemer, and Charles Nungesser. What de Rose might have accomplished beyond Verdun is unknown, for this aggressive air leader, very much in the mold of a

Boelcke, perished in a flying accident in May. Gifted individual German pilots, like Boelcke, continued to score—within ten days of his arrival at the Verdun front, Boelcke had shot down four planes—but the losses were but a trickle to the French air forces in the skies over Verdun. On April 13, for example, Navarre, a brilliant and daring pilot, shot down four German planes. The French also found a novel means of dealing with the plump, sausage-like *Drachen* that hung in the eastern sky and spied upon French forces: they shot them down with rockets, heralding the birth of the air-to-air missile. Heavily protected by antiaircraft emplacements, the *Drachen* were no easy targets, for ordinary machine-gun bullets just pierced the envelope starting small gas leaks, and the pilot who stayed too long while trying to destroy one was almost certain to be shot down himself. What was required was some sort of "stand-off" weapon. An aerial rocket, propelled by a black-powder mixture, seemed the ideal solution to Y.P.G. Le Prieur, a French naval officer; he designed a small rocket that could be mounted on the V-struts of a Nieuport and fired electrically from the pilot's cockpit. A Nieuport could carry six or even eight of the unguided rockets, which closely resembled the familiar fireworks rocket. Launched in a salvo within a hundred yards of a balloon, the rockets would streak forward, ripping through the balloon's skin. The fiery exhaust ignited escaping hydrogen gas from the balloon, which usually roared down in flames. The observers fortunately had parachutes—unlike pilots of airplanes—and thus could usually escape by leaping from their observation baskets. In one day over the Verdun front, no less than five of the costly *Drachen* erupted into fireballs under the attack of de Rose's airmen. Later, undoubtedly inspired by the French example, Germany experimented with similarly-armed Halberstadt fighter biplanes, forming a special experimental *Raketentrupp* (rocket squad), and pilot Rudolf Nebel, later a German rocket pioneer in the interwar years, claimed to have actually shot down two British aircraft with rockets. But the German experience with rockets was not as felicitous as the French; Le Prieur rockets became a standard armament for French and British "balloon busters," and took a heavy toll of German observation balloons until superceded by incendiary bullets. As such, they represented a further refinement of the fighter's armament and were the ancestors of the unguided and guided missiles carried by today's warplanes. Germany would not make its mark on rocketry until a second and even more terrible world war.[8]

As the spring of 1916 arrived, then, fighting at Verdun remained a stalemate on the ground, but there was undoubtedly an Allied victory aloft. Fresh from combat, du Peuty—who had flown and fought alongside his fellow pilots—wrote to Trenchard concerning the French experience. The message heartened Trenchard considerably, for it solidified his belief in the airplane as an offensive weapon and also cemented his faith in the strategic air offensive. Du Peuty examined the ways combat aircraft could be employed: first, the traditional strategy of keeping fighters close to reconnaissance and artillery spotters, and next the more radical doctrine of letting the two-seaters "fend for themselves so that the combat machines can do their real job of fighting."[9]

Du Peuty summarized the Verdun experience. The French air service had gone on the offensive from the outset, leaving the two-seaters on their own. As a result, they overwhelmed the Germans' *Luftsperre*, forcing the Germans even more to the defensive, by making the German airmen protect their own two-seaters from the depredations of the nimble Nieuports. With air supremacy assured, du Peuty and others next made a big mistake; they yielded to the pleas of the reconnaissance and artillery spotters who felt uncomfortable without close protection. Trying to provide close protection against German airmen now trying to go on the offensive, the French quickly found that they "were barely able to hold our own with the enemy."[10] So du Peuty directed a return to offensive air policy with predictable results: the inferior Fokkers were driven from the battle area, and the French army corps commanders "protested shrilly at being left in the lurch," despite few casualties.[11] The only serious problem, du Peuty concluded, was the "acute nervous strain" on the Nieuport pilots and pilots of bombardment aircraft as they carried the war into the enemy's rear areas. He concluded, "Our losses in the air may be heavy, but they are much less than those we are inflicting on the enemy. And our air mastery is proving of enormous advantage to the troops on the ground."[12] In sum, du Peuty learned that the best way of defending one's reconnaissance and cooperation aircraft lay in destroying the enemy's fighter forces away from the front over the enemy's own territory. (Sadly, du Peuty perished in combat in March 1918, ironically, leading a force of Zouaves in a ground attack against a German position.)

In the hot crucible of combat over Verdun, many German airmen recognized the weakness of the *Luftsperre* and the necessity of reorganizing fighter employment as a result of the bitter losses being experienced. It fell to a 41-year-old air service captain, Hauptmann Wilhelm Haehnelt, to do something about it. This creative officer served as staff officer for aviation *(Stabsoffizier der Flieger,* abbreviated *Stofl)* for the German Fifth Army then assaulting Verdun. A former infantry officer from Posen, he had learned to fly at Johannisthal in 1913, and had served as the commander of a field flying detachment before joining the Fifth Army as *Stofl* in September 1914. Haehnelt immediately recognized that the French fighter *escadrilles* possessed infinite superiority over any German flying units. At this time, each field flying detachment usually possessed four single-seat fighters (*Kampfeinsitzer,* virtually all Fokker or Pfalz *Eindecker* fighters) for the protection of the detachment's two-seaters or for air fighting duties. But flying singly or in pairs, the Fokkers, and occasionally armed two-seaters, were no match for the more maneuverable Nieuports, which usually had a numerical advantage as well. Accordingly, Haehnelt decided to combine all of his fighter aircraft — approximately thirty planes — into two combat groups. These two units he designated *Kampfeinsitzer Kommando Nord* (based at Bantheville), and *Kampfeinsitzer Kommando Sud* (based at Avillers). Previously, in 1915, the German Sixth Army *Stofl* had established three fighter commandos, designated *KEK* 1, 2, and 3, along the British front. But these earlier *KEK* seem to have had little effect upon the day-to-day operations of the field flying detachments, and pilots remained with whatever detachment they had been assigned. Boelcke and Immelmann, for example, were nominally members of *KEK* 2 at Douai when they began their careers as fighter pilots. Haehnelt's *KEK Nord* and *KEK Sud* were the first serious attempt by the Germans to group fighters together for tactical superiority. At the same time, Boelcke, now on the Verdun front, sought and obtained Haehnelt's permission to establish a two-plane roving fighter detachment of his own based at Sivry-sur-Meuse.[13]

Haehnelt's reorganized fighter forces attempted to offset the tactical and numerical superiority the French now possessed, but while they forced heavier losses upon du Peuty's airmen, the outnumbered and technologically inferior Fokkers accomplished little. Through the ten long months of the Verdun struggle, the French jealously kept their superiority aloft and never relinquished it to Germany's airmen. Haehnelt's efforts were not wasted, however. *KEK Nord* and *KEK Sud* became the forerunners of the German fighter squadrons (*Jagdstaffeln*) that appeared after the opening of the British Somme offensive. If Imperial Germany had been slower to realize the value of fighter units than the British and French, the shock of Verdun ended forever this blundering shortsightedness.

Verdun offered four clear lessons. First, the success of the strategic air offensive convinced both Britain and France that it constituted the best method of employing aircraft, both to ravage the enemy and to protect one's own control of the air. From Verdun onwards, the Allies pursued an unrelenting air offensive against Germany. Secondly, Germany realized the futility and inherent weaknesses of the *Luftsperre* and abandoned it as a fighting doctrine. Though the Germans did not initiate a strategic air offensive themselves, their adoption of centralized fighter forces did enable them to conduct their defensive air operations with greater efficiency, and paved the way for the emergence of true fighter squadrons, the *Jagdstaffeln*. Thirdly, the value of the fighter and the fighter formation had been demonstrated to both German and French satisfaction. By now, the fighter had emerged as a full-fledged partner of the reconnaissance and bomber aircraft. Fourth, the Verdun operations led to increased cooperation between the French and British air services. Remembering Trenchard's generous response to du Peuty's requests for material aid, the French were quick to assist their British ally in whatever way they could. Good will between the two services lasted throughout the remainder of the war, much of it due to the constant efforts of Trenchard's aide Maurice Baring. This gracious linquist played no small part in ensuring that a spirit of friendly and willing cooperation existed at the highest levels of both air services.

So the lithe Nieuport, flown in roving *escadrilles* by skilled and aggressive pilots, had mastered the Fokker over the French front. Now it remained for Trenchard, with the benefit of the French experience and with his own new combat aircraft and tactics, to whip the Fokker two hundred miles further north.

One morning in February 1916, a young newly-fledged RFC pilot, Cecil Lewis, watched a squadron leave the training field at Gosport, England, for the front in France. It was a sight that moved him deeply, and he recollected it vividly in an excellent memoir published decades later: "I can hear the strong engines and smell the tang of the burnt oil. I can see them as they came hurtling up, their goggled pilots and observers leaning down to wave a last farewell before they passed in a deafening flash of speed and smoke fifty feet overhead."[14] Impressive, certainly, and of ominous portent for Germany's air service, for the twelve aircraft Cecil Lewis saw leave that cold winter's morning were of a new generation. The F.E. 2b two-seat fighters built by Britain's Royal Aircraft Factory would wrest the skies away from the Fokker over the muddy Somme. And they were but one of several new types that the RFC would place in service to combat the heretofore fearsome *Eindecker*.

None of these new types had been expressly designed to defeat the Fokker, but all were well suited to do so. The Nieuport 11 entered service with Britain's Royal Naval Air Service (RNAS) in January 1916, about the same time it first appeared in France's fighter *escadrilles*. An advanced development, the nose-heavy Nieuport 16, and the superlative Nieuport 17, both of which retained the general lines of the earlier *Bébé*, would enter service with the RFC over the summer of 1916, sealing the Fokker's doom. To one RFC pilot soon to make his own reputation over the Western Front, Canada's Billy Bishop, the elegant little Nieuport "had an extremely lethal look about her, as if she were the mistress of some nabob of the Quai d'Orsay on her way to shoot her lover."[15] There were three other types as well that brought the era of the Fokker scourge to an abrupt end, and all of these were indigenous British designs. Two, the De Havilland D.H. 2 and the Royal Aircraft Factory F.E. 2b, were pushers—concessions to the problems of mounting an unsynchronized gun on a tractor airplane. The third, Tommy Sopwith's so-called "1½ Strutter," was a tractor two-seater that featured a synchronized gun for its pilot as well as defensive armament for the observer.

Like the *Eindecker,* the D.H. 2 and the F.E. 2b were basically wartime developments of prewar conceptualizations. But whereas the basic *Eindecker* had been conceived as a high-speed liaison and observation aircraft, the D.H. 2 and F.E. 2b were intended from the outset to be combat aircraft carrying machine guns. The design of both aircraft had been well in hand when the war broke out, and, in fact, the prototype D.H. 2 arrived in France for operational evaluation in July 1915, even before the Fokker scourge erupted. Unfortunately, it crashed in German territory in early August, probably as the result of engine failure, killing the pilot. German technical evaluators dismissed the type as a "Vickers single-seater," thinking it was a variation of the previously encountered Gunbus. (Parenthetically, one might question the wisdom of risking a prototype at the front. Britain delivered a lot of new aircraft to the Germans for technical evaluation because of mischance landings in German territory, including the D.H.2, the Vickers Gunbus, the F.E. 2b, and even the Handley Page O/400 heavy bomber, all of which arrived in German hands before beginning their operational careers in British service!) A few early production D.H. 2's reached France late in 1915. A predecessor of the F.E. 2b, the slightly more complex and slower F.E. 2a entered limited service with one RFC squadron as early as May 1915. Clearly, then, the D.H. 2 and F.E. 2b were not drawn up as hasty responses to the *Eindecker.*[16]

Both designs benefitted, however, from the single-purpose intent to which their creators had designed them: air fighting. Both were purposeful, sturdy aircraft. The D.H. 2 was a single-seater powered by either a Gnôme or Le Rhône rotary engine, and its pilot operated a single Lewis gun. At first, the gun was affixed to a flexible mounting on the left side of the cockpit, but a centralized mounting with the gun installed on a rotating pivot directly in front of the pilot proved more useful. Unfortunately, higher command dictated that the gun be moveable, despite the problems of firing such a weapon and flying an airplane at the same time. Most pilots in combat, as typified by Major Lanoe Hawker, preferred to treat the gun as a semi-fixed weapon, and flew the D.H. 2 as they would fly later fighters, maneuvering the plane to change the gun's aim. Unlike the single-seat D.H. 2, the F.E. 2b was a two-seater, with one or even two moveable machine guns. With an observer who could handle the guns in combat, and with its powerful Beardmore engine, the F.E. 2b was a very dangerous opponent. Both aircraft were maneuverable, the D.H. 2

especially so, and at least as fast as the *Eindecker* (something the earlier F.E. 2a had not been). Nevertheless, as was true of most aircraft of that first war in the air, they were not without their vices: the D.H. 2 and F.E. 2b had a nasty habit of departing from controlled flight during abrupt maneuvers and entering spins. At a time when the behavior of an aircraft in a spin was still imperfectly understood, and spin training was not a part of a student pilot's curriculum, this led to tragic losses of aircraft and aircrew. Additionally, the failure of a propeller blade or a cylinder could be disastrous, for the horizontal and vertical tail surfaces of a pusher aircraft were supported by thin and vulnerable tail booms. On at least two occasions, a cylinder hurled from the disintegrating rotary engine severed the tailbooms of a D.H. 2, the plane subsequently crashing and killing its unfortunate pilot. But such were the risks of flying in 1916. Overall, the D.H.2 and F.E. 2b represented an excellent interim solution to the problem of trying to develop practical fighter aircraft, pending the development of satisfactory synchronizer mechanisms that could be fitted to more practical tractor aircraft.

The Sopwith 1½ Strutter, however, was a different case altogether — a truly remarkable design that had a profound impact on the subsequent development of both multimission fighter and bomber aircraft. Its odd name stemmed from the unusual "W" bracing strut arrangement attaching the top wing to the fuselage. Designed for the British Admiralty as a two-seat, multipurpose aircraft, the 1½ Strutter embodied all the elegance of line that came to characterize Sopwith aircraft. A graceful tractor monoplane with equal-span wings, the 1½ Strutter set the standards for the heavy multipurpose fighter, later typified by the Bristol F.2A. For the first time, the pilot of a two-seater had a fixed, forward-firing gun connected to a synchronizer gear — the new Scarff-Dibovsky mechanism — while his observer had a defensive gun as well. Coupled with the 1½ Strutter's Clerget radial engine, rugged structure, and reasonable agility, the advanced armament installation guaranteed the success of the 1½ Strutter when it appeared over the Somme in RNAS and RFC service in the summer of 1916. Yet the 1½ Strutter, despite its numerous aerial successes against the remaining Fokkers and German two-seaters, would become best known as a long-range reconnaissance and strike aircraft, even serving as a single-seat bomber with an internal bomb bay for four small 65-pound bombs, and as a "home defense" single-seat night fighter on anti-Zeppelin and anti-bomber patrols. The 1½ Strutter deserves greater attention than it has received, for it anticipated the concept of the multimission fighter aircraft as it evolved over subsequent decades.[17]

Of all of these British aircraft, the Nieuport and 1½ Strutter embodied the future trend in combat aircraft design. The streamlined Nieuport, for example, flew faster than the D.H. 2, and took but half the time required by the British pusher to reach 10,000 feet. The 1½ Strutter performed better than the F.E. 2b, a comparable type, being faster, capable of climbing twice as fast, having a higher operational ceiling, and more efficient armament. Though other pushers would appear (such as the ill-fated single-seat F.E. 8, a type comparable to the D.H. 2), the future, even as discerned in the murkiness of mid-1916, clearly belonged to the tractor airplane. The D.H. 2 and F.E. 2b were aircraft whose historical time had come in the summer of 1916, and when the next generation of German fighters appeared—the Halberstadts and Albatros—they would quickly pass into eclipse. But if their moment was brief, they nevertheless made the most of it.

In February of 1916, the RFC's first single-seat fighter squadron, No. 24 Squadron, arrived in France. Equipped with twelve of the new D.H. 2's and commanded by the dashing Lanoe Hawker, who held the Victoria Cross for his single-handed daring attack on three armed German two-seaters the previous July, 24 Squadron, soon dubbed "Hawker's Squadron," eagerly awaited combat. They spent the first few weeks familiarizing themselves with the front, patrolling the lines north of the Somme. The unit's baptism by fire came on April 2, when Lieutenant D.M. Tidmarsh shot down a German plane near Bapaume. Three weeks later, on April 25, a group of Fokkers bounced an eight-plane reconnaissance flight consisting of a B.E. 2c escorted by four other B.E. 2c planes and three of 24 Squadron's new De Havillands. The three D.H. 2's wheeled after the Fokkers, and soon sent one crashing to earth.[18] In the succeeding weeks, the sturdy D.H. 2 proved itself master of the *Eindecker*. During May, Trenchard's airmen noticed a marked decrease in Fokker aggressiveness and by the end of the month the Fokker rampage had ended. Though it still took an occasional toll of British planes, the loss rate was much smaller and reconnaissance and bomber crews could fly with more confidence in their safety. The changed situation caused General Sir Henry Rawlinson, the commander of the British Fourth Army, to write on May 23 that:

> It was about the first week in May that we sent out our reconnaissance over Bapaume escorted by the de Havilland machines. . . . I cannot speak too highly of the work of these young pilots, most of whom have recently come out from England, and the de Havilland machine has unquestionably proved itself superior to the Fokker in speed, manoeuvre, climbing, and general fighting efficiency.[19]

More importantly, perhaps, the average RFC pilot now recognized that the Fokker was overrated. Myth and rumor had endowed the Fokker with almost magical properties; as Cecil Lewis recollected, "Rumor credited it with the most fantastic performance! It could outclimb, outpace, and out-manoeuvre anything in the R.F.C. You were as good as dead if you as much as saw one . . . and so on. In short our morale wanted bucking up."[20] Morale did receive a "bucking up," and in a most dramatic fashion. In early April 1916, a German pilot ferrying a brand-new *Eindecker* mistakenly landed it in perfect condition behind Allied lines. The RFC transported it to the aircraft depot at St. Omer, where it underwent comparative flight trials with various Allied aircraft. A Morane Type N monoplane (like the *Eindecker*, a prewar design) handily mastered it, to the pleased delight of observers, including many British airmen. There remained little doubt which way the air war over the Somme would go when the *Eindecker* clashed with the newer aircraft in British service.[21]

The fighting that summer was predictably sharp and vicious. One example is the experience of an F.E. 2b from 20 Squadron on patrol with four other "Fees" deep inside German territory early one morning, back and forth between Armentières and Lille. Its pilot, Harold Hartney, a Canadian in British service, spotted two *Eindeckers* making for one of his fellow pilots, and fired a Very flare to warn the flight it was under attack. The two Fokkers made a high pass on the other Fee, which adroitly maneuvered out of the way: one Fokker turned for another pass, but the second, seeing Hartney's Fee approaching, broke for home. The remaining Fokker now came under attack by the Fee it had jumped; the RFC pilot had half-rolled off the top of a loop and now his gunner had the Fokker in range. As Hartney watched, the other Fee's gunner "with wonderful coolness . . . literally butchered that poor single seater light rotary-engined Fokker monoplane. In a few seconds the Hun was belching smoke and flames and was on its way to the ground."[22] Now Hartney, still a neophyte to front flying, found himself separated from the flight, with neither British nor German planes in sight, and down to 8,500 feet. Climbing slowly at 60 miles per hour, he looked back over the top wing, unhooking his seat belt and standing up, holding the engine's radiator cap to brace himself as he peered over the tail. And there, lining him up, was another *Eindecker* — perhaps the one that had previously broken away from the first combat. Frantically, Hartney got his gunner's attention, and the gunner, sitting in his cockpit ahead of the pilot, hung on through Hartney's defensive maneuvering. A quick climbing turn to reverse direction, and Hartney discovered the Fokker "streaking like hell" slightly below and in front of the angry Fee. His gunner riddled the *Eindecker* and its pilot; the Fokker burst into flame, nosed upwards, and then dove to earth. Hartney headed west, his gunner testing his Lewis guns by firing short bursts to make certain they were still in firing condition. Ahead, he could see three of the Fees from his flight, but so high as to preclude his forming-up. Where was the fourth? Hartney wondered about this, and also about enemy airplanes. Suddenly his gunner pointed over the tail of the Fee at another Fokker approaching. Hartney was still ten miles behind enemy lines, and low on fuel; he skidded out of the way of the attacking Fokker, and then chased it around the sky, his gunner snapping bursts at it. Now a second Fokker pounced onto the Fee's tail, and the dogfight was two-on-one; Hartney alternated zooming and diving, gaining a little altitude each time. One Fokker presented an easy target to his gunner, who riddled it, sending it earthwards. The other turned and fled. Hartney resumed course for the lines, but again his doughty Fee was bounced by two Fokkers, from front and behind. Again it developed into a turning, swirling dogfight. His gunner, worried about the low state of his ammunition, held his fire until he had a clear sight and sent a third Fokker down streaming smoke. Now Hartney was within five miles of the lines, but the prevailing winds had blown him far south off course. Near Armentières two more Fokkers bounced the Fee, and this time, their accurate fire damaged the engine and sent a stream of bullets through the crew nacelle, fortunately without injuring Hartney or his gunner. A Fokker approached from head-on to deliver a *coup de grace*, and Hartney's gunner was helpless: the guns had jammed. Hartney drove straight for the German, hoping to ram the Fokker with the Fee's heavy landing gear. The Fokker pilot, reading Hartney's intentions and possibly thinking him mad, dove away and disappeared. With a smoking, sputtering engine, Hartney and his gunner crossed the lines at less than 1,000 feet, force-landing without injury among Australian troops He returned to base to discover that one of the flight's Fees had indeed been shot down, but the crew had survived and landed, like Hartney, in friendly territory. It had been an eventful morning.[23]

Another Fee combat, on the evening of Sunday, June 18, dramatically affirmed the meteoric fall of the Fokker. That day, while British General Headquarters readied final plans for the long-awaited Somme offensive that would open on the first of July, the airmen of 25 Squadron patrolled over the front. In the afternoon, this veteran squadron had suffered the loss of one F.E. 2b in a swirling dogfight with seven Fokkers, but the remaining two Fees of the flight had destroyed an *Eindecker* apiece, chasing the rest away. At approximately nine o'clock that evening, Lieutenant G.R. McCubbin and his observer-gunner, Corporal J.H. Waller, spotted three Fokkers cruising near Annay just as the Fokkers spotted the Fee. One of the monoplanes dived for home, but the remaining two, presuming, apparently, that McCubbin posed no immediate danger, attacked another unwary Fee cruising in the evening. As one of the *Eindeckers* came within range, Waller opened fire with his machine gun, and the German monoplane disintegrated, falling swiftly to earth. The victorious crew turned to assist the other Fee, but neither it nor the attacking Fokker (which had, in fact, shot it down, the crew being taken prisoner) were to be seen. McCubbin and Waller returned to base; not so Oberleutnant Max Immelmann, holder of the *Pour le Mérite*, instigator of the Fokker scourge, legendary inventor of the Immelmann turn, recently appointed commander of *Kampfeinsitzer Kommando 3*, and victor of fifteen air combats.[24]

Immelmann's death has always been one of the mysteries of the First World War, along with the deaths of fellow pilots Guynemer and von Richthofen. Whether Waller's fire broke up his monoplane, or whether it failed structurally of its own accord will probably never be known for certain. The official German report on his death concluded that the "Eagle of Lille" had shot off one of the blades of his propeller when the synchronizing mechanism of the Fokker failed to function properly. The resultant vibration caused progressive structural failure of the airframe. This was a plausible explanation, for earlier Immelmann had indeed shot off the blades of his propeller when a synchronizer failed; that time the ace had been able to glide to a safe landing.[25] Anthony Fokker, eager to clear the reputation of his plane and mechanism, claimed the *Eindecker* had been shot down by German antiaircraft fire. He cited as evidence the plane's control wires, which were cleanly cut, and not stretched as one might expect in a structural failure.[26] Oswald Boelcke blamed the synchronizer.[27] Clearly, no absolute cause would satisfy all parties. If one accepts Fokker's statements about the control wires as accurate, and the improbability of antiaircraft fire as the cause of Immelmann's death, together with the indisputable fact that Waller had Immelmann's machine under fire, then the RFC's traditional claim that Waller shot down Immelmann is not only plausible, but probable.

Germany greeted the news of Immelmann's death with the same sense of national loss that followed the announcement of Manfred von Richthofen's death two years later. The airmen with their daring deeds had given the public of all the combatant nations a new hero, the air warrior. In contrast to the unspectacular and often gloomy news from the Western Front, aviation (and to a lesser extent the U-boats) presented a wholly new aspect of combat, war in three dimensions. In the absence of glorious victories and stunning enemy defeats, the actions of Germany's *Fliegertruppen* were given full play in the press; their true value was often overplayed. The airmen became the recipients of decorations, citations, titles, property, and fan mail. Immelmann, above all others, had been the symbol of Germany's aerial might for everyone from the Kaiser to the man in the street. After his eighth victory, he had been awarded the *Pour le Mérite*; after his twelfth, he received the Commander's Cross of the Saxon Order of Heinrich, and Kaiser Wilhelm II ordered that a special message of personal congratulations be sent to the pilot. After aides had drawn up the document and as the Kaiser started to sign it, news arrived that Immelmann had shot down his thirteenth victim. "Immelmann shoots faster than one can write," the Kaiser remarked to an aide, personally altering the text.[28] At his funeral, the crown princes of Bavaria and Saxony, twenty generals, and his friend Oswald Boelcke paid homage to this early airman whose charismatic public appeal stood in ironic contrast to his quiet personality.

So Immelmann died, and with him the remnants of the Fokker menace. The vacancy left by his death did not remain unfilled for long, for the German public soon transferred its adulation to an airman of exceptional ability whose fame — on both sides of the front — soon outshone even that of the Eagle of Lille: Oswald Boelcke.

IV.
Boelcke and the *Jagdflieger*

Oswald Boelcke, a major figure in the development of air fighting doctrine and tactics, entered the air service from a German army communications unit. Boelcke's grandfather had been state secretary of Brandenburg, and his father the rector of a German evangelical school in Buenos Aires. Born on May 19, 1891, the third of five brothers, in Giebichenstein (near Halle), young Oswald soon moved with his family to Dessau where he attended the *Gymnasium*, studying history, natural science, mathematics, and physics. Sports attracted his greatest attention, however, and he excelled in athletics, especially swimming. When his older brother Wilhelm received an army commission, the younger Boelcke determined to follow in his brother's footsteps. With a directness that characterized his entire life, he wrote to the Kaiser requesting permission to become a cadet. The first that his parents heard of his letter was the notification that a cadet vacancy did exist. But only a third-former, Boelcke had to complete his secondary education and pass his *Abitur* before he could accept the cadetship. In due course he got his wish, and in 1911, at the age of twenty, he received posting as an officer cadet to a telegraph battalion at Coblenz, where he found military life to his liking. Following commissioning, Leutnant Boelcke joined a communications unit at Darmstadt, and received his first taste of flying.[1]

Boelcke had noticed the *Tauben* that the German air service maintained at a flying field near Darmstadt, and he soon made many friends among the airmen, who encouraged his interest in flight. He applied and received assignment to the Darmstadt *Fliegerschule*, and completed his flight training shortly before the outbreak of the war. Following brief duty in Darmstadt and Trier, he arrived at the front on September 1, 1914, joining his brother Wilhelm, who was an observer. By the spring of 1915, Boelcke had proved himself an able and daring pilot. He received the Iron Cross 1st class for reconnaissance sorties over the Argonne and Champagne sectors of the front, and in April 1915, joined *Feldfliegerabteilung 62* as it formed at Doberitz, near Berlin, moving with it shortly afterwards to its combat station at Douai. Here Boelcke found himself piloting the new L.V.G. C I two-seat reconnaissance biplane, the first German aircraft equipped with a machine gun for its observer. Favoring more active duties than reconnaissance, Boelcke and his officer observer sought out enemy aircraft. Early one Sunday, the two airmen spotted a French Morane Type L parasol monoplane also on a reconnaissance sortie, and gave chase. They closed within fifty yards of the Morane, and opened fire. The French observer fired back as his pilot, the Comte de Beauvicourt, desperately maneuvered to escape. For twenty minutes the two aircraft wheeled high over the French countryside; then the German observer found his target, and the Morane, with its crew dead, glided down to a crash landing—on Beauvicourt's own estate. Shortly thereafter, Fokker arrived at Douai with his *Eindecker*, and Boelcke launched his career as a fighter pilot.[2]

Boelcke's career proceeded apace of Max Immelmann's, with an important exception: Boelcke made as favorable an impression on his foes as he did on his countrymen. In August 1915, for example, Boelcke saw a French boy fall into a canal and disappear; he dove into the water, searched about under the surface, and brought the unconscious youth to the surface. He then revived him, and after the boy regained consciousness, chided the youth for being too lazy to learn to swim. The boy's townspeople subsequently requested (without success) that the French government in Paris reward Boelcke for his humanitarian deed; eventually he did receive a German lifesaving medal.[3] Boelcke was at the Verdun front when Immelmann perished, and the Kaiser, shocked by the hero's death, ordered Boelcke out of combat after his eighteenth aerial victory. Restricted to non-combat flying, Boelcke received notice to prepare for a tour of the middle European front, including an inspection and morale-boosting trip to Germany's shaky ally, Turkey. Boelcke did not retire willingly, and while still in the Verdun sector, shot down a French plane over Fort Douaumont. He did not claim it, but the news that a French plane had crashed near the German-held former French strongpoint cast immediate suspicion on Boelcke, and the secret was soon out. Boelcke departed on his tour, and while he was abroad a series of events occurred that soon released him to fight once more.[4]

The airplane in 1916 was not the decisive weapon (in the sense of determining a war's outcome) that it would be three decades later. For that reason, though Germany had lost air supremacy over the Verdun front, on the ground this colossal battle had reached a stalemate. In truth, it was a slaughterhouse, as its architect, the chief of the German general staff General Erich von Falkenhayn, had intended. Von Falkenhayn had given the operation its name: *Gericht*, which meant both a judgment and a place of execution. But despite the most appalling casualties, France's army refused to collapse—that would come a year later, in the Nivelle debacle—and in bitter irony, Verdun proved a drain on both aggressor and defender. By the summer of 1916, the Allies were ready to make their own offensive, to relieve the pressure on Verdun, and also to bring greater stability and consolidation to the northern portion of the front in France and Belgium. British generals lived in fear of a German drive to the sea, because the front ran but a mere fifty miles from the Channel. A joint Anglo-French drive on the Somme sector of the front—an area of hills and marshlands—had been in the planning stage; now, the terrible losses at Verdun made an Allied offensive even more urgent. Sir Douglas Haig, a personally courageous but unfortunately unimaginative officer who had replaced Sir John French as the commander of the British Expeditionary Force, hoped that this offensive would restore the war of movement that had ended with the establishment of the deadly trenches, and result in a general breakthrough along the entire Somme front. Hugh Trenchard's Royal Flying Corps went into the Somme battle with three not inconsiderable advantages: the technology of the Nieuport, the new pushers, and the 1½ Strutter; the experience of du Peuty's airmen proving that an offensive air policy worked best; and, finally, the numerical advantage of 185 RFC airplanes over 129 German ones.[5]

The great offensive began on July 1, 1916. Because of heavy commitments to the Verdun fighting, the French involvement in the Somme battle—which would last nearly five months—did not approach the intensity of British involvement. The Somme offensive constituted the greatest battle that Great Britain ever fought, and its casualties indicate its terrible cost and scope. On the *first* day, the British Army sustained nearly 60,000 casualties (the RFC lost five men that day). Rather than a stunning breakthrough, the Somme offensive proved a heartbreaking disappointment. The front changed by approximately one mile but even where this limited gain was made, German forces maintained the integrity of their secondary defenses, and quickly consolidated. More importantly, the Somme offensive resulted in an important shift in the character of the war; gone was the last hope for a negotiated peace.[6] Germany recognized that France constituted a less serious threat than Great Britain, and (especially following the breaking of the Nivelle offensive in April of 1917), the war became a conflict between Great Britain and Germany; for this reason, after the Somme, the German air service always measured its abilities and tested itself not against the *Aviation militaire*, but against the drab-colored aircraft of Britain's Royal Flying Corps. Thus, the air war over the Western Front took on an increasingly Anglo-German character.

In the air, however, everything went Britain's way. The "Fees," De Havillands, and Nieuports pressed and harried enemy aircraft wherever they came across them. On the ground German infantry smarted under artillery barrages called by British aircraft and impromptu strafing attacks by low-flying planes. Exposed to these threats, the troops felt deserted by their artillery and air force, and some even grumbled, "God punish England, our artillery, and our airmen," an unjustified slur, for the overworked Fokkers and overwhelmed reconnaissance aircraft could make little impression on the massive British air offensive.[7] As Maurice Baring recollected, "a German machine scarcely could put its nose this side of the line."[8] Many German troops grudgingly complimented the RFC: "Every day one can scarcely show oneself in the trenches owing to the English airmen. It is a wonder that they don't come and pull one out of the trenches so low do they fly," wrote one unknown German diarist.[9] Another recalled thinking, "The English artillery—the English army—the masses of English aeroplanes over our heads always. We are finished. . . ."[10]

In fact, however, all certainly was not lost, for already seeds were germinating that would result in a resurgence of German airpower over the Western Front. A technical advance in airframe design, resulting in the introduction of more powerful, more agile, and more heavily-armed aircraft, lay in the near future; coupled with changed tactics, it augered far better for Germany's combat air situation than even the most sanguine of German airmen could have predicted. Several new aircraft types typified the new trend, notably the Roland C II reconnaissance plane; and three new fighter biplanes—the Fokker D I, D II, and D III series, the Halberstadt D II, D III and D V, and the Albatros D I and D II. How had this promising situation come about?

Not, certainly, through the efforts of the German *Idflieg*, the Inspectorate of Military Aviation; this critical office, responsible for technical procurement, had continued to order Fokker and Pfalz *Eindecker* fighters (220 in February 1916 alone) long after it should have dispassionately reexamined the worth of these aircraft. In fact, the new aircraft types resulted from the initiative of private German aviation companies, possibly with the active encouragement of experienced air fighters from the front such as Immelmann and Boelcke. To understand the position these new aircraft types came to occupy one must look into the various "generations" of fighter aircraft built during the First World War.

Arguably there were five generations of fighter aircraft that appeared during the Great War. The first generation, typified by the *Eindecker* and such other aircraft as the Morane Type L and N, represented prewar designs hastily modified for air combat. They lacked the advantages of being designed specifically for air combat, and constituted rather successful compromises. They lacked the handling qualities, performance, payload, and design refinements of later aircraft; most, for example, made use of Wright-derived wing-warping for lateral control rather than the more efficient moveable ailerons. The first generation fighters served as late as September 1916 and then quickly disappeared from the front, many continuing in service at training establishments.

The second generation of fighters represented a more diverse collection of aircraft, interestingly, none of which was of monoplane configuration. These single or two-place tractor or pusher aircraft ranged from the Vickers F.B. 5 to the Nieuport 11 and the Fokker D I/II/III biplane fighters of 1916. Many of these aircraft, too, could trace their origins to prewar projects (such as the F.B. 5 Gunbus), but they had been designed from the outset as gun-toting combat aircraft. In any generation there are "early" and "late" aircraft, this generally (but not always) translating directly into "less sophisticated" and "more sophisticated." Certainly, for example, the F.B. 5 was a less sophisticated and useful aircraft when compared, say, to the Nieuport 11 *Bébé*. Second-generation aircraft, it must be stressed, did not owe their origins to the Fokker scourge. The initial second-generation fighters appeared over the Western Front as early as February 1915, and remained in service as late as August 1917, by which time they were deathtraps for their crews. Then they too passed from the front to home training units.

The third generation of fighters appeared in the late spring and summer of 1916. These were the first generation of combat aircraft designed with the lessons learned from maneuvering air combat over the Western Front. These aircraft were generally much more powerful than either the first- or second-generation aircraft, with more efficient armament systems (as exemplified by a trend towards twin synchronized machine guns firing forwards and rotating and traversing "ring"-type gun mounts for an observer), improved structural design, and great attention to reducing aerodynamic drag and streamlining. The initial third-generation fighters entered service in April 1916; some of the later examples of this generation were still in service (though clearly obsolescent) at the end of the war. Within this generation, some "families" evolved, such as the Albatros fighters of Germany, and the Nieuport 17 through 27 family of fighters in French service (the Nieuport 28 constitutes a special case not that closely related to the previous Nieuport "family tree"). Two more generations, the fourth and fifth, appeared in 1917 and 1918, respectively, and will be examined subsequently. The following is a breakdown of the first through third generations showing aircraft type and dates of operational service (month and year):

FIRST GENERATION

Sopwith Tabloid	8/14 through 4/15
Bristol Scout	9/14 through 9/16
Martinsyde S.1	11/14 through 6/15
Morane Type L	3/15 through 10/15
Morane Type N	6/15 through 9/16
Fokker E I/II/III/IV	7/15 through 9/16
Pfalz E III/IV	10/15 through 7/16

SECOND GENERATION

Vickers F.B. 5/F.B. 9	2/15 through 6/16
Nieuport 10/12	2/15 through 6/16
F.E. 2a	7/15 through 9/15
De Havilland D.H. 2	12/15 through 6/17
Nieuport 11/16	1/16 through 8/17
F.E. 2b/2d	2/16 through 8/17
Fokker D I/II/III	7/16 through 12/16
F.E. 8	8/16 through 6/17

THIRD GENERATION

Sopwith 1½ Strutter	4/16 through 10/17
L.F.G. Roland C II/IIa	4/16 through 5/17
Halberstadt D II/III/V	6/16 through 12/17
Nieuport 17/23/17bis	6/16 through 9/17
Albatros D I/II	8/16 through 9/17
Spad 7	8/16 through end of war
Sopwith Pup	9/16 through 9/17
L.F.G. Roland D I/II/III	10/16 through 7/17
Siemens-Schuckert D I	12/16 through 6/17
Albatros D III	1/17 through 9/18
Sopwith Triplane	2/17 through 11/17
Nieuport 24/27	5/17 through 3/18
De Havilland D.H. 5	5/17 through 1/18
Albatros D V/Va	6/17 through end of war
Hanriot H.D. 1	8/17 through end of war
Fokker Dr I	9/17 through 8/18
Pfalz D III	9/17 through end of war
Nieuport 28	3/18 through 6/18
Fokker D VI	4/18 through 8/18

During 1915, largely at the instigation of German air chief Thomsen, the army granted ever-increasing priority to the growing German aviation industry, recognizing that mastery of the air required large numbers of mass-produced aircraft. The fighting at Verdun and later on the Somme in 1916 spurred on army efforts to increase production of new and more ef-

ficient types, because, quite simply, Germany lacked the numbers to confront the Allied powers on anything approaching parity. For example, in
addition to the 185 RFC aircraft opposing the 129 German aircraft at the
opening of the Somme offensive, the French could add 201 of their own.
Strident calls from German airmen for machines capable of battling the
Nieuport and the British pushers, especially Oswald Boelcke's suggestion
that the German aircraft industry concentrate on producing light, agile,
and fast-climbing biplanes, encouraged Germany's more advanced
aeronautical engineers to depart from proven prewar configurations in
favor of ones more suitable to the combat conditions of 1916. Even as the
D.H. 2's and Fokkers battled it out over the Somme in the months prior to
July 1, promising new designs were undergoing flight testing, particularly
four types that would go on to service ranging from satisfactory to excellent: the Roland C II "escort" and reconnaissance airplane, and three
fighters, the Fokker D I/II/III, the Halberstadt D II/III/V, and the
Albatros D I/II. The Roland C II epitomized the growing German fascination with streamlining as a means of improving the aerodynamic performance — and hence speed — of combat aircraft. Its fuselage completely
bridged the gap between the upper and lower wings, and was, like the
prewar Deperdussin Monocoque racer, a lightweight plywood monocoque
shell. Somewhat portly despite its smooth lines (including a completely
enclosed 160-horsepower Mercedes engine in the nose), the C II and its
successor the C IIa quickly received the nickname "*Walfisch*" (whale). A
small fighter cousin, the similar but single-seat Roland D I, appeared in
October 1916 and was named *Haifisch* (shark), but did little subsequently
to prove worthy of so formidable a nickname. The two-seat C II, intended
for reconnaissance or the escort of other reconnaissance craft, had an
observer-fired machine gun, as well as a synchronized forward-firing gun
operated by the pilot. Faster than a Nieuport *Bébé* (by almost 10 miles per
hour), the *Walfisch* could prove to be a deadly opponent for the unwary.
The first *Walfisch* appeared at the Verdun front in April 1916. By the end
of August 1916, fifty were in service, most facing the British on the
Somme.[11]

Unlike the elegant Roland, the first of Germany's new fighters, the Fokker and Halberstadt biplanes, had more conventional structures using
fabric-covered frames and extensive bracing. The Halberstadt appeared
first but it was easily the most advanced of the two types, and would remain in service for well over a year. Indeed, while the Halberstadt was
clearly a third-generation fighter aircraft, the Fokker biplane was just as
clearly a second-generation machine; although it did not appear until the
summer of 1916, it still relied on wing-warping for lateral control. It really
represented the last vestige of Fokker's dependence on the prewar Morane-

derivative *Eindecker*, to which it bore an unmistakable relationship. Though it entered service and proved a satisfactory fighter, Anthony Fokker's first fighting biplane definitely ranked third behind its Halberstadt and Albatros compatriots. The Halberstadt had a deceptively fragile appearance for it could dive steeply and maneuver with abandon, possessing excellent responsiveness and handling qualities. *Idflieg* ordered 104 of the new Fokker and Halberstadt biplanes in May of 1916. The first of the Halberstadt fighters arrived at the front in late June, and Boelcke flew this aircraft at Douai shortly after Immelmann's death. During the flight he approached an unsuspecting British B.E.2c, exploiting the Halberstadt's vaguely B.E.2-like side profile to get close, and then attacked. Fortunately for the RFC crew, a jammed gun prevented him from carrying out the nasty surprise to its predictable finish, and the B.E. 2 managed to return to its own side of the line. The Halberstadt fighter owed much of its design to a training biplane the firm had previously constructed. Combining the synchronized machine gun with excellent flying characteristics and a rugged structure, the Halberstadt D II, and its successors the D III and V, was Germany's first fighter with performance equal or superior to that of the *Bébé* or the British pushers.[12]

It was the Albatros, however, that would go down in history as the deadliest of this new breed of warplanes. Like the Halberstadt a third-generation design, the Albatros shared with the Roland the streamlined advantages of the monocoque wooden shell. Sleek, purposeful-looking airplanes, the D I and D II Albatros fighters had two wings of equal span and chord (in contrast to the sesquiplane layouts of the later D III and D V/Va). The Albatros came to typify Germany's aviation at mid-war as the *Eindecker* had typified the early war years and the Fokker D VII, the final months. Powered by a 160-horsepower Mercedes engine, the Albatros had a maximum speed of 110 miles per hour, roughly 20 miles per hour faster than the *Eindecker* it replaced. It mounted two synchronized Spandau machine guns. The D II differed from the D I primarily in having the upper wing slightly shifted to improve visibility from the cockpit; later, the D III introduced at the beginning of 1917 dispensed with the equal-span and equal-chord lower wing in favor of a Nieuport-like narrow lower wing to improve the pilot's downward visibility. (This modification also introduced an unsatisfactory feature of the Nieuport—namely, its problems with structural failure of the lower wing, particularly during dive recoveries.) With well-harmonized controls, a high maximum speed, an excellent armament system, and good maneuverability, the Albatros would soon pose a major threat to British control of the air over the Western Front. It made its first appearance in September 1916 in the hands of Oswald Boelcke and his "cubs."[13]

It is true, of course, that while these new German designs were underway, the Allied powers had equivalent designs on the drawing board. The famous French Spad fighter, for example, entered service concurrently with the Albatros, as did the British Sopwith Pup. By and large, however, because of problems in the procurement of British military aircraft, it was not until late spring of 1917 that the first British fighters capable of matching and even exceeding the Albatros's performance — the S.E. 5/5a and the Sopwith Camel — entered RFC service. Until then, British fliers had to make do with the Pup, some Spads sent by the French to help Trenchard out (together with some Nieuports), and the Royal Naval Air Service's Sopwith Triplane. Germany thus had an interval of approximately eight months — September 1916 through April 1917 — in which to make a bid for air superiority over the Western Front. Her airmen owed their opportunity more to the creative efforts of individual German design engineers than to the master planning of the German aviation inspectorate.

Interestingly, both German and British military aviation procurement officials seem to have favored a conservatism in aircraft design that often hampered genuine initiative and creativity, resulting in unsatisfactory aircraft or even slavish copies. Three stories, one British and two German, serve to illustrate this: the stories of the B.E. 12 "fighter" for the RFC, the Siemens-Schuckert D I "German Nieuport," and the Fokker Dr I triplane. All illustrate the dangers of designing to overcome a specific threat, without trying to anticipate the next stage that that threat will reach. The results were designs that were obsolete or obsolescent with respect to fighters on the front when they entered service.

Faced with the threat of the *Eindecker* monoplanes in the fall of 1915, the Royal Aircraft Factory of Great Britain undertook to develop an aircraft capable of defeating the *Eindecker* in combat. Unfortunately, those entrusted with this task had imperfect vision and insight. They clearly recognized the synchronized machine gun to be an advantage, but did not recognize the equal importance of speed and maneuverability. As a result, they simply modified the slow and unmaneuverable B.E. 2 reconnaissance airplane by fairing over the observer's position and adding a 150-horsepower engine to replace the standard 90-horsepower engine used on the type. After the addition of a single forward-firing Vickers machine gun equipped with a Vickers synchronizer mechanism, the design received the designation B.E. 12, and was optimistically classified as a fighter. Predictably — one might say inevitably — the development of this lash-up arrangement took longer than planned, and it did not appear for service until the time of the Somme offensive. After a month of sharply rising losses as the newer Fokker, Halberstadt, and Albatros biplane fighters entered the inventory of German fighter squadrons, Trenchard announced plans to withdraw the B.E. 12 from service, and it soon ceased being employed as a fighter. The RFC attempted to use it instead as a single-seat fast bomber, but after further casualties, this most unwarlike fighter finally left the Western Front for good in February of 1917. It did score a few successes as a home defense nightfighter, protected by the cloak of darkness, its pilots carefully choosing the time and place of combat: a B.E. 12 shot down the German Zeppelin L 48 over England. The B.E. 12 episode demonstrated to the Royal Aircraft Factory that merely giving an airplane a synchronized machine gun did not turn it into a fighter; agility and speed meant life in the 1916 skies over France.[14]

In the summer of 1916, stunned by the reversal of German fortunes in the skies over Verdun, the *Idflieg* ordered German aircraft manufacturers to study captured Nieuport fighters with a view to copying them. The result was a trim little fighter that was virtually indistinguishable from a Nieuport 17: the Siemens-Schuckert D I. It entered service at the very end of 1916, and served briefly on the Western Front. Like the B.E. 12, the D I took so long to produce that it had but limited utility when it finally saw combat. For a while, it scored some successes, largely because Allied pilots and observers tended to mistake it for a Nieuport. But by the late spring of 1917, it was clearly an obsolescent design, and quickly passed to the Russian Front, where it had a better chance of both making a contribution and surviving. Meanwhile, those who studied what made the Nieuport a good fighter — such as excellent control harmonization and a narrow-chord lower wing that gave the pilot good visibility below — incorporated these ideas and concepts in their own designs, but not by blindly copying the entire plane. The Albatros D III, arguably the finest fighter in the war until the emergence of the S.E. 5 and the Camel in mid-1917, benefited from the technical analysis of the captured Nieuports, but was undeniably an indigenous German design. Ironically, after the disappointing D I experience, Germany proceeded to repeat it with the Fokker triplane. This over-rated and over-glamorized fighter stemmed from examination of the Sopwith Triplane, introduced to the Western Front with great success in February of 1917. Again, copying the design formula took so long that when the Fokker triplane finally entered service, British pilots were already aware that the days of the triplane had passed (as will be subsequently examined). The Fokker triplane never achieved for the German air service what its designers and adherents had hoped. Following the usual initial successes (Allied pilots and observers apparently mistook it for its inspiration, the Sopwith Triplane, as happened with the D I), Fokker triplane pilots found that all too often they could not engage or break off combat at will. The Allies, flying the higher performance Spad, S.E. 5a and Camel, gradually reduced the triplane "menace" to a mere nuisance.[15]

These three examples notwithstanding, when the British and German aircraft industries were left to their own devices, without the benefit of official "design by committee," the results were often spectacular aircraft, or at least ones that did quite well, such as the Camel, S.E. 5a, Fokker D VII, and Siemens-Schuckert D III and D IV. Subsequent aviation history is replete with similar examples.

Within a month of the July 1 Somme offensive, German and British third-generation fighters and cooperation aircraft were battling it out in combats involving Rolands, British Nieuport 17's, and Sopwith 1½ Strutters. Then, as July passed into August, the first Halberstadts and Fokkers appeared in numbers; September would bring the Albatros and Britain's Sopwith Pup. The combats were predictably violent. At first the most numerous of the German aircraft were the Rolands, flying singly or in formations. With its high speed, the Roland offered the D.H. 2 a difficult and elusive target. The RFC's De Havilland pilots did discover that they could outmaneuver the heavier and faster Roland in a straight dogfight, if the German pilot unwisely chose to fight that kind of battle. Pilots of Hawker's 24 Squadron fought a memorable contest with a mixed formation of Rolands, Fokkers, and L.V.G.'s on July 20, 1916, near Flers, four D.H. 2's against five L.V.G.'s, three Rolands, and three Fokkers. The two Rolands and a Fokker sent crashing to earth were all outmaneuvered.[16] But the Roland had a definite edge in speed over the D.H. 2, and could engage or break off combat at will. Slightly slower (by about three to five miles per hour) than the Nieuport 17, the Roland, if flown properly, could force a Nieuport pilot to engage in a fruitless tail chase. It had a roughly ten miles per hour advantage over the older Nieuport 11. If a group of Rolands operated in pairs, the combination of speed, forward firing guns, and armed observers could make an attacking British or French pilot think carefully about his approach.

Albert Ball, one of the emerging RFC fighter pilots, developed his own method for dealing with the Roland. He dove upon them from high altitude, using the extra speed to overtake the faster plane, zoomed underneath to the Roland's blind spot, and fired a short but deadly burst from his Nieuport before breaking away. Ball, a former B.E. 2c pilot who had joined 11 Squadron flying Nieuports in May of 1916, came to typify the image of the dashing "lone wolf" fighter pilot of the mid-war period. Many of these did not survive the war, for air combat increasingly demanded teamwork and careful tactics. Ball's tactics were simply to spot a large formation of German aircraft, dive straight into them, use his extraordinary accuracy and marksmanship to get a kill, and then plunge away from the combat. (One commentator has called him "the worst air combat tactician of the war.")[17] For the time his "tactics" worked, and by October 1916, in the complicated scheme that the RFC used to assess air combats, he had shot down ten German airplanes, forced twenty to land, driven another down out of control, and probably downed eighteen others — an astounding record of marksmanship. Odds did not bother him; on August 22, for example, he dove into a formation of seven Rolands and shot down two of them. On several occasions he used Le Prieur rockets, designed for use against balloons, to break up Roland formations, particularly if he was being attacked head-on by them. During one flight, Ball and a fellow pilot spotted a Roland and an L.V.G.; Ball fired his rockets and just missed the Roland, then closed to twenty yards and fired nearly two drums of Lewis bullets into it. The Roland entered a spin and crashed. His colleague fired his rockets at the L.V.G., and one of them shot into the fuselage of the German two-seater, sending it flaming to earth.[18]

The third-generation aircraft were far more capable than their first-generation and second-generation predecessors, and they undertook combat missions and duties of ever-greater sophistication and value. For example, on August 6 an offensive patrol of 1½ Strutters, from 70 Squadron left on an evening sortie from Fienvillers. Near Gouzeacourt, the two planes bounced an Albatros two-seater and forced it back to German lines. Next, the two attacked a formation of ten German two-seaters near Bapaume. The leader of the Sopwiths broke away to return to Fienvillers for more ammunition; his partner and observer kept harassing the ten German planes. Eventually, all ten two-seaters abandoned their mission and landed at Hervillers airfield.[19] (One can imagine the exasperation of the crews.) Episodes such as this confirmed the plans of the German air service to restructure its fighter forces into specialized squadrons called *Jagdstaffeln*: hunting packs. And these plans, which grew out of the bitter lessons of Verdun and the Somme and the implicit promise of the new technology of the Fokker biplanes and the Halberstadt and Albatros fighters, resulted in an order to Hauptmann Boelcke, then touring the Turkish front: he was to return home and form a *Jagdstaffel* of his own picked pilots to take into combat on the Somme.[20]

Nothing could have pleased Boelcke more, and the German pilot decided before his return to visit his brother Wilhelm, now a reconnaissance pilot stationed at Kovel, on the Russian front. Boelcke arrived at Kovel on August 12. His impressive reputation as the Fatherland's leading fighter pilot and holder of the coveted *Pour le Mérite* had spread wherever German airmen flew. Plied with eager questions, the affable pilot described his trip to the Balkans and Turkey, but soon came to the point. He would be leaving for the Somme to command a single-seat *Jagdstaffel*; he wanted pilots, the very best in the *Fliegertruppen*. The atmosphere grew more serious, as each pilot realized he was a candidate for Boelcke's select band, even then being evaluated by the master's appraising looks. After an evening of conversation with his brother, evaluating potential pilots, Boelcke made his choice. The next morning, Boelcke appeared at the hut of two of the unit's pilots and asked, "Want to come to the Somme with me?" Leutnant Erwin Böhme and Ulanenleutnant Manfred von Richthofen quickly assented.[21]

Boelcke wanted good pilots, and these two were among the very best. Böhme, at 37, was older than his contemporaries by as much as fifteen years, but Boelcke recognized that age does not necessarily lessen proficiency, and the older pilot's stabilizing influence on the younger ones would be desirable. He also wanted aggressive pilots, airmen who sought combat with the enemy, and it was this hunting trait that he had seen in von Richthofen. Leutnant Manfred Freiherr von Richthofen was 24 when selected by Oswald Boelcke for his Somme *Jagdstaffel*. An avid outdoorsman who enthusiastically hunted boar and other game all his life, von Richthofen had been a cavalry lieutenant when war broke out, and soon revealed himself as an eager and aggressive *Uhlan* leader. Lack of skill and his constant yearning for battle sometimes led to impetuosity. For example, early in the war he stumbled upon French cavalry in a wood. Instead of reporting the strength and position of the French *cuirassiers* to his commander, von Richthofen led his troops in a rash attack that cost him several men. Horse-mounted cavalry soon proved virtually useless in the war for fighting purposes, and, like many cavalrymen, von Richthofen found himself serving as a supply officer behind the lines. Such duties grated on his nature, and he applied for a transfer to the German *Fliegertruppen* as an observer, brashly writing to his commanding general, "*Liebe Exzellenz,* I have not gone to war to gather cheese and eggs, but for an entirely different purpose."[22] Shortly afterwards, his bold request was approved.

Von Richthofen flew as an observer on the Eastern front, and then departed for Ostend for posting to the *Brieftauben-Abteilung Ostende,* ostensibly a carrier pigeon group but in reality a fledgling long-range bombing unit. Here he helped crew a so-called *Grosskampfflugzeug* (large battle plane), armed with a swiveling machine gun. Imbued with an eager desire to do battle, he directed his pilot to attack enemy aircraft whenever the opportunity presented itself. Finally, flying an Albatros reconnaissance plane over the Champagne front, the German crew came across a French Farman two-seater. Von Richthofen's pilot steered the Albatros close alongside, while von Richthofen in the rear cockpit opened fire with his machine gun. The French and German observers traded fire, but von Richthofen's aim was the deadlier. The Farman spiraled earthwards, crashing approximately three miles behind French lines, preventing confirmation and official recognition of the air victory. Nevertheless, the young baron was more than proud of his accomplishment.[23]

Boelcke's meeting with von Richthofen at Kovel was the second time the two men had met, for nearly a year before, on a railroad train, they had had a chance meeting and a long conversation. The young observer had asked Boelcke how he shot down his victims. Boelcke, von Richthofen recalled later, "laughed loudly," and answered, "Well, it's very simple. I fly quite close and aim carefully, then he falls downwards." That conversation determined von Richthofen to become a pilot and fly fighters.[24] Following acceptance and completion of flight training, von Richthofen joined an Albatros reconnaissance unit on the Verdun front, where, in the words of fellow pilot Erwin Böhme, he proved himself "audacious and reliable."[25] While at Verdun in the spring of 1916, von Richthofen affixed a machine gun on a makeshift mount, Nieuport-style, above the Albatros' wing and he managed to shoot down a Nieuport with the weapon, possibly a tribute less to his ability than to poor tactics on the part of the unfortunate French pilot. In the summer, with the launching of the ill-fated Brusilov offensive by Czarist Russian forces, his unit left for Russia, and there he met Boelcke for the second time. When Boelcke met the young von Richthofen on August 12, he recognized him as the eager airman he had met the previous October. For his part, von Richthofen "dared not ask him to take me with him."[26] He did not need to; Boelcke remembered him, and saw in him the type of pilot he required: aggressive, a hunter, a man with determination. The mission of the new *Jagdstaffeln* would be to destroy opposing fighters so that German two-seaters could go about their observation and artillery spotting tasks unmolested, as well as to destroy Allied two-seaters on similar duties; it would demand the fierce zeal embodied in pilots such as von Richthofen. Von Richthofen's lack of technique and experience did not trouble Boelcke, for to him, all his pilots were pupils and he the master. Three days after their meeting, von Richthofen and Böhme boarded a train on the first stage of their journey to the Somme. At the station, one of von Richthofen's friends called out, "Don't return without the *Pour le Mérite!*" Von Richthofen, soon to become Boelcke's star pupil, would not disappoint his comrades; as the train sped eastwards, he believed himself to be embarking upon "the finest period of my life."[27]

Boelcke returned to the Western Front in late August, formally establishing *Jagdstaffel 2* (2nd Fighter Squadron, abbreviated *Jasta 2*) at Lagnicourt by the end of the month. On September 1, the first fighters arrived, two Fokker D III's and an Albatros D I. Boelcke had determined to instruct his pilots in the technique of air fighting, so he appropriated one of the two Fokkers for his own, and while cruising over the front the next day he spotted a B.E. 2 escorted by three D.H. 2's. Boelcke dove at the B.E., but the scouts wheeled upon him and attacked, and he turned away from the fight, one of the British machines following. Boelcke next slowed his retreat, luring the D.H. deeper into German territory, and as it drew closer, he suddenly turned upon it, using the Fokker's superior rate of climb and speed. The two pilots entered a grim turning contest; Boelcke won, getting on the tail of the D.H. and thoroughly riddling it. Its pilot, Captain Robert Wilson, brought off a successful forced landing, and escaped from the plane just as it burst into flames. His captors brought Wilson to Lagnicourt, where Boelcke showed Wilson his new *Staffel* and dined with him; such personal touches were a hallmark of the courtly German ace.[28]

Boelcke's pilots discovered that the master had no intentions of letting them fly in combat until they had received thorough instruction in the art of combat flying as he had developed it. In the first weeks of September, he took the time to teach them tactics and air combat strategy, analyzing his own victories as case studies. Basically, he taught eight rules. First, a pilot should secure as many advantages for himself *before* entering a fight as possible; this meant, above all, keeping the sun behind him. Secondly, a pilot should be decisive; if he started an attack, he should carry it through to its conclusion. Thirdly, firing at long range at indistinct targets wasted ammunition and effort; a pilot should fire a well-aimed burst from close range. Fourth, a fighter pilot must ever be on the alert for ruses, and must constantly keep his eyes on his opponent. Fifth, the best method of attack was a diving approach from behind. Sixth, if attacked by a diving opponent, a pilot must not try to dive away or engage in unnecessary and useless aerobatics such as looping or rolling; he should turn into the attacker, and keep turning, being careful not to lose height during the turns relative to the attacker, and try to close on the attacker's tail. Seventh, a pilot should never forget the line of retreat, particularly if over enemy territory. Eighth, pilots should attack as a team in groups of four or six, taking care that several did not dive after one opponent. There were other tricks of the trade as well, such as thoroughly understanding the technology and performance characteristics of one's fighter. Boelcke picked out a number of rendezvous points behind the front and instructed his pilots that if they were separated from him during a dogfight they should fly to one of those points immediately and await other separated pilots, then return home. Under no circumstances would a pilot go out patrolling on his own, nor should a fighter pilot be oblivious to the cloud conditions in the sky. Above cloud, a plane was visible for miles against its white background, like a bug on a wall. Just below cloud, however, a pilot could circle in relative immunity from attack. Boelcke drilled his men until they knew these rules as well as he did. And always he interspersed his instruction with practical experience; on September 15, he lured Captain Guy Cruickshank, a noted

British fighter pilot who commanded A Flight of 70 Squadron, into combat, and shot down Cruickshank's 1½ Strutter from a distance of twenty
yards, killing both Cruickshank and his observer. A Flight, on the same
sortie, lost one other Sopwith and its crew, and the surviving two aircraft
returned with one observer wounded and the other dead. But it was the
events two days later, September 17, that really signalled that Boelcke's
"cubs" had graduated from school and were ready for service.[29]

That Sunday, Boelcke and five of his pupils lifted off the field at
Lagnicourt and climbed towards the lines. Soon he spotted a mixed formation of B.E. 2c's and F.E. 2b's below. Though Boelcke could not know it,
the eight B.E.'s each carried a single 112-pound bomb as well as four
smaller 20-pound bombs, and their target was the Marcoing railroad station. As Boelcke turned after the British planes, the B.E.'s reached the station and bombed it thoroughly; it caught fire and a large secondary explosion sent up a dense cloud of smoke. Then Boelcke's gaggle of Albatros
burst upon the British planes. The bounce caught the British by surprise,
and the German and RFC airplanes mixed it up in a violent dogfight. In
the midst of the confusion, as the chocolate-brown British aircraft dueled
with the shark-like Albatros, seven more German fighters joined the fight.
The Albatros had it all their own way, the six escorting "Fees" being harried and destroyed as they strove to protect the lumbering B.E.2c's. Von
Richthofen closed on one F.E. 2b, but it was a clumsy attack, and the
British crew evaded his approach. He circled back unnoticed, closed from
astern and below, and riddled the F.E., which nosed earthwards, its crew
mortally wounded. He had scored his first official victory as a fighter pilot,
the first of an eventual eighty. Boelcke and the other German pilots had
done as well; all told, four of the F.E.'s and two of the B.E. 2's had fallen.
The battered formation had been saved from further depredations by the
arrival of an offensive patrol from 60 Squadron; Boelcke wisely extracted
his planes from the fight, and *Jasta 2*'s patrol returned to Lagnicourt in
high spirits; the "cubs" had done well.[30]

Other German pilots quickly repeated the success of September 17, and
the obvious superiority of the Albatros, which was entering service in growing numbers, led to a marked increase in the aggressiveness of German
airmen. The Albatros maintained its superiority until the late spring of
1917. To this technological supremacy were added the benefits of careful
pilot tutelage. Boelcke's success in teaching tactics made itself manifest in
the rising victory scores of his airmen; at the same time, operational training within the Royal Flying Corps began a gradual decline that reached its
nadir in early 1917. While the experience and operational skill of German
fighter pilots rose, the average experience and skill level of RFC pilots
declined, to the discomfiture of British squadron commanders. Lanoe

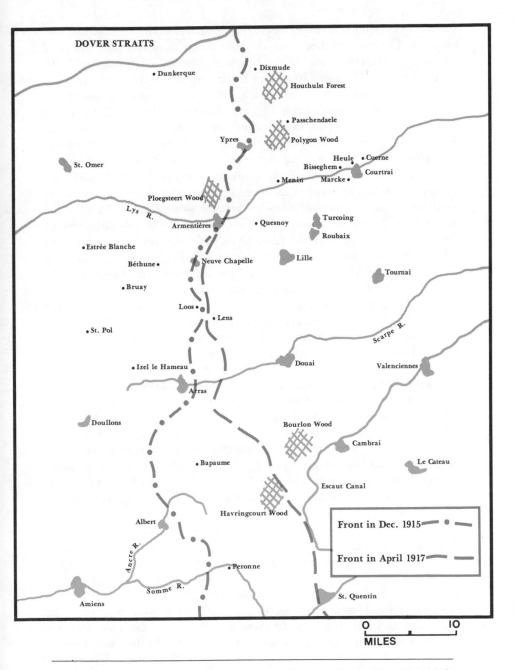

The RFC vs. the Luftstreitkräfte: The Scene of Battle, 1916-1917

Hawker of 24 Squadron, for example, recognized not only the inferiority of his D.H. 2's in comparison with the new Albatros scouts, but the poor training of replacements for his veteran pilots in 24 Squadron.[31] In September, the RFC lost 170 airmen in air combat, nearly three-quarters of these in the last half of the month following the introduction of the Albatros and other new German fighters, and the initiation of *Jagdstaffeln* operations. Trenchard, anxious, drafted a memo for Haig to send General Sir William Robertson, the chief of the Imperial General Staff, concerning the latest state of the Somme fighting. Referring to the new German fighters and their tactics, the Haig memo conceded that the RFC had been unable to conduct as many of its operations behind enemy lines, with the result that German two-seaters, emboldened, now ventured right up to the British lines, "and a few cross them."[32] As the toll of RFC casualties rose in October, the average life expectancy of an RFC pilot at the front dropped to a mere three weeks.[33] The need for new Allied fighter aircraft to meet the Albatros and Halberstadt on equal ground increased accordingly.

Fortunately, the Allied aircraft industry had generated some new combat types that represented a clear advance over the already obsolescent F.E. 2b, D.H. 2, and the earlier Nieuports. France had new and improved models of the Nieuport fighter entering service, notably the Nieuport 17. With greater wing area, a more powerful engine, and various structural refinements, the Nieuport 17 eventually equipped every French fighter *escadrille*, and Britain's RFC and RNAS ordered well over a hundred of the new planes starting even before the Albatros menace had appeared, in July of 1916. Eventually, the Nieuport 17 came to symbolize all of Gustave Delage's trim fighters, and it is the plane that most often comes to mind when "Nieuport" is mentioned. In addition to the Nieuport, however, France had also introduced a new fighter type destined to take its place among the front-rank of World War I combat aircraft, to generate its own family of spin-offs: the Spad 7. Unlike the saucy and exquisitely Gallic Nieuport, the Spad 7 had an angular and rugged appearance that bespoke its great strength and power. Like the Albatros, the Spad 7 typified the trend towards more powerful aircraft, for it had a liquid-cooled 150-horsepower Hispano-Suiza engine designed by Marc Birkigt. Designed by Louis Bechereau, who had given aviation its first wooden monocoque structures with the prewar Deperdussin racer, the Spad did not have a complex plywood monocoque shape, as might have been expected, but rather a traditional "built-up" fuselage of stringers and formers. Its great strength ensured the safety of even the most ham-fisted pilot, and it could be flung around the sky with relative abandon, unlike many of its contemporaries. The Spad 7 first fired its guns in anger on August 23, 1916, when French fighter pilot Armand Pinsard shot down a German plane. It quickly became the favorite mount of *Les Cigognes* (replacing even the Nieuport in their affections), including *Le Grand Chasseur* himself, Lieutenant Georges Guynemer. British interest in the Spad dated almost to the time of its design, and the appearance of the Albatros and Halberstadt fighters accelerated Trenchard's desire to acquire the new machine for the RFC.

Britain had followed a completely different design philosophy with its own Sopwith Scout, more popularly known as the "Pup." The graceful Pup had a delicacy of line that showed an obvious resemblance to the earlier 1½ Strutter; in fact, the Scout, in the eyes of its pilots, was the 1½ Strutter's "pup," hence its popular (but officially frowned-upon) nickname. Designed by Herbert Smith, who had created the earlier two-seater, the Pup constituted a masterpiece of careful and creative design. Its two equal-span wings and well-harmonized controls endowed it with superlative handling characteristics; for the sheer pleasure of flying, the Pup stands apart as the finest flying machine of the First World War. And it did it all on a mere 80 horsepower furnished by either Le Rhône, Clerget, or Gnôme rotary engines. Because of Sopwith's close affiliation with the Admiralty, the Pup, like the 1½ Strutter before it, first entered service with the RNAS, in September 1916. It was in combat before the end of the month; on September 24, for example, naval pilot S.J. Goble, flying from Dunkerque, shot down an L.V.G. two-seater near Ghistelles. Eventually the Pup entered widespread service with the RFC as well.[34]

All of these machines were forward-firing tractor biplanes that had provisions for synchronized machine guns (though the Nieuport most often flew with its now-standard machine gun mounted above the wing). Yet despite their merits, all had their share of problems that, at times, limited their usefulness. The Nieuport had a poorly designed structural interface between its lower wing spar and the circular fitting through which the spar passed. As a result, it could shed its lower wing during aerobatics or a high-speed dive, often with disastrous effects for the unfortunate pilot. The Spad had an unusual problem; unlike most aircraft, which had trouble keeping their engines running cool, the Spad had problems with its engine not running hot enough! This limited its combat effectiveness until adequate radiator designs and engine cowling shapes appeared (often jury-rigged in the field) that kept the engine temperature high enough for combat efficiency. The Pup, despite its excellent performance, was clearly an underpowered machine: the same basic design formula, with more power, was used for Sopwith's next fighter, the war-winning (but brutish) Camel. Finally, all three aircraft were single-gun machines, at a time when Germany had standardized the twin-machine gun armament. Not until the Camel appeared in the summer of 1917 would Britain field its first fighter designed for a twin-synchronized machine gun installation.

The RFC had to await deliveries of the Spad and Nieuport from French stocks, and this logistical problem, coupled with over-optimistic French production predictions, delayed the arrival of both fighters in British units. Indeed, it was not until the early part of 1917 that either of these fighters reached high levels of service with the RFC.

By the fall of 1916, Trenchard forecast a need for twenty RFC fighter squadrons, increasing the ratio of fighters to British reconnaissance and cooperation aircraft to two to one.[35] On October 17, Lord Curzon, the president of Britain's Air Board, requested from the war cabinet that Trenchard's urgent need for fighters be met with aircraft from the Royal Naval Air Service. Throughout 1916, the RNAS had proven itself a most cooperative service in supporting the needs of the RFC, and it did likewise now, in Trenchard's hour of need. At Dunkerque, the RNAS had eighty aircraft, half of which were classified as fighters. The navy decided to assemble a composite fighter squadron comprising a six-aircraft flight from each of the three naval air wings at Dunkerque, thus establishing the new unit with a complement of Pups, Nieuports, and 1½ Strutters. Designated No. 8 (Naval) Squadron, and popularly known as "Naval Eight," the new unit arrived at its base at Vert Galand near Amiens in late October. By the end of the year, Naval Eight had wisely replaced its Nieuports and 1½ Strutters with the better Pup, and had used the little fighter to shoot down twenty German planes (four others had fallen to the Nieuports and none to the already obsolescent 1½ Strutters). On December 24, the first RFC unit equipped with the Pup, 54 Squadron, arrived in France, probably the best Christmas present British fighter squadrons could have gotten.[36]

With the introduction of the Albatros and Halberstadt fighters, Germany once again stood poised on the threshold of air supremacy over the Western Front. But this time, with the dramatic downfall of the Fokker firmly in mind, the individuals commanding and directing the development of German airpower determined not to stop with the introduction of a new type. Answering the call of many service pilots, they undertook to change the very structure of the *Fliegertruppen* itself. There had been early signs of this; in July 1916, the German *Kriegsministerium* had appointed the immensely capable Major Wilhelm Siegert as the new *Idflieg*. Moreover, the sacking of the chief of the German General Staff, von Falkenhayn, architect of the bloodbath at Verdun, in favor of the astute Paul von Hindenburg elevated an officer with a keen appreciation for airpower: Hindenburg's deputy Erich Ludendorff. Both Hindenburg and Ludendorff realized that the former's victory at Tannenberg had stemmed from German aerial reconnaissance; aviation would come to occupy a key section in Hindenburg's plan for total industrial mobilization that would go into effect over the fall and winter of 1916-1917. Ironically, by demanding standardization and reduction of the numbers of different types of fighters and other aircraft being produced, the plan would eventually result in over-reliance on the Albatros long past the time when it should have been replaced with more advanced designs. The design initiative would pass to the Allies, and Germany would not regain it before the end of the war.[37]

But first came the reorganization of the fighting service itself, which took place in October 1916, largely as the result of the efforts of Oberstleutnant Hermann von der Lieth-Thomsen, the German *Feldflugchef*. A photograph of Thomsen resembles Dürer's engraving of Desiderius Erasmus, the great northern humanist of the sixteenth century; one can see the same forceful personality, the same tenacious intellect. Ludendorff, in his memoirs, praised Thomsen for his "dynamic creative powers," and for his part, Thomsen always remembered their work together before the war, noting particularly the strong support that then-Oberst Ludendorff had given to his suggestions and programs.[38] As early as March 1916, Thomsen had concluded that the air services of the German army and navy, together with all aviation establishments and other organizations, should be centralized under a single authority, preferably an imperial air ministry. Such a proposal did not appeal at all to the Germany navy, but the army followed his call with interest. The Somme offensive swept aside all doubts; the glaring weaknesses of the army air service were evident to all, and on October 8, Kaiser Wilhelm II issued a decree that made Thomsen's proposals the core of a new organization. The decree placed all army aviation units at home and abroad, including antiaircraft forces, under the authority of a commanding general of the air forces. The Kaiser appointed Generalleutnant Ernst Wilhelm von Hoeppner, a professional cavalry officer, to this position, abbreviated *Kogenluft*, and he held it through the end of the war. Thomsen's position as *Feldflugchef* was abolished, and he became Hoeppner's right-hand man as chief of staff, and was soon promoted to Oberst. The ever-capable Siegert, promoted to Oberstleutnant, remained as *Idflieg*, where he could do the most good.[39]

This triumvirate, Hoeppner, Thomsen, and Siegert, ran the *Luftstreitkrafte*, the Imperial German Air Service, until its defeat in 1918. The reorganization had not in a true sense created an independent air force, such as the *Luftwaffe* was in Hitler's Germany, and the *Luftstreitkräfte* remained, as did the RFC, an appendage—but a most important one—of the army. (Great Britain would become the first nation to organize an independent air force with the creation of the Royal Air Force on April 1, 1918, merging the RFC and the RNAS, to the general happiness of both services.) The three men believed that the technological superiority of the

Albatros would enable the *Jagdstaffeln* to quickly gain ascendancy over the British and French, provided — and this was Siegert's task — that they were available in sufficient numbers to match the numerical strength of the Allies. Hoeppner wanted no less than thirty-six *Jastas* in service on the Western Front by the spring of 1917. Germany's *Kriegsministerium* did not formally announce the reorganization of the German air service until November 20, 1916. By that time, the three men and their staffs were busily at work, having recognized, as Hoeppner subsequently recollected, that "numbers, leadership, fighting spirit, and the technical excellence of fighter aircraft themselves would increasingly determine the outcome of the struggle for air superiority." The months ahead would be filled with bitter fighting, combat, ironically, that Oswald Boelcke would miss.[40]

V.
The Resurgence
of the *Luftstreitkräfte*

On Saturday, October 28, 1916, British air activity kept Boelcke's airmen busy. The master himself flew four sorties over the front, despite rain and heavy overcast, in the morning. In the afternoon, the pilots sat in readiness in their quarters at Lagnicourt, waiting for orders to scramble. Ernst Böhme, the unit's "old man," had just begun a chess game with Boelcke when, at approximately four o'clock, a call came from ground observers at the front: British aircraft had crossed the lines. Chess forgotten, Boelcke, Böhme, von Richthofen, and three other pilots raced to their waiting fighters; slipping over the rainy field, the six Albatros left the earth behind and disappeared to the west. Soon, cruising near Pozieres, the six came upon two De Havilland D.H. 2's from Hawker's squadron. At once, Boelcke dove to the attack, and the alert RFC pilots began evasive action. Von Richthofen picked out one D.H. 2 as his victim, but had to break off his attack when one of his fellow pilots flew into his way. The cubs were forgetting the leader's cautious rules in their eagerness for a kill. Böhme and Boelcke both closed on the other D.H. 2 when suddenly the second De Havilland cut across their path. To avoid a collision, both Boelcke and Böhme banked sharply and, in so doing, lost sight of each other, the wing surfaces blocking the pilots' view. Then, only yards away, Böhme saw Boelcke's Albatros closing quickly on his own. Mutually surprised, the two men maneuvered to clear each other, Böhme starting a climb, and Boelcke diving away. But the two planes were too close, and with only the briefest and lightest of impacts, Böhme's undercarriage struck Boelcke's upper left wing, crumpling the outermost portion and tearing away one side of Böhme's landing gear. The two British pilots saw the collision. Then six more German fighters joined the melee, and only by violent maneuvering were the D.H. 2's able to avoid being shot down. As the two damaged

Albatros fell away, Böhme recovered after dropping "a few hundred meters" and steered for home. He saw Boelcke's fighter in a gentle easterly glide; it passed through a thin cloud layer and, apparently buffeted by gusts, plunged down in an ever-steepening dive, crashing near a German artillery battery. Böhme, Boelcke's closest friend, tried to land by the wreck, but many shell craters and trenches made it hopeless. Filled with anxiety, he returned to Lagnicourt, where he landed safely, though the damaged landing gear threw the plane on its back in a wild somersault. The D.H. 2's survived, against all odds. But Boelcke did not. Unsecured in his fighter by a restraint harness, he was fatally injured when it struck the earth; secured, he might have lived.[1]

The death of Boelcke shocked the German fighter community in a way that none other—not even Immelmann's—had. Only the death of Manfred von Richthofen in 1918 would have as profound an effect. As befitted a holder of the *Pour le Mérite*, his funeral service was held in the cathedral of Cambrai, his parents and brother escorting his remains back to Dessau for internment. At the funeral, an RFC airplane flew overhead and dropped a laurel wreath by parachute with the inscription, "To the memory of Captain Boelcke, our brave and chivalrous foe. From the British Royal Flying Corps." One of his victims, Captain Robert Wilson, shot down on September 2, brought a wreath of his own. The Kaiser, by Imperial decree, renamed *Jasta 2 Jasta Boelcke*, his life to serve as a model for all aspiring fighter pilots. Greatly saddened, Böhme continued combat flying, eventually rising to command the *Jasta Boelcke* in August 1917 before being shot down and killed over the Zillebecker Teich near Ypres in late November of that year.[2]

Boelcke's spirit lived on, as did the example of his remarkable chivalry. He was one of the few authentic courtly figures in the often over-romanticized history of World War I combat flying. His combat *dicta* became the official air tactical doctrine of the German fighter forces. It is impossible to say what turn his career might have taken had he lived; possibly, indeed probably, it was inevitable that he should perish in combat, as did so many of the other "greats" of the First World War. Without question, Boelcke deserves recognition as the first great fighter tactician, and his grasp of tactics might have manifested itself in other ways as 1916 led into 1917. Ludendorff is alleged to have remarked upon the death of von Richthofen that the "Red Baron" was worth three divisions; perhaps so, in a war where divisions were thrown away so carelessly.[3] But von Richthofen was in no sense the tactician or air leader that his mentor had been. Indeed, though all paid lip service to the Boelcke *dicta*, the leading German fighter pilots, like the leading French ones, seemed more concerned with running up large individual scores than with training pools of skilled pilots. Though the German air service ran fighter transition schools through which rated pilots passed before being posted to a combat *Jasta*, the careful tutelage in the *Jasta* that Boelcke gave his cubs quickly became a thing of the past with his death. Through mid-1917, the average German fighter pilot had more flying experience when posted to the front than did his British counterpart. But after mid-1917 this changed. By the end of the war, the balance had gone the other way; RAF flight commanders took pains to ensure that their pilots were ready for front flying before sending them across the lines. German pilots' memoirs, on the other hand, give the impression that newcomers were often thrown straight from the replacement pool into combat — as the RFC pilots had been in 1916-1917. It is hard to imagine this situation existing had Boelcke lived, for his position and record would have assured him great administrative responsibility for the development of German fighter forces, especially in the dark days of 1917-1918.

Boelcke was dead, and the air war went on. Von Richthofen mercilessly demonstrated the technological gap between the Albatros, with its sleek, powerful, streamlined design, and the ungainly D.H. 2 pusher on November 23, when he shot down and killed Lanoe Hawker, V.C., commander of 24 Squadron. Hawker had crossed the lines that morning as one of a flight of four D.H. 2's led by Captain J. C. Andrews. Andrews led the patrol in an attack on six of *Jasta Boelcke*'s Albatros. Just then, one of the De Havillands developed engine trouble, a not uncommon occurrence, and turned away. Hawker and the other two unwisely pressed on, but an Albatros damaged Andrews' engine with a well-placed burst, and the leader himself had to limp away, escorted by the third De Havilland for safety. Whether the Albatros pilots were busy chasing Andrews, who made a successful forced landing behind Allied lines, or whether by choice they let Hawker duel it out with von Richthofen will remain a mystery; perhaps the recent tragedy of the Böhme-Boelcke collision was uppermost in their minds and they felt that the eager von Richthofen would easily dispose of the Englishman. In any case, the individual combat that broke out was one of the most memorable — if tragic — of the war. High over Bapaume, where Boelcke had fallen less than a month before, von Richthofen and Hawker pirouetted in a deadly ballet. Each strove to get on the other's tail, and if Hawker was perhaps the better pilot, von Richthofen undoubtedly had the better machine. First they turned twenty times to the left, then thirty times to the right. Von Richthofen realized he was up against a tenacious opponent, one who showed no desire to break away. The D.H. 2 could out-turn the faster Albatros in a straight turning contest, but von Richthofen's fighter could out-climb and out-dive it with ease. As they circled and turned, Hawker occasionally waved to the German pilot as if saying, von

Richthofen later wrote, "Well, well, how do you do?" The business-like von Richthofen had no time for such frills, and instead concentrated on getting the D.H. 2 in his sights. The prevailing west wind, a natural ally of Germany throughout the war, blew Hawker's fighter deeper and deeper behind German lines; von Richthofen knew that Hawker would soon have to break for home or run out of fuel over German territory. By this time, the fight had descended from over 10,000 feet to less than 1,000 feet; in vain endeavor to evade the German, Hawker looped several times. The effort failed, and as a last resort, Hawker nosed down just above the ground and began zigzagging for British lines. With his superior speed and armament, it was the opportunity the German had been waiting for. In a flash his Albatros was after Hawker's plane, its twin Spandau guns firing constantly. Momentarily von Richthofen's Spandaus jammed, but he cleared them and resumed firing; his following burst killed Hawker, and the D.H. 2, with its dead pilot, stalled at one hundred feet and then plunged to earth. Always an avid trophy hunter, von Richthofen tastelessly claimed Hawker's Lewis machine gun from the wreckage and mounted it over the door of his room in the family home at Schweidnitz.[4]

The death of "the English Boelcke" (as von Richthofen dubbed him) dramatized the changes that had taken place in air fighting since the summer. "There is nothing resembling the fighting that took place in the second half of July during the present time," wrote one D.H. 2 pilot; indeed there wasn't, for the tables had again turned.[5] The German observation planes, again emboldened by the success of the Albatros fighters, resumed flights across the lines, to the consternation of Trenchard and British airmen. Reflecting on those days, another D.H. 2 pilot, James T. B. McCudden, who would become a legendary British ace only to die in a flying accident before war's end, wrote of the superiority of the Albatros over the D.H. 2. Remembering how German reconnaissance machines droned high over Allied lines, he penned "Oh! How I envied the other squadrons who were also at Le Hameau and had Nieuports with their wonderful climb."[6] Unfortunately, until mid-April of 1917, the majority of British fighters on the front would be the same mix of D.H. 2's and F.E. 2b's that had mastered the Fokker over the Somme. They were no match for the Albatros of 1916, and certainly not for the advanced Albatros that entered service at the end of that year.

During December 1916, thirty-nine RFC airmen died over the front; of the twenty-seven aircraft downed, seventeen fell over British lines, an ominous sign to Trenchard, who feared a major switch in German tactics.[7] Air casualties paled into insignificance beside the thousands on the ground, but the RFC's pilots constituted only two percent of that service, and the RFC itself a mere three percent of the total British Expeditionary

Force in France. Proportionally, then, deaths among airmen approached one in four, a ratio closely comparable to the loss rate among infantrymen on the ground.[8] Moreover, if the British fighters could not prevent German fighters from marauding among the RFC's cooperation, reconnaissance, bombing, and artillery-spotting aircraft, the air defeats might have a decisive impact upon the conduct of the war on the ground as well. Trenchard visited London in mid-December to ask for an immediate increase in the RFC's fighter strength, arguing that he had only two squadrons (including Naval Eight) capable of matching the Albatros, and could expect only a further nine squadrons capable of matching the Albatros to enter service before the end of March, far short of the twenty squadrons he believed were really needed. Some historians have blamed Trenchard in part for the RFC's problems at this stage of the war, accusing him of tardiness in alerting London to the problems he faced. But, in fact, Trenchard had alerted the War Office and cabinet of his difficulties, as evidenced by the previous cited memo from Haig to Sir William Robertson sent in September, 1916, about two weeks after Boelcke's cubs had initiated the era of the Albatros. And in addition, Trenchard's problems could only be resolved by the introduction of new and more capable aircraft. He looked to the new year in the hope that his fighter squadrons would receive a host of new aircraft, including more Pups, the new Bristol F.2A two-seat fighter, and other designs. Above all else, Trenchard feared technological obsolescence, for it could destroy the RFC. Already, by the end of 1916, the excellent Albatros D II had replaced the earlier D I, and even it was giving way to the new Albatros D III, which incorporated a sesquiplane layout based on the Nieuport, giving it a distinctive "V-strut" appearance (but endowing the previously rugged design with the same weak lower-wing that had plagued the French fighter). When W. Sefton Brancker, Britain's director of air organization (essentially the manager of all RFC equipment), informed Trenchard in mid-January 1917 that factory labor disputes had delayed the completion of the new Bristol F.2A's, preventing their being sent to France, Trenchard exploded in frustration, accusing Brancker of not acting on his previous warnings and expecting the RFC to fight into 1917 with machines outdated by the end of 1916. He predicted that, "We shall be hopelessly outclassed . . . there will be an outcry from all the pilots . . . what I have asked for is absolutely necessary."[9] (The F.2A's entered service by April.)

The same win-the-war-in-this-year optimism that had prevailed at the beginning of 1915 and 1916 prevailed in 1917 as well. Looking forward to the spring of 1917, the Allies hoped to mount an offensive along a hundred-mile sector of the Western Front, from Arras south to the Aisne River. If all went well, British troops would attack north at Arras, while

French troops under the command of General Robert Nivelle would swarm across German positions at the southern sector of the front, ending the stalemate and bringing the conflict to a quick close. Nivelle, a charismatic but fatally flawed military leader whose popularity crested with his text-book recapture of Fort Douaumont at Verdun, proposed to duplicate the earlier feat along an entire front. First, a massive artillery bombardment would saturate German positions with high explosives. Next, French infantrymen would advance under a creeping barrage, smashing through German lines and then driving deep behind them. Overhead, the French and British air services would support this Allied thrust with reconnaissance and cooperation missions. Unfortunately, through both French carelessness and chance, the Germans knew all about the proposed offensive, and it was destined to failure.[10] With the RFC facing serious supply and equipment shortages, Field Marshal Haig doubted that Trenchard's airmen could provide the offensive with the necessary support, and as January passed into February, he repeatedly urged the war cabinet to get new aircraft into the RFC's fighter squadrons. While Germany did not yet possess aerial superiority over the Western Front, January had been a month of increasingly bitter fighting as the *Luftstreitkräfte*'s aggressiveness grew. Forty-one RFC airmen were killed or missing. Haig wrote to the war cabinet, warning that Germany would continue to enjoy a qualitative superiority over British aircraft — and might gain a quantitative superiority as well — in the weeks ahead. He prophesied that "we cannot expect to gain supremacy in the air in April, and it is even possible that it may pass to the enemy."[11]

German air strength grew steadily, as indicated by the numbers of Albatros and Halberstadt fighters in service over the entire front:

Month	Halberstadt	Albatros
September 1916	25	7
November 1916	55	78
January 1917	104	266
March 1917	83	315

Halberstadt strength declined as the newer D III Albatros entered service. In January 1917, only 13 of the 266 Albatros at the front were D III's; in March, 137 of the 315 were D III's.[12] Together with the changes in the strength of the *Luftstreitkräfte's Jagdstaffeln* came changes in personnel and command that also exerted a profound influence on subsequent events. In January 1917, von Richthofen was ordered to leave *Jasta Boelcke* and assume command of *Jasta 11*, a unit that so far had failed to down a single Allied airplane. Almost simultaneously, he received notification of the award of the *Pour le Mérite*. Since his sixteenth victory, the German airman had fretted at not having the Blue Max; both Boelcke and Immelmann had received theirs much earlier in their careers. The news eased somewhat the pangs of leaving his old *Jasta* for the responsibilities of commanding his own. Like Boelcke — but without Boelcke's all-consuming interest in training — von Richthofen instructed the pilots of *Jasta 11* in the tactics of air fighting. Many of them — Karl Allmenröder, Karl Schaefer, and Kurt Wolff in particular — soon developed a deadly proficiency as a result of von Richthofen's tutelage. The von Richthofen flair for action manifested itself from the first day the new *Jasta* commander took over. He shot down an ungainly F.E. 8 pusher fighter, breaking the unit's scoreless record; on his second day, he downed an F.E. 2b. Von Richthofen had embarked on what would soon appear to be a one-man war against the Royal Flying Corps.[13]

With the improvement of flying weather in March 1917, the intensity of air fighting, which had eased from November through January before picking up tempo, increased dramatically. In March, the RFC lost 120 aircraft, divided almost equally between machines shot down over German lines and British lines. In these combats, the Albatros generally proved supreme, though chance still played a more than adequate role. On March 9, for example, nine F.E. 8 pushers, awkward and slow single-seat fighters having no advantage over the earlier D.H. 2, met a group of aggressive Albatros led by von Richthofen. In the action that followed, the German pilots shot down four of the F.E.'s, and severely damaged all of the remaining five, which had to be force-landed. Thus, in one combat, 40 Squadron lost roughly three-quarters of its effective strength. Ironically, in this combat, one Albatros was seen to fall earthwards; its pilot was von Richthofen, who, in the midst of the dogfight, smelled petrol. Fearing the worst, he quickly switched off the engine and glided to a safe landing, finding afterwards that his fuel tanks had been pierced by fire from the F.E.'s. Had he allowed himself to get into a vulnerable position? For all of his expertise, many of von Richthofen's victims were slow two-seaters, and he occasionally blundered when attacking fighters — as he did in his last, fatal combat in April 1918. Perhaps the F.E. pilots had been lucky, or perhaps it was a random shot whining through the airspace. In any case, had it been an incendiary bullet, the subsequent history of the air war on the Western Front might have been considerably different.[14]

Trenchard now found himself in virtually the same position he had been in during the period of the Fokker scourge a year before. Somehow he had to cut rapidly mounting losses, but if he did not continue to press the Germans in the air, they could ravage over the front with ease. In preparation for the imminent Arras offensive, he had to continue reconnaissance sorties far behind German lines, especially following Germany's shrewd withdrawal of forces behind the so-called Hindenburg line in mid-March, which negated the potential value of Nivelle's reckless gamble. The Hindenburg line was a network of no fewer than three trench systems with concrete fortifications and shelters hewn from limestone deposits, linked with a ridge, the Chemin des Dames, soon to be drenched with the blood of Nivelle's troops.[15] Haig needed information on German defenses east of the Hindenburg line, in preparation for Britain's Arras offensive. As the demand for reconnaissance missions drove flying hours up, the average time flown per casualty dropped, reflecting the rapidly mounting losses. An examination of RFC aircrew losses by month, together with the average flying time in hours per casualty, and RFC monthly operational flying time clearly indicates the quandary confronting Trenchard:[16]

Month	Aircrew KIA/MIA	Total Hours Flown	Hours/Casualty
October 1916	75	13,500	186
November 1916	59	10,600	179
December 1916	39	5,200	133
January 1917	41	10,500	256
February 1917	65	12,000	183
March 1917	143	14,500	101

In a bid to conserve strength and still maintain some element of surprise in the British Arras offensive, Trenchard ordered the seven squadrons of the RFC's Ninth Wing to cease operations until a mere five days before the planned offensive. But ground commanders had such a pressing need for reconnaissance that the Ninth Wing could not afford to stay on the ground, though efforts were made to minimize its activities. Predictably, as the recon aircraft winged their way deep into German-held territory, they were badly mauled by waiting German fighters. On March 24, for example, 70 Squadron dispatched six 1½ Strutters on a reconnaissance mission to Valenciennes, a place one Australian fighter pilot recollected as "the most Hun-infested region in the north of France."[17] Twelve Albatros bounced the formation near Oisy, shooting down two of them and so badly damaging the remaining four that they had to break off the mission to return home. Only one of the four was flyable the next day, when the squadron attempted to repeat the mission with another six aircraft. That day, a formation of Albatros from *Jasta* 5 and *Jasta* 6 met the 1½ Strutters, and shot down five of the six — the sixth survived; it had turned back earlier with engine trouble.[18] In less than a year, the 1½ Strutter had gone from being a fearsome opponent to being a relatively easy kill for German fighters. The two 1½ Strutter units, 70 and 45 Squadrons, became known as the "Suicide Club." So great were the casualties among aerial gunners that the RFC was forced to recruit volunteers from infantry on the ground; as a result, not only were "green" pilots with relatively little air-time embarking on combat missions, their observer-gunners were often equally unseasoned and uncertain of what to do in a dogfight. Typical is a story related by RFC pilot Frank Courtney, who flew as a flight commander with 70 Squadron. A volunteering ex-infantry gunner arrived at the front; during his briefing, he asked what kind of a joke had prompted the replacement pool personnel to dub the unit the Suicide Club. The following afternoon, he was posted missing.[19]

According to Haig's plan, the British First and Third Armies would bear the brunt of the fighting in the upcoming Arras offensive. Over this front, the RFC had an active strength by April 1917 of twenty-five squadrons, made up of approximately 365 serviceable airplanes, of which approximately a third were fighters. On paper, this gave the RFC a numerical advantage in fighters over the *Luftstreitkräfte* units supporting the German Sixth Army on the opposite side of the line, for the German air service had a total of only 195 aircraft on that sector of the front, approximately half of which were fighters. And over the entire British front from Lille to Peronne, the RFC had an even greater numerical advantage. Facing approximately 264 German aircraft, of which 114 were fighters, the RFC could muster 754 aircraft, including 385 fighters. (A preponderance of German fighter strength was deployed against French forces in anticipation of the Nivelle offensive.)[20]

But numerical superiority can be deceptive, and lead to false optimism. The Albatros fighters then at the front, especially the new D III, were superior to any British fighter then in service. Flown with skill, the Sopwith Pup, Spad 7, and Nieuport 17 could give an Albatros trouble, and the two squadrons of the new Sopwith Triplane would give the *Jagdstaffeln* a nasty shock. Trenchard placed great faith in the Bristol F.2A and the Royal Aircraft Factory's S.E. 5 to keep the Albatros in check, and eventually these two great aircraft—representatives of a fourth generation in Great War fighter design—would do just that. But meantime, both were untried in combat, and the S.E. 5 would not undergo its baptism by fire until April 23. Much of the air fighting in April would fall to the F.E. 2b's and 2d's, a few F.E. 8's, and even a few remaining D.H. 2's—Hawker's old squadron would soldier on with the D.H. 2, at heavy cost, until its replacement in May by the unsatisfactory D.H. 5. At the beginning of the Arras offensive,

Trenchard could count on the following squadrons to attempt to stave off the Albatros on somewhat equal terms:

54 Squadron	Sopwith Pup
66 Squadron	Sopwith Pup
3 Squadron (Naval)	Sopwith Pup
1 Squadron (Naval)	Sopwith Triplane
8 Squadron (Naval)	Sopwith Triplane
19 Squadron	Spad 7
23 Squadron	Spad 7
48 Squadron	Bristol F.2A
1 Squadron	Nieuports
29 Squadron	Nieuports
40 Squadron	Nieuports
60 Squadron	Nieuports
6 Squadron (Naval)	Nieuports

Trenchard urgently acquired as many Nieuports as possible, for though this fighter was obsolescent and, in fact, slightly inferior to the Sopwith Pup, it could give an Albatros a stiff fight. On St. Patrick's Day, 1917, the French transferred sixty Nieuports to the RFC in return for thirty 1½ Strutters (there is little doubt who received the better deal). The trade was a tribute to the strong bonds between the *Aviation militaire* and the RFC, the result of the long-standing Trenchard-du Peuty partnership that had worked so well at Verdun. Trenchard also sought Spads, but though some were eventually forthcoming, the type never equipped more Western Front RFC fighter squadrons than the two with which Trenchard began the Arras offensive.[21]

Next to equipment, training is everything in air combat, and here, for this moment at least, the *Jagdstaffeln* had a priceless advantage; the average German fighter pilot had longer flying experience than the average British pilot. Faulty training methods and outdated aircraft conspired to produce pilots not ready for the rigors of combat flying. Until Robert Smith-Barry's so-called "School of Special Flying" at Gosport demonstrated the desirability of specially training flight instructors, most instructors were pilots returned from the front for a badly needed rest. They lacked any formal training in how to teach flying. Training was not altogether safe: British training establishments averaged a crash per 155 flights; more than half of all RFC pilot fatalities during the Great War occurred during flight training. (In contrast, German training deaths were but a quarter of those in the war.) The need for pilots at the front led to a drop in the RFC's already mediocre standards, so that by early 1917, the average RFC pilot arrived at the front with about fifteen hours solo time, including two night landings—and less time was not uncommon. Frank Courtney recalled one fighter pilot who joined his squadron with a mere four hours solo time. The average German pilot passed through a fighter transition school at Valenciennes giving him lead-in experience that greatly enhanced his chances of survival. In contrast, the average RFC pilot was more often than not thrown into the fray after a perfunctory flight check by his squadron or flight commander. As historian Alan Morris has bluntly noted, "those who learned quickly would survive long enough for their replacements to reach France."[22]

Gordon Taylor, a newly-arrived Australian pilot with 66 Squadron was one of these ill-trained replacements; his second mission, flown in March 1917, was nearly his last. Near Douai he lost formation amid some light cloud, not having been thoroughly trained in formation flying. Alone over German lines, he spotted an Albatros formation. Overconfident, Taylor nosed his Sopwith Pup towards an Albatros straggling behind the rest of the formation, and then opened fire while still hopelessly out of range. The straggler easily evaded the clumsy attack, and the rest of the Albatros formation turned on the lone Pup as Taylor frantically maneuvered to escape. It was a rude awakening to the limitations of not only his combat skills, but the underpowered if agile Pup as well. Already a gifted pilot—he would survive the war and become a noted long-distance air explorer—Taylor kept maneuvering constantly, and was able to avoid being shot down for twenty minutes, until the Albatros had either shot off all their ammunition or reached the limits of their fuel. Shaken, he returned to his base at Vert Galand, convinced that "only by cunning and unfailing alertness could I survive."[23]

The Aisne offensive got off to a delayed start. Nivelle pushed the date back from April 1 to April 5, then to April 10, and finally settled on April 15. Haig had, meanwhile, set the date of his own Arras push for April 9, Easter Monday. Trenchard decided the RFC would go to battle five days before Haig's general offensive, and, accordingly, made plans for intensive flight operations to begin on the 4th. The month's fighting for von Richthofen actually began on April 2, when his orderly awakened him amid the sounds of pounding feet and roaring engines with, *"Herr Leutnant*, the English are here!" A group of B.E. 2d's from 13 Squadron were raiding his field. Von Richthofen ran to his all-red Albatros D III, and, accompanied by his squadron mates, took off in pursuit of the obsolete British planes. One of them gamely attacked von Richthofen who, in his memoirs, generously labeled it a "two-seat fighter," but it was not, and von Richthofen was no easy mark. He planted his sleek Albatros on the tail of the B.E. and hung on through a wild low-level chase towards the front.

Finally, the B.E. 2d's pilot flew too low, and with the observer still firing at von Richthofen's fighter, the British plane ploughed into a block of houses in the little village of Farbus. Before day's end, he had shot down yet another British plane, a 1½ Strutter. Von Richthofen had destroyed the first two of the more than twenty aircraft he would down that month, a period not inappropriately remembered by RFC veterans as "Bloody April."[24]

Trenchard's air offensive had hardly begun when the RFC received a severe shock that, fortunately, proved but a temporary setback. On April 5, a formation of six of 48 Squadron's new Bristol F.2A two-seat fighters left on a patrol over German lines. Designed by Frank Barnwell, the F.2A had been intended at first as a reconnaissance and general-purpose airplane powered by the new Rolls Royce Falcon 190-horsepower engine. As it emerged, however, the F.2A was quite a different airplane indeed, with a synchronized forward-firing gun, a Lewis gun on a Scarff mounting for the observer, and excellent handling qualities. The power of the Falcon gave this large biplane the maneuverability of a single-seat scout; later models, the F.2B, had an even more powerful 275-horsepower Falcon and served until 1932, soldiering with the Royal Air Force. The location of the pilot and observer facilitated good crew coordination, and the F.2A can be said to have constituted the first true two-place multimission fighter. Evaluation flights over the winter of 1916-1917 drew enthusiastic endorsement from pilots and observers with frontline experience, and Haig and Trenchard had decided to keep the F.2A away from combat until the opening of the Arras offensive when, it was hoped, the Bristol would come as a nasty surprise to the German air service. But, through tactical misuse rather than technological inferiority, the nasty surprise fell upon the RFC.

Captain W. Leefe Robinson, V.C., led 48 Squadron's first offensive patrol in the type on April 5. Leefe Robinson had attained fame the previous summer when, as a nightfighter pilot over London, he shot down a German army airship. It was a measure of the terror in which dirigibles were held that he was awarded the V.C.: Reginald Warneford also received one for downing a Zeppelin over Belgium in the summer of 1915. His experience in flying fighters against other fighters was, however, negligible, and his inexperience, coupled with poor tactical doctrine and an unfounded rumor that the F.2A would not stand up to combat maneuvering (in fact, it was an exceptionally robust airplane) led to disaster. Standard doctrine for two-seaters held that in a dogfight, the pilot should maneuver the airplane to give the observer the best possible chance of hitting an attacker. Thus, the doctrine was basically a defensive one. It did not take into account that the F.2A was ideally suited for offensive operations, in which the pilot does the attacking, flying it like a single-seater, and the

WESTERN FRONT: APRIL 1917

observer-gunner takes care of anyone unwise enough to attack the plane from behind. So, when Leefe Robinson's patrol ran across von Richthofen and four other *Jasta 11* Albatros near Douai, they immediately went on the defensive, flying a roughly straight course and trying to let the observers have a clean shot at the attacking Germans. The Albatros treated them like any other two-seater; apparently none of the RFC pilots attempted to get into position to use the forward-firing Vickers machine gun, and four of the Bristols fell, including Leefe Robinson's. The remaining two returned to base, riddled with bullets. Taken prisoner, Leefe Robinson's health deteriorated rapidly in captivity, and he died only two months after the armistice from influenza. The loss of the Bristols was a stunning setback for Trenchard's hopes that the F.2A would turn the tide over the Western Front during April. But it had a beneficial outcome. Von Richthofen dismissed the F.2A as an airplane of little consequence (he subsequently changed his opinion dramatically), thus dooming many German fighter pilots who encountered it. Knowing how *not* to fly the airplane caused RFC crews to exploit its maneuverability to the fullest, so that by the end of April they were already beginning to fly the plane more aggressively, using the gunner for defense and the forward-firing gun for offensive purposes. Even as late as the summer of 1918, the Bristol Fighter was in a class by itself among two-seaters, leading one German pilot, Rudolf Stark, to pen in his diary that "we are amazed to see how nimble they are." The Bristol Fighter typified the fourth generation of World War One aircraft, fighters such as the Spad 13, S.E. 5, and Fokker D VII: rugged, exceptionally well thought-out, very powerful aircraft capable of long years of productive and useful service dating far beyond the armistice of 1918. One shudders to think how the potential of this fine fighter, the first true multirole combat aircraft, might have been wasted had the faulty tactics of April 5, 1917, persisted much longer.[25] (It is also interesting, in passing, to note the lessons from the F.2A experience that were unlearned; in the 1930s, the Royal Air Force sponsored development of the Boulton-Paul Defiant two-seat fighter, its only armament being a four-gun turret operated by a gunner sitting behind the pilot. Defiants scored some early victories over German pilots who mistook them for Hurricanes and attacked them from above and behind; but once the secret of its lack of forward-firing armament was out, they were butchered by marauding Messerschmitts: so much for learning from the past.)

The bitter fighting with which April opened continued unabated throughout the month. The RFC pilots in their Pups, Nieuports, Sopwith Triplanes, and Spads quickly recognised the inferiority of having but a single forward-firing machine gun; pilot accounts abound with references to the frightening rasp of an Albatros's twin Spandaus compared to the gentler drumming of the single Lewis or Vickers. Given the opportunity to fly a captured Albatros D II a few weeks after Bloody April, Gordon Taylor thought the Albatros "a war machine, a weapon of ruthless efficiency"; in contrast he viewed the Pup as suitable for sport flying after the war. There was no doubt in his mind in which airplane he would have preferred to go to war.[26] While the Pup had an edge in maneuverability over the Albatros in turning combat, especially above 17,000 feet (even in that era of non-oxygen-equipped flying many patrols and dogfights were fought that high), it could seldom pick and choose the circumstances in which it fought the much more powerful and faster Albatros. Invariably, the RFC pilots, committed to an offensive air strategy, went looking for combat. Just as invariably, the German pilots used the superior performance of the Albatros to engage or break off combat at will, on their own terms.[27] Trenchard's Nieuports took very heavy losses. On April 7, for example, six of 60 Squadron's Nieuport 17's were bounced by von Richthofen and four other Albatros. The German fighters wheeled about and shot down two Nieuports, and the remaining four were unable to maneuver into firing position; only one of the surviving machines returned undamaged. Indeed, in the first three weeks of April, the RFC lost fifty-five Nieuports, and by the end of the month nearly another fifty were in depots for repair of combat damage—reminding one of the very heavy losses and maintenance workload inflicted upon Israel's air force during the 1973 Yom Kippur war.[28]

Occasionally, the scout pilots of the RFC could claim victories over the Germans. On April 6, for example, four Halberstadts dove on a formation of B.E. 2's over Bourlon Wood. Five escorting Pups pounced on the German fighters, shooting down all of them. There was no question that the day of the Halberstadt was quickly drawing to a close, and after a few similar incidents the *Luftstreitkräfte* completed its rapid phase-out in favor of the Albatros. The Pup was not so fortunate: it soldiered on long after it should have been retired to training establishments.[29] For a brief period, the Siemens-Schuckert look-alike copy of the Nieuport 17 caused consternation; several RFC airplanes fell victim to it, the crews mistaking it for a friendly Nieuport. On the whole, however, it proved a disappointment and certainly not equivalent to the superlative Albatros D III then entering service with most *Jagdstaffeln*, and it quickly disappeared from the front.[30]

Britain's Sopwith Triplane proved an exceptionally fine fighter. This intriguing design subsequently spawned the famed German Fokker triplane popularized by such aces as Werner Voss and von Richthofen. The Sopwith Triplane owed much to the Sopwith Pup, but in place of the Pup's two equal-span and broad-chord wings, the Triplane featured three narrow-chord wings having pronounced stagger, as well as a much more powerful 130-horsepower Clerget rotary engine. Sopwith test pilot Harry Hawker convincingly demonstrated his faith in the machine by looping it almost immediately after its first take-off, a fitting way to introduce it to the air, for the trump card of the "Tripehound" was its superlative rate of climb and exceptional maneuverability. Slightly faster than the Pup, the Triplane shared the Pup's relatively outdated single-gun layout. Its narrow-chord wings gave the pilot excellent visibility. As a result of complex negotiations between the Admiralty and the War Office, the Triplane saw service only with the RNAS, and its gestation from drawing board to operational squadrons was slow. Naval One and Naval Eight squadrons had them in hand in February 1917. Its introduction to service came in a dramatic encounter early in April, when a naval pilot brashly attacked a formation of eleven German fighters; though so hard-pressed he was unable to shoot any of them down, he nevertheless managed to out-maneuver them, thanks to his flying ability and the Tripehound's design, though not to his common sense. In the middle of the month, Roderic Dallas (a pilot whose name is inextricably connected with the exploits of Sopwith's three-wing fighter) and his wingman attacked a formation of fourteen Albatros fighters and D.F.W. C V two-seat reconnaissance aircraft heading for Amiens. Using the Tripehound's superior rate of climb to zoom away from the Albatros, the two pilots made side attacks on the D.F.W.'s, sending three of them spiraling earthwards; the remainder, demoralized and disorganized, turned for home. Episodes like these, coupled with the fortuitous capture of a Sopwith Triplane, convinced the *Idflieg* that the triplane configuration possessed inherent advantages for fighters, and a number of triplane projects resulted, only one of which, Fokker's famed Dr I, saw front-line service. In fact, the moment of the Triplane was all too brief, and though it was not yet outclassed, the RNAS began removing it from service over the summer of 1917, replacing it with that whirling dervish of a fighter, the two-gun Sopwith Camel. When the Dr I entered service—late like the Siemens-Schuckert D I—the triplane as a fighter was clearly on the wane. And yet, in the hasty world of fighter development during the Great War, some designers, clearly out of the mainstream of technical progress (and out of touch with reality) proposed quadriplanes having four wings—no doubt following the mistaken logic that if two wings are good and three are better, then four must be excellent.[31]

By mid-April, RFC casualties were soaring, particularly among the crews of the hopelessly outclassed B.E.'s, the outdated 1½ Strutters, and the Nieuports. Out of a formation of seven 1½ Strutters, for example, 45 Squadron lost three to a mixed group of Albatros and Halberstadts over

Tournai. The remaining four, riddled, regained their base, where the harassed formation leader exclaimed, "Some people say that Sopwith Two-Seaters are bloody fine machines, but I think they're more bloody than fine!" His remarks, Norman Macmillan recalled, "brought about his transfer to Home Establishment with loss of acting rank" — a sad commentary on the price of telling the truth.[32] Squadron commander W. Sholto Douglas recollected that his unit, 43 Squadron, took over 100 percent casualties among its 1½ Strutter crews during April; replacements arrived just in time to be shot down, and out of thirty-two pilots and observers authorized for the squadron, 43 Squadron took thirty-five casualties. "Six or seven" of the original crews that started the month survived it, Douglas recalled.[33] Nieuport losses were almost equally severe. In two weeks, 60 Squadron lost thirteen pilots, forcing the squadron commander to halt offensive patrols until the squadron could be again brought up to strength. Those that survived advanced rapidly. Billy Bishop, a gifted and daring pilot in the mold of Albert Ball, flew his first offensive patrol on March 24, and shot down his first Albatros on his second sortie, the next day. Within two weeks he shot down a further five planes and was promoted to the position of flight commander, already an "old hand." (Ironically, on his very first patrol, he crashed his Nieuport on landing; a watching British general recommended that the young Canadian return to flying school for more instruction.)[34]

In the first four days of Trenchard's air offensive, from April 4 to April 8, the RFC lost seventy-five aircraft in combat, with casualties among aircrew of nineteen killed, thirteen wounded, and seventy-three missing. A further fifty-six aircraft crashed in accidents, due in part to pilot strain and insufficient training. Muddled tactical thinking caused unnecessary losses. In 1917, the RFC introduced the Royal Aircraft Factory's R.E. 8, a two-seat reconnaissance biplane bearing an obvious lineage from the earlier B.E. 2e. The R.E. 8, destined to become the standard RFC-RAF reconnaissance airplane during the latter half of the war, had little to commend it, being tricky to fly, unmaneuverable, slow, and prone to burst into flames in any crash landing. On the morning of April 13, six R.E. 8's from 59 Squadron left Bellevue for a morning reconnaissance from Drocourt to Queant. Since the mission took them right through airspace challenged by von Richthofen's *Jasta* at Douai, only two of the R.E.'s were detailed for reconnaissance, the other four being for escort (a pathetically naive notion). Six F.E. 2d's from 57 Squadron and three Spad 7's from 19 Squadron would fly top cover, and a formation of 48 Squadron's Bristol Fighters was instructed to watch for the R.E. 8's. At this point, command and control fell apart. The three Spads left base twenty minutes late, and never made the rendezvous. The six F.E.'s crossed the front, lost formation, were bounced by Albatros, and in the combat with the German fighters, two of the British pushers were shot down. The Bristol Fighters saw nothing. The R.E. 8's, like lambs led to slaughter, crossed the front, met six Albatros led by von Richthofen himself, and were all shot down, only two of the total of twelve crewmen surviving.[35] (Trenchard felt compelled to call on the men of 59 Squadron after this debacle, for their spirits were reported to be "mutinously low." He dined in silence with them, then left; as they gave vent to their pent-up emotions, he flung open the mess door and, characteristically, boomed, "There's nothing wrong here. I've been watching you. Now go to work properly and give the Hun hell in your R.E. 8's." Trenchard acutely felt the loss of his crews—but such "up and at 'em" pep talks could not disguise nor remedy the realities of the situation.)[36] Once scoreless, von Richthofen's *Jasta 11* loomed as the most dangerous single *Jasta* facing the RFC; as *Kogenluft* von Hoeppner later wrote, "Boelcke's spirit lived on."[37] What it meant to the RFC was simply this: during the month of April, a British pilot could look forward to flying ninety-two hours at the front before being posted missing or dead.[38]

But the casualties in the air were but a trifle compared to the casualties on the ground. Haig's ground offensive had opened on April 9, Easter Monday, and by the 14th, had accomplished all its immediate objectives, including the capture of Vimy Ridge in a gallant assault by Canadian troops.[39] Now it was up to Nivelle's forces to sweep through German lines and break German resistance. But as many feared, Nivelle's offensive ended in utter disaster. Lacking the necessary artillery for the bombardment, neglecting the hard-learned lessons of the futility of close mass assaults, still blinded by the pernicious prewar doctrinal notion of "*élan vital*," and with the details of the proposed assault known to the Germans, Nivelle's plan collapsed amid bloody slaughter. The French army, blooded in the frontier battles of 1914, crippled at Verdun in 1916, was broken on the Aisne in 1917 before the formidable Chemin des Dames. Ahead lay mutinies affecting over fifty divisions of French troops, disgrace for the assault's perpetrator, and the slow and painstaking rebuilding of the French army under Henri Petain.[40] In the north, Haig now knew additional pressures as he desperately renewed the Arras battle to keep the German army occupied so that it could not bring its full weight to bear against the remnants of Nivelle's troops.

The air war raged on. Trenchard found himself in a situation analogous to the period of the Fokker scourge. So many escorts had to be detailed for reconnaissance and bombing formations—at least five fighters to every recon airplane, and two fighters for every bomber—that the numerical advantage the RFC possessed over the *Luftstreitkräfte* was effectively nullified. For their part, the German fighter forces switched tactics, using cloud masking to shield fighters from RFC high patrols, and then popping up through these clouds to attack British aircraft. Von Richthofen presented such a threat that special measures were taken to try to shoot him down. On April 29, for example, von Richthofen was spotted leaving Douai on patrol. Orders flashed to 19 Squadron to intercept the Baron in their Spads.

Nineteen Squadron's commander was none other than H. D. Harvey-Kelly, who had been both the first RFC pilot to land in France, and the first to force down a German airplane as related earlier. Now he took off from Vert Galand with two other Spads and headed for the front. Back at the airfield, Trenchard and aide Maurice Baring unexpectedly arrived to visit Harvey-Kelly, one of the general's favorite pilots. They decided to wait for his return. East of Douai, the three Spads spotted the six Albatros droning below; in the distance were six naval Sopwith Triplanes. Confident of their help, Harvey-Kelly dove on the formation. Von Richthofen, leading the Albatros, was not to be caught. He clawed around in a climbing turn, fixed himself on the tail of one of the Spads, and riddled it, sending it in a flaming spin to crash in a marsh at Lecluse. A wandering band of Albatros came across the Triplanes and engaged them before they could come to Harvey-Kelly's aid. The second Spad was likewise shot down and its pilot taken prisoner. Harvey-Kelly, like Lanoe Hawker before him, fought on, until wounded by Kurt Wolff. He crash-landed his fighter, but died of his wounds three days later. Back at Vert Galand, lunchtime came. The Spad trio were now overdue and Trenchard and Baring left, the general publicly expressing his regrets at missing Harvey-Kelly. But Trenchard was a realist, as was Baring, and neither man, as Baring recollected, was ever in doubt as to why Harvey-Kelly was late. His Spad had become one of the twenty-one aircraft that von Richthofen would shoot down that terrible month.[41]

At the end of the month came another switch in German tactics, and a portent of the mass German fighter operations that came to characterize German air tactics through the end of the war. On April 30, four German *Jagdstaffeln*, 3, 4, 11 and 33, combined forces and, in two formations totaling twenty aircraft, left Douai on a patrol along the front. Combat was not long in coming. The Albatros pounced on seven F.E. 2d's and shot down three; they would have destroyed the formation except for the timely arrival of three Sopwith Triplanes from Naval Eight that prevented further carnage. The Albatros formation turned for easier prey; they came across a formation of six Bristol Fighters on a reconnaissance sortie, escorted by Sopwith Triplanes, and in a twenty-minute running fight forced the Bristols to break off the mission and fight their way home. Three of the new S.E. 5's of 56 Squadron intervened, one being shot down in flames.

Still on the prowl, the German formation jumped eight F.E. 2b's on a reconnaissance mission, shooting down two of them. The appearance of the gaily colored Albatros in mass formation led RFC pilots to christen the group the "Richthofen Circus." In fact, the April 30 formation was not under von Richthofen's command, and the true "Flying Circus," (*Jagdgeschwader I, JG I*) did not emerge until June 1917. For all it accomplished, the "Circus" of April 30 was not really an efficient fighting formation. Too loosely organized, it suffered from a lack of discipline that resulted in pilots milling about, having no clear idea how to employ their mass formation to best advantage. The risk of collision was high. Nevertheless, with more practice, it is likely that the formation would have taken a higher toll of British planes. On this note, Bloody April 1917 ended.[42]

VI.
The Evolution of the Fighter, 1914-1918: A Photographic Essay

The Militarization of the Airplane, 1908-1914

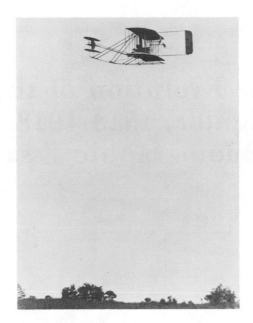

In 1908, five years after Kitt Hawk, Orville Wrigh demonstrated the Wrigh Military Flyer to the U.S Army Signal Corps in a series o trials at Ft. Myer, Virgini. Though marred by an acciden that killed Lieutenant Thom: Selfridge, the tests clearl demonstrated the utility of th airplane for reconnaissance an scouting. *NASM, Smithsonia Institution*

In August 1909, Orville Wright went to Germany and completed a number of demonstration flights of a Wrig Type A Flyer at Tempelhof and Potsdam. These flights were witnessed by many dignitaries, including the Empre of Germany, standing with this group as Wright passes overhead. *NASM, Smithsonian Institution*

Great Britain, designers such as Geoffrey de Havilland of the Royal Aircraft Factory were busily trying to ...velop practical military machines. This S.E. 1 biplane, powered by a pusher propeller and a canard ("tail first") ...sign, proved unsuccessful, and de Havilland subsequently pursued more conventional designs with greater suc- ...s. *NASM, Smithsonian Institution*

...e Wright-inspired canard configuration soon disappeared in favor of so-...led "tractor" biplanes and monoplanes that had the engine driving a pro-...ler at the front of the airplane, and the elevator control surfaces at the rear ...the machine. One major trend-setter was France's 1912 Deperdussin ...nocoque Racer, designed by Louis Bechereau, the first airplane to exceed ...) miles per hour. Its wooden shell fuselage construction and streamlined ...pearance anticipated later aircraft. *NASM, Smithsonian Institution*

The Deperdussin *Military Monoplane* constituted a "spin-off" of the technology demonstrated by the highly refin*Monocoque Racer*. It anticipated the high-speed "fighting scouts" that appeared in the World War. *NASM Smithsonian Institution*

Fliegerschule: RUMPLER Luftfahrzeugbau, Flugplatz - Johannisthal.

Meanwhile, the graceful Rumpler-built *Taube* (Dove) typified Germany's growing military airpower. This elega aircraft, shown here with a group of officers at the Rumpler factory at Johannisthal before the war, was the sing most important German aircraft in service at the outbreak of the war. *NASM, Smithsonian Institution*

In France, Louis Blériot's Model XI monoplane, an early version of which had been the first airplane to fly across the Dover Straits in 1909, equipped many scouting *escadrilles* of the *Aviation militaire,* and some Royal Flying Corps units as well. Here a group of French Blériots stand ready for flight at an airfield on the Western Front. *NASM, Smithsonian Institution*

eat Britain's Royal Flying Corps made extensive use of de Havilland's B.E. 2 family of scouting and recon-
ssance aircraft. This B.E. 2b typifies the kind of "advanced" aircraft that the RFC possessed on the eve of the
r. Slow and unmaneuverable, the B.E. 2 family nevertheless did yeoman service on scouting, artillery observa-
n, and even bombing duties, but at great cost in aircrew killed, wounded, and captured. *NASM, Smithsonian
titution*

The Airplane at War,
1914-1916

This British-flown but French-designed Morane-Saulnier Type L "parasol" monoplane typifies the pre-war designs hastily modified for combat duty. Though one of these aircraft exploded a German Zeppelin while flown by Royal Navy pilot R. A. J. Warneford in 1915, such successes reflected more on the individual abilities of the pilots than on the practicality of these designs for "fighter" duties. Roland Garros scored his victories in a Morane Type L. *Imperial War Museum*

Potentially far more valuab[le] were such aircraft as the Vicke[rs] F.B. 5 "Gunbus," a two-se[at] pusher with an observer perch[ed] in the nose of the airpla[ne] equipped with a machine gu[n.] This design influenced t[he] layout of subsequent push[er] fighters, all of which utilized t[he] pusher layout to off-set the la[ck] of a synchronizing mechanis[m] that would enable a machi[ne] gun to fire forward through t[he] propeller. (This particular Gu[n]bus is a meticulously craft[ed] reproduction built in 1965 [by] the British Aircraft Corpora[-]tion. Note the turning of t[he] rotary engine.) *Jarrett Colle[c]tion*

Likewise, this German Ago C II pusher biplane had an observer-operated machine gun in the nose of the aircraft, but its poor maneuverability hindered its usefulness, and it disappeared from the Western Front by mid-1916. *NASM, Smithsonian Institution*

ck of synchronizer mechanisms seriously impaired otherwise excellent designs, such as this Bristol Scout C of the
yal Flying Corps. The Bristol Scout anticipated the highly agile biplane fighters of the mid-war period, but lack
a gun synchronizer forced pilots to make do with carbines, rifles, or machine guns mounted at awkward angles to
ar the propeller arc. Lanoe Hawker won his V.C. for an air action while flying a Bristol Scout. *NASM, Smith-
nian Institution*

Two German fighter pilots and their ground crew pose with an *Eindecker* in the summer of 1916. By this time, the *Eindecker* was well past its prime. Just visible in the left of the photograph are the tail surfaces of a Halberstadt fighter biplane, with which the *Fliegertruppen* began re-equipping after the debacle at Verdun and the Somme. *U.S. Air Force Museum*

The Fokker *Eindecker* (monoplane), equipped with a synchronized forward-firing machine gun (or two) threatened to seize air superiority from the French and British air services in 1915-1916. It represented an ideal interim weapon: an essentially pre-war design with a single trump card, the synchronized gun. This particular E III model is shown being examined by British troops after its pilot became disoriented and landed by mistake on the British side of the lines. It subsequently underwent detailed flight evaluation in France and England, losing much of its *mystique. Jarrett Collection*

Verdun, the exquisitely Gallic Nieuport 11 *Bébé* handily proved the master of the *Eindecker*. France overcame e lack of a gun synchronizer by installing the Nieuport's Lewis gun above the wing center section. This particular .euport is shown equipped with eight launch tubes for carrying the stabilizing sticks of Le Prieur rockets used for alloon busting." *NASM, Smithsonian Institution*

The even more advanced Nieuport 17 entered service with the *Aviation militaire* in the summer of 1916. It proved [a] favorite mount of many French and British pilots, including Guynemer, Nungesser, Ball, and Bishop, befor[e] leaving service over the summer of 1917, by which time it was clearly obsolescent. Here one is shown warming u[p] prior to flight. Note the blurred image of the speeding rotary engine. Engine cowlings on rotary engine aircra[ft] were intended primarily as oil traps rather than for streamlining, and, unlike later engine cowlings, were seale[d] around the back to prevent oil from blowing back in the face of the pilot. *NASM, Smithsonian Institution*

Pending development of a British gun synchronizer, the RFC made do with more advanced pusher aircraft. This d[e] Havilland D.H. 2 proved decisive in sweeping the Fokker from the skies during the Somme offensive, but it was o[f] only brief value, for the arrival of the Albatros immediately rendered it obsolete. *NASM, Smithsonian Institution*

The two-seat F.E. 2 series could be dangerous opponents in a brawl because of their power and the observer's free-firing gun position in the nose. Often equipped with two machine guns, one firing forward and the other firing aft, the F.E. 2 scored some surprising successes in spite of its relative lack of speed and maneuverability. "Fee" crews shot down von Richthofen on one occasion, and shot down and killed Max Immelmann. Introduced in late 1915, the "Fee" soldiered on as night bombers and interdictors long after their usefulness for day-fighting had ended. This is an F.E. 2a, predecessor of the more widely used F.E. 2b and F.E. 2d series. *NASM, Smithsonian Institution*

The introduction of the Sopwith 1½ Strutter, a two-seat fighter-reconnaissance aircraft, marked a new stage in the evolution of the fighter: a relatively agile two-seater with a synchronized forward-firing machine gun and a defensive machine gun to protect the craft from stern attacks. This concept received its fullest expression in the First World War with the Bristol F.2B. The 1½ Strutter entered service in time for the bitter Somme fighting that spelled the end of the period of Fokker supremacy. Reflecting the pace of aeronautical development, however, the 1½ Strutter was completely obsolete by the following spring. *NASM, Smithsonian Institution*

The Struggle for Air Superiority, 1916-1917

With the introduction of the Albatros D I (shown here) and D II fighters, coupled with the formation of the new *Jagdstaffeln* (fighter squadrons), Germany regained the initiative in the air war. The sleek, streamlined Albatros, with a powerful Mercedes engine and twin-gun armament, had a major technological edge over opposing Allied fighters through the opening months of 1917. *U.S. Air Force Museum*

The Albatros D III, introduced into German fighter squadrons at the end of 1916, featured various design refinements, including a Nieuport-inspired "V-strutter" sesquiplane wing configuration that offered the pilot better visibility. The same structural weakness of this wing configuration that plagued the Nieuport now in turn plagued the Albatros D III and D V series aircraft through the rest of the war. *NASM, Smithsonian Institution*

April 1917, when this photograph was taken, the Albatros was at the peak of its effectiveness against Allied arplanes. Here a mixed group of D II's and D III's of *Jasta 5* are lined up on their "ramp." Such line-ups made elcome targets for British fighter pilots operating on ground attack sorties. *U.S. Air Force Museum*

ven while the Albatros held technological superiority, the British and French had aircraft entering service or eing designed that promised to overcome the inferiority of the out-dated pushers and Nieuport scouts. The opwith Pup, though underpowered and armed with but a single machine gun, performed with good effectiveness gainst the speedier Albatros, forming the genesis of Sopwith's subsequent family of fighters, the Triplane, Camel, nipe, and Salamander. *NASM, Smithsonian Institution*

The Sopwith Triplane enjoyed a
brief but spectacular career as a
fighter, inspiring Germany's
own Fokker Dr I Triplane.
British planners wisely recognized that fighter trends pointed
towards more multipurpose
machines rather than such
specialized designs. *British
Aerospace Aircraft Group*

France's Spad 7, a contemporary of the Albatros but
slower to enter service in quantity, started the trend towards
the multimission heavy single-
seat fighter, as typified by later
Spads and such aircraft as the
S.E. 5a. Fast and rugged, the
early Spad was handicapped by
engine problems and its single-
gun armament as well as
deficient handling qualities, but
it became the mainstay of
fighter *escadrilles* in the
*Aviation militaire. NASM,
Smithsonian Institution*

After a disastrous start, the two-seat Bristol Fighter became the finest all-around fighter aircraft of the First World War, performing admirably in the fighter, attack, and reconnaissance roles. Here is the F.2B, the best-known version of this versatile warplane. Note the close placement of the pilot and rear gunner, which facilitated crew coordination, always a concern in multiseat fighters. The agility of the "Brisfit" constantly surprised even veteran German fighter pilots. *Jarrett Collection*

The Bristol Fighter's reputation reached across the Atlantic to the United States, which attempted to produce an American version powered by the 290 horsepower Liberty 8 engine. The Liberty-powered machines, one of which is shown here, proved disappointing. This photogaph gives a good indication of the gunner's excellent wide field of fire. *NASM, Smithsonian Institution*

The fourth-generation Bristol Fighter, in conjunction with three fourth-generation single-seaters, the British S.E. 5/5a and Sopwith Camel, and the French Spad 13, spelled the end to the Albatros's supremacy. Here a factory-fresh S.E. 5a is shown at Farnborough in November 1917, before being posted to an operational RFC squadron. Note the Lewis machine gun mounted Nieuport-fashion above the upper wing, and the ring and bead sight visible between the center-section struts. The rugged S.E. 5a, Britain's equivalent to the Spad, was flown by a number of leading British fighter pilots, such as Mannock, McCudden, Maybery, and Jones. *NASM, Smithsonian Institution*

The nimble Sopwith F.1 Camel, Britain's first fighter to feature a synchronized twin-gun armament, had vicious handling qualities that caused the death of many an inexperienced or careless pilot, but which also endowed it with astounding maneuverability, making it a formidable dogfighter and excellent fighter-bomber as well. *NASM, Smithsonian Institution*

The Camel's success inspired development of the similar Sopwith Snipe, which nevertheless differed in several important respects from its predecessor. The Snipe was a tamer machine than the brutish Camel and had much improved visibility for the pilot and greater horsepower. Following its introduction into the service in the late summer of 1918, the Snipe continued the Camel's mastery of German fighters. *British Aerospace Aircraft Group*

In turn, the Snipe gave rise to Britain's most sophisticated ground-attack fighter, the heavily armed and armored Sopwith Salamander "trench fighter." Surprisingly maneuverable, the Salamander was just entering service at the war's end; it featured a 650-pound armored box for protection of the pilot and fuel tankage, and 2,000 rounds of ammunition for its twin Vickers machine guns. The Salamander constituted the ultimate spin-off from the Sopwith Pup planform and the Camel. *British Aerospace Aircraft Group*

Not all of the new fighters the Allies introduced proved combat-worthy. The de Havilland D.H. 5, with rearwa stagger on the upper wing to enhance pilot visibility, was an undistinguished fighter, despite performing valuab (though costly) service as a fighter-bomber during the Battle of Cambrai. *NASM, Smithsonian Institution*

American designers looked to France and Great Britain for inspiration, and, while not destined to produce a fighter design that would see combat on the Western Front, they nevertheless were quick to seize upon the now-established single-seat scout formula typified by Britain's Sopwith Pup and France's Nieuport. Here is the Thomas-Morse Scout, a fighter-trainer of 1917; its European legacy, from rotary engine to general layout, is obvious. *NASM, Smithsonian Institution*

The *Luftstreitkräfte's* Final Effort, 1917-1918

Growing recognition of the Allies' technological parity and then superiority led *Idflieg* to an unwise and inappropriate response: standardization on "improved" versions of the Albatros formula, the Albatros D V and D Va. The prototype, shown here, first flew early in 1917; but the D V/Va proved little better than its D II predecessor, and it possessed the same wing flaw inherited from the Nieuport that had plagued the earlier German fighter. The D V/Va remained in service through the end of the war, by which time it was hopelessly outclassed by the fourth-generation Allied fighters. *NASM, Smithsonian Institution*

An even greater disappointment was the much-awaited Fokker Dr I triplane, inspired by the successful (but transitory) Sopwith Triplane. First flown in service by a few "star turn" pilots such as Werner Voss (whose own triplane, with its distinctive "face" insignia on the engine cowling, is shown here) . . . *U.S. Air Force Museum*

. . and then by whole
agdstaffeln such as *Jasta 26,*
hown here with their triplanes
nd Oberleutnant Otto Esswein,
was a dangerous, impractical,
nd ultimately unrealistic air-
raft for the air war of
917-1918. *U.S. Air Force
Museum*

ven as Germany's fighter forces languished with new aircraft built to old formulas, individual technologists were
nerating often surprising and trend-setting designs. Here co-developer Otto Reuter proudly stands before Dr.
ugo Junkers' prototype J I all-metal attack aircraft, which with other two-seaters such as the Halberstadt C1 II
d Hannover C1 II established the first standards for armored ground-attack aircraft. *NASM, Smithsonian
stitution*

A Halberstadt Cl II, shown on the Western Front in 1918, displays the trim fighter-like lines of this impressive ground-attack aircraft, which entered service in time for the Battle of Cambrai. Note the traversing ring mounting for the rear machine gun. *Raidor Collection*

Die Flugze

he Halberstadt fighters were
easy pickings, as many an
llied fighter pilot learned to
s sorrow. Here Germany's
ost successful two-seat fighter
ew, pilot Friedrich Huffzky
d gunner Gottfried Ehmann
Schlasta 15, pose for the
mera; in June and July of
18, this team shot down nine
llied aircraft. *Raidor Col-
ction*

it Maschinengewehren, Signalpatronen und
ndgranaten ausgerüstet

BRÜNHIL

Here a Halberstadt C1 II crew
pose with their aircraft, named
after the Wagnerian heroine
Brünhilde. Note the close placement of the pilot and gunner,
which facilitated crew cooperation, and gave this ground-
attack fighter an "extra pair" of
eyes. Note, too, the gunner's
Parabellum machine gun, stick
grenades, and, on the aft
fuselage decking, cartridges for
a signal flare gun. *Raidor
Collection*

Finally, in early 1918—largely as a result of the insistence of von Richthofen and other leading fighter pilots—Germany fielded the finest single-seat fighter of the war—the Fokker D VII. Here Hermann Göring, future head of Hitler's *Luftwaffe* and the last wartime commander of *Jagdgeschwader I,* is shown taxiing to takeoff on a sortie in his all-white Fokker D VIIF. *NASM, Smithsonian Institution*

Entering service later than the Halberstadt ground-attack fighter, the portly Hannover Cl II and Cl III, with their unique biplane tail — a feature designed to decrease the over-all width of the tail surfaces, thus reducing the plane's "blind spot" behind and below it — featured fighter-like agility and speed despite being designed for battlefield close air support. This Cl III force-landed in Switzerland. *Raidor Collection*

st D VII's, such as this captured example shown after the war at Langley Field, Virginia (note the background of rtin Bombers), sported a complex low-visibility and image-distorting lozenge camouflage pattern over their lage and wings. Pilots often expressed their individualism by replacing this somber and practical scheme with lly flamboyant schemes — such as Göring's all-white machine, or Ernst Udet's candy-striped red-and-white D . *U.S. Air Force Museum*

Complementing the D VII were a host of new fighters indicative of future trends in design — streamlined monoplanes with internally braced wings and tail surfaces, and good power-to-weight ratios as well as metal structures. Some, including the wooden-winged and underpowered Fokker E V (D VIII) "Flying Razor" (such as this one shown in Germany after the war), proved disappointing, and were obsolescent by the time they entered service. *NASM, Smithsonian Institution*

Two other new German planes, built by a Junkers-Fokker consortium, might have proven very successful, but both entered service too late (partially as a result of official disinterest, and partially as a result of developmental and production difficulties) to affect the fighting in the air or on the ground. Here is Junkers' trim J-7, the prototype of the world's first all-metal low-wing monoplane fighter, the Junkers D I, a "fifth-generation" warplane. *NASM, Smithsonian Institution*

By war's end, a ground-attack "spin-off" of the D I design philosophy, the two-seat Junkers Cl I, was just enteri
service with the *Schlachtstaffeln*. (Ironically, it later formed the inspiration for Junkers' first commerc
transports, which eventually culminated in the world-famous Ju 52 trimotor). *NASM, Smithsonian Institution*

VII.
The Fighter
Comes of Age

The tempo, the frantic urgency that had marked the air war in April, soon slackened. Bloody April had been the pinnacle of Germany's air strength, her last chance to utterly destroy the RFC, and the *Luftstreitkräfte* had failed. True, wherever the Albatros appeared, it generally secured local air superiority. But German fighter operations still remained essentially defensive, and there was not the aggressive bombing effort or penetration deep within enemy lines that so characterized RFC operations. More significantly, Germany's technological edge was steadily eroding. New aircraft representing a fourth generation of fighter design were entering service. Blending greater horsepower with strong structures, more sophisticated armament, and refined handling qualities and maneuverability, these were true multimission vehicles capable of air fighting, ground attack, interception and fighter reconnaissance. They had the potential for years rather than months of useful service. They set performance standards more typical of the late 1920s and early 1930s than of 1914-1918. Obsolete types such as the B.E. 2 soon disappeared for good from British combat units, as did the remaining F.E. 2 and D.H. 2 pushers, followed by the obsolescent Sopwith 1½ Strutters and the elegant though outdated Nieuports. In April, shortages had put Trenchard's back against the wall, and Haig dreaded for the future. The supply tangle finally cleared: In January and February, Trenchard had received only 250 new aircraft; in March and April the total had been 612; in May and June, the figure rose to 757. But more important, the majority of these newly-produced aircraft were of new design as well. Casualty figures indicated that the RFC had a new lease on life, that the peak of German depredations on Britain's flying service had passed. In April, the RFC had lost 316 aircrew killed or missing in the course of flying 29,500 operational flight hours. In May, the RFC flew 39,500 hours, losing 187 men killed or missing. In June, 165 men were killed or missing in 35,500 flying hours over the front.[1]

What had saved the Royal Flying Corps in late 1916 and early 1917 from destruction? First and foremost was failure of the *Luftstreitkräfte*'s commanders to exploit the technological sophistication of the Albatros and other aircraft by operating them offensively over the British side of the lines. Had the Albatros established air superiority not only over its own side of the line but over the British side as well, raiding airfields and shooting down British aircraft over Allied territory, it would have had a tremendous effect. It would have forced large standing defensive patrols, reduced the number (as well as the effectiveness) of aircraft available to the RFC for offensive work over the front, and demoralized the British flyers. There are those who disagree and point to the disparity of numbers between the RFC and the *Luftstreitkräfte*, alleging that the Germans possessed too few fighters to conduct offensive operations. In fact, the Albatros's technological sophistication acted as a force multiplier, largely negating the RFC's numerical advantage. By not taking advantage of the technological gap between the German and British aircraft, the leadership of the German air service threw away a priceless eight-month advantage in which they could have seized air superiority over the front. Because of Germany's fatal fascination with the defensive air war, with "letting the customer come into the store" (as German fighter pilots phrased it), of reacting to British moves, the *Luftstreitkräfte* found itself confronting large formations of British aircraft as well as annoying single and two-ship sorties, penetrating German airspace all along the front. It was a "target-rich" environment, and there were simply too many aircraft to shoot down. Britain swamped the defenses, at heavy cost. The large-formation tactics that eventually spawned the German fighter wings (*Geschwader*) comprising several fighter *Jasta* represented an attempt to confront these varied assaults and attain air superiority over important sectors of the front, the *Jagdgeschwader* being shifted from one sector to another as circumstances demanded. Again, however, the aircraft would have been more effective making offensive fighter sweeps into enemy territory, rather than passively filling the sky and waiting for the arrival of British strike, reconnaissance, and fighter aircraft. In sum, right up to the war's end Germany continued to miss the big lesson, the need to conduct offensive air operations over enemy territory.

After April 1917 Germany was never again in a position to contest seriously for control of the air because British fighter technology caught up with and eventually surpassed that of Germany. In part this was because of a fatal error in judgment on the part of the *Idflieg*. The decision to standardize on the Albatros fighter formula caused German fighter technology to level off in a fatal hiatus with the Albatros D III and its derivatives, the D V and Va (which entered service in May of 1917), and the rugged but generally disappointing Pfalz D III (itself a design that typified the Albatros formula). The hasty and ill-thought-out decision to copy the Sopwith Triplane (a decision influenced by the *Jasta* pilots themselves) further crippled development, and caused German fighter technology to remain at the third-generation level long after British craft, both in prototype and in service at the front, had passed into the fourth generation. Britain introduced the fourth generation of fighter aircraft in March 1917, with the Bristol Fighter. Germany, in contrast, did not reach the same level until January of 1918, when the Siemens-Schuckert D III arrived in limited numbers at the front. (Ironically, Germany fielded fourth-generation two-seat cooperation aircraft — the Halberstadt and Hannover — several months earlier.) Obviously some standardization is desirable, but instead of artificially introducing standardization via unimaginative planning, Britain introduced a plethora of types (largely through failures within her own planning process), and the crucible of war provided the real standardization tests. As a result of combat experience and aircrew preference, the standard RFC-RAF fighters in service to the end of the war were the Sopwith Camel, the Royal Aircraft Factory S.E. 5a, and the Bristol F.2B — all fourth-generation types. It was with these aircraft that Great Britain won the air war over the Western Front. In contrast, not until the introduction of Germany's own fourth-generation fighters in the early months of 1918 did the *Luftstreitkräfte* again possess aircraft that were equivalent, plane for plane, to their British counterparts.

The following were the fourth-generation fighters that appeared in service on the Western Front in 1917 and 1918:

Bristol F.2A/B	3/17 through end of war
S.E. 5/5a	4/17 through end of war
Spad 13	4/17 through end of war
Sopwith Camel	6/17 through end of war
Halberstadt Cl II/IIa/IV	10/17 through end of war
Hannover Cl II/III/IIIa	12/17 through end of war
Siemens-Schuckert D III/IV	1/18 through end of war
Sopwith Dolphin	2/18 through end of war
L.F.G. Roland D VIa/VIb	4/18 through end of war
Fokker D VII	4/18 through end of war
Fokker E V/D VIII	8/18 through end of war
Pfalz D XII	9/18 through end of war
Sopwith Snipe	Entered service 9/18
Sopwith Salamander	Entered service 11/18

A fifth generation of all-metal monoplane fighters, two types built by Junkers, entered service at the very end of the war; these were the single-seat Junkers D I and the two-seat Junkers Cl I. German wartime procurement policy may have been deficient, but German research was not, as these two aircraft indicate—a situation analogous to that at the end of the Second World War, when German aerodynamic and jet propulsion research advanced even as the German fighter forces tottered onwards to destruction. Indeed, a strong case can be made that at the very end of the war Britain had gone about as far as it could in extending the lineage of Sopwith fighters—Pup to Camel to Snipe and Salamander. The future certainly belonged to metal-structured aircraft, with fabric or wood-covered metal frames or all-metal construction. In another bit of irony, Great Britain's attempt to standardize on the dreadful A.B.C. Dragonfly radial engine might have seriously damaged the combat effectiveness of the Royal Air Force had the war lasted longer. Proponents of systems standardization—now as then—should move with great caution, keeping ever before them the examples of the Albatros and the Dragonfly.

There is a remarkable document from a uniquely qualified critic of German fighter development that illustrates the decline that afflicted the German fighter forces between the success of late 1916 and early 1917 and the final searing plunge into *Götterdämmerung* in March of 1918. It is a letter written by none other than Manfred von Richthofen to a close friend serving on Ernst von Hoeppner's staff, on July 18, 1917. At the time, von Richthofen was recovering from a near-fatal head wound encountered in a fight between a group of new Albatros D V's and some old F.E. 2d's. The F.E. 2d could be a dangerous opponent in a swirling brawl because of the observer's free-firing gun, and von Richthofen had received a bullet wound that creased his skull, splintering the bone. Barely conscious, he managed a good forced landing; his convalescence took several months, though he never fully recovered. Even allowing for his condition and a pessimism possibly resulting from his near-fatal wound, the letter is a clearly written and forthright indictment of *Idflieg*'s obsessive endorsement of the Albatros monopoly from a *Luftkämpfer* of unquestioned skill. In part it reads:

> I can assure you that these days it is no longer enjoyable being the commander of a *Jasta* . . .
> . . . the English . . . can fly whither they wish, with absolute command of the air not only over their own lines, but over the entire countryside. And they are not shot down, at least not in proportion to their number. . . .
> Now comes another matter that I wish to discuss with you: Our aircraft are inferior to the English in an absolutely laughable fashion. The [Sopwith Triplane] and the 200 hp Spad, as with the [Sopwith Camel] play with our D V's. And in addition to better quality of aircraft, they have greater numbers. Thus, our fine

FIVE GENERATIONS OF FIRST WORLD WAR FIGHTERS

I
FOKKER E III (1915)
Speed: 87.5 mph
Ceiling: 12,000 feet
Endurance: 1.5 hrs.
Horsepower: 100
Armament: twin synchronized machine guns
Weight (gross): 1,342 lbs.

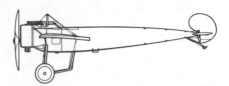

II
NIEUPORT 11 (1916)
Speed: 97 mph
Ceiling: 15,000 feet
Endurance: 2.5 hrs.
Horsepower: 80
Armament: one machine gun
Weight (gross): 1,210 lbs.

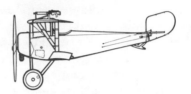

III
ALBATROS D III (1917)
Speed: 103 mph
Ceiling: 18,000 feet
Endurance: 2 hrs.
Horsepower: 160
Armament: twin synchronized machine guns
Weight (gross): 1,949 lbs.

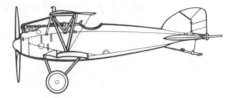

IV
SOPWITH F.1 CAMEL (1917)
Speed: 104.5 mph
Ceiling: 19,000 feet
Endurance: 2.5 hrs.
Horsepower: 130
Armament: twin synchronized machine guns
Weight (gross): 1,482 lbs.

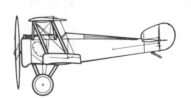

V
JUNKERS D I (1918)
Speed: 115.5 mph
Ceiling: 19,680 feet
Endurance: 1.5 hrs.
Horsepower: 180
Armament: twin synchronized machine guns
Weight (gross): 1,841 lbs.

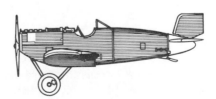

Drawings by Ken Baas

fighter pilots are nevertheless lost! The D V is so out-dated that one does not risk anything with it. And the people at home, for nearly a year, have developed nothing better than this lousy [lit. *lausigen*] Albatros, remaining with the Albatros D III with which I fought last fall.

. . . English single-seaters climb better and are faster than us, and the English even have already [the Bristol Fighter], a two-seater, that can overhaul an Albatros, easily overpowering us in turns, against which one is virtually powerless. . . .

You would not believe how bad the morale among the fighter pilots serving at the front is because of their terrible machines. Nowadays, nobody wants to become a fighter pilot. . . .

Before our pilots receive their flight badges and some decorations, fifty percent are shot dead.*

Von Richthofen's subsequent influence upon German fighter development is interesting, and characterized by two critical decisions, one questionable, and the other certainly not. In this same letter, von Richthofen enthusiastically endorsed the development of Tony Fokker's lightweight Dr I triplane interceptor, inspired by the Sopwith Triplane. Von Richthofen recognized that its high rate of climb suited it to the defensive nature of Germany's air war over the Western Front where, more often than not, the German fighter *Jagdstaffeln* awaited word from the *Flugmeldedienst* (the German air warning network of reporting stations along the front) of British incursions before hopping into their aircraft and taking off to intercept the "Tommies." Subsequently, he became much less enthusiastic, though Germany continued to favor fast-climbing interceptors, lightweight and powered by rotary engines: a design philosophy that spawned not only the Fokker triplane, but also the Fokker E V and the D VIII "Flying Razor," which was outdated almost from the moment that it arrived for service on the Western Front. By January of 1918, von Richthofen recognized that Germany required an aircraft of a very different sort. By this time, the D Va Albatros had proven less capable than the D III it was to have replaced, and it had the wing weakness inherited from the Nieuport via the D III that caused the death of many a German fighter pilot. (Nevertheless, it was the available plane; by May of 1918, nearly fifty percent of all German fighter aircraft at the front would be D Va machines.)[2] The Dr I triplane had lost much of its allure, proving incapable of choosing its own terms of combat, though its superlative agility made it a much respected opponent in an out-and-out dogfight. At this time, for a variety of reasons, some of which were political, and others of which stemmed from the apparent problems Fokker had in designing structurally sound aircraft (his triplane had killed several pilots, including the well-known ace Heinrich Gontermann, through in-flight structural

---

*Translated and reprinted with permission from the Peter M. Grosz Archive.

failure), Tony Fokker was essentially out of favor with the *Idflieg*. But von Richthofen, as well as other aces such as Ernst Udet, remained loyal to him, because, like them, he was a capable pilot who always emphasized developing aircraft that had superior handling qualities and maneuverability. Now, largely at the insistence of von Richthofen, Fokker was permitted to enter the January 1918 fighter competition held at Adlershof, the German flight test center. For this competition, Fokker had produced a prototype designated the V 11, a biplane bearing a vague family resemblance to the firm's earlier designs, but with a powerful 160-horsepower Mercedes inline engine. Just before the competition commenced, Fokker decided the plane was a bit too tricky for the average pilot, so he lengthened it, increasing its stability during a dive. The fighter pilots invited to fly twenty-two designs entered in the trials, including von Richthofen himself, so enthusiastically endorsed the V 11 that *Idflieg* opposition collapsed, and Fokker left the competition with orders for 400 of the new plane, to be designated D VII. Albatros, to Fokker's satisfaction, was instructed to undertake license production. The first D VIIs arrived at the front in April 1918, a few days after von Richthofen fell in combat. Nearing the end of his life, then, von Richthofen provided the German fighter community with his greatest, though least-recognized, service: supporting development of a superlative fourth-generation aircraft that probably would have died at birth had it not been for his enthusiastic and determined endorsement. Indeed, as historian John H. Morrow has written, "To Richthofen's sponsorship of the Fokker D VII, which appeared too late to save him, many a German combat pilot of 1918 owed his life."[3]

At last, Germany had returned to the correct path in fighter aircraft design, and there is little question that the Fokker D VII was the finest single-seat fighter of the war. Many make a strong case for the Sopwith Camel, but the Fokker case is more persuasive, because it was a better, safer, and more rugged all-around aircraft. Its excellent handling qualities, high-lift wing, refined aerodynamic design, good power-to-weight ratio, and good visibility enabled a pilot to concentrate on flying the mission, not flying the plane. Its twin-gun installation, agility, and speed made it a fearsome opponent, and Allied airmen quickly recognized that the nature of the air war had changed yet again. They were particularly impressed with the ability of the Fokker to hang on its prop while the pilot hosed bullets at his opponents; one S.E. 5a pilot reported a combat in which the Fokker pilot "just hung right there and sprayed me with lead like he had a hose. All I could do was to watch his tracer and kick my rudder from one side to the other to throw his aim off. This war isn't what it used to be."[4] Successfully fighting the Fokker was grueling, hard work, and the Allied powers had no doubt as to the value of this angular fighter;

Article IV of the armistice terms specifically directed the surrender of *"alle Apparate D VII. . . ."*

Through the spring of 1917, the function of fighters had been primarily to destroy opposing two-seaters, and to clear the air of opposing fighters so that one's own two-seaters could function without molestation. There had been, of course, the occasional use of fighters to intercept long-range enemy aircraft, and sometimes pilots flying low over the front sprayed a few bullets at the troops crouching below. But it was only in 1917 and 1918 that the fighter's functions dramatically enlarged to include organized air defense duties against day and night long-range bombers, and operations in a fighter-bomber role against front-line targets and targets just behind the forward edge of battle. In addition, a naval fighter tradition was emerging, including the use of aircraft carriers and coastal patrol fighters. By the time of the climactic battles of 1918, the fighter had matured and its contributions over the battlefield could not be denied.

To Germany, France, and Great Britain, air defense in 1914 meant primarily defense against the threat of gas-filled airships. Only Germany had a fleet of militarily useful rigid airships, but even in that country fear of airship attack caused aircraft pioneer August Euler to propose a machine-gun-armed *Zerstörer* (destroyer) before the war. Similar fears helped spawn the Vickers "fighting biplane" that evolved into the F.B. 5 Gunbus.[5] Eventually, in fact, the rigid airship bomber did make a combat appearance, and for a while proved an elusive enemy. But the introduction of higher-performance interceptors, and especially the introduction of explosive incendiary bullets, stripped it of its invulnerability and rendered it a flaming deathtrap. Thereafter, strategic and tactical bombardment remained exclusively the province of the airplane.[6]

At the beginning of the war, Germany's military airships (most of which were Zeppelins, but others of which were wooden-framed Schütte-Lanz dirigibles) were divided between the army and the navy. Although both services stressed the advantages of the hydrogen-filled rigid airships for reconnaissance and bombardment, prewar fears had credited them with a military effectiveness all out of proportion to their true worth, and it is astounding how many fell victim to weather and especially to intense ground fire in the opening months of the war. For example, conventional rifle and machine-gun fire holed the gas cells of four army airships, the Z V, Z VI, Z VII, and Z VIII, sending them sinking slowly to earth; they were lost before the end of August 1914.[7] Still, the appeal of the dirigible airship as a bombardment vehicle lingered, and the Kaiser approved raids on England beginning in January 1915. The first raid, by four navy Zeppelins, took place on January 19, 1915. Despite their intent to strike only "docks and military establishments," imprecise and crude targeting systems coupled with generally by-guess-and-by-God navigation resulted in indiscriminate strikes that most often did little more than kill British civilians — and aroused an understandable public outcry both in Great Britain and in neutral nations abroad, notably the United States. Nevertheless, Germany persisted with the ethically questionable raids. Naturally, this forced a British decision to take appropriate countermeasures.

As early as September 1914, anticipating that the Zeppelins would probably be used to attack British targets, the Royal Naval Air Service had undertaken a daring series of raids on airship bases at Düsseldorf and Friedrichshafen, using small biplanes armed with four small 20-pound bombs — forerunners of the "bomb-loaded fighters" Great Britain would field in quantity in 1917 and 1918. One Zeppelin, the Z IX, was burnt in its shed by a well-placed bomb dropped by Flight Lieutenant R. L. G. Marix from a Sopwith Tabloid. After the airship raids on England started, RNAS aviators at Dunkerque were briefed to attack German Zeppelins using incendiary darts and small bombs. An air strike by two Henri Farmans, an almost laughably primitive prewar pusher, blew up LZ 38 in her shed. Naval pilot R. A. J. Warneford, flying a Morane Type L armed with six 20-pound bombs, encountered LZ 37 in the air over Belgium, stalked it over an hour, and managed to drop his bombs on it, sending it earthwards in a ball of exploding hydrogen. In recognition of his courage and skill — the LZ 37's explosion had nearly destroyed his own plane — he was awarded the Victoria Cross.[8]

Warneford's attack clearly indicated the vulnerability of airships to airplanes — if they could be attacked. When a Zeppelin was at its bombing height, about 10,000 feet, it was all but immune to attack from the primitive aircraft of the day. Further hampering defense against them was the lack of genuine explosive or incendiary ammunition. Warneford, indeed, had been following the official doctrine in his attack when he flew above the ill-fated LZ 37 — he had to, for like most early Zeppelin interceptors, he was armed only with gravity weapons. John Slessor, a young RFC pilot on "home defence" duty at Joyce Green aerodrome outside London, has left a humorous and informative account of flying in those early days. On October 13, 1915, the future marshal of the Royal Air Force was ordered to undertake an anti-Zeppelin patrol at 10,000 feet. As he climbed to altitude in his straining B.E. 2c armed with incendiary bombs, the nightlights of London (there was no blackout) illuminated the giant shape of Zeppelin L 15, commanded by Kapitänleutnant Joachim Breithaupt. Slessor subsequently compared his vision of the droning Zeppelin to "a cod's eye view of the *Queen Mary.*" As he strained to reach the almost motionless Zeppelin, Breithaupt's crew spotted the plane, and at once the Zeppelin dropped ballast water, and as Slessor recalled, "cocked its nose up at an incredible angle and climbed away from me." Slessor eventually lost track of the German airship, and then realized that he must take stock of where he was. He managed to locate his airfield, and as he descended through a thick Thames fog, a searchlight operator, trying to be helpful, flashed his light on the plane, causing Slessor to lose his bearings and land heavily, damaging the plane but fortunately not himself.[9] Slessor's sortie illustrated many of the problems of operating against the Zeppelins: having to climb above them, flying underpowered aircraft that had to rely on stealth to arrive within firing range, and, finally, the difficulties of navigating and flying blind during the night missions.

However, the days of the Zeppelin bomber were numbered. John Pomeroy, J. F. Buckingham, and F. A. Brock had all developed explosive and incendiary ammunition suitable for destroying airships, and by the spring of 1916, one million .303-caliber rounds of Brock, Pomeroy, and Buckingham were on hand for use by home defense fighter units. On the night of September 2, 1916, Leefe Robinson exploded the Schütte-Lanz wooden airship SL 11 over Cuffley in full view of Londoners and arriving German airships; the demoralized crews of the other ships beat a hasty retreat. On the night of October 1, L 31, commanded by Kapitänleutnant Heinrich Mathy, fell in flames before the guns of W. J. Tempest, carrying "the greatest airship commander of the war" (as RAF historian H. A. Jones subsequently wrote) to a Wagnerian death.[10] With Mathy's death, interest in risking the vulnerable airships to intercepting fighters ended. With the reorganization of the *Luftstreitkräfte* under von Hoeppner, Thomsen, and Seigert, Zeppelin advocates within the army lost all remaining support. The torch passed to long-range bombers. The German navy pressed on, largely due to the fanatical determination of Fregattenkapitän Peter Strasser, the director of the German airship service. In 1917, Germany introduced a series of "height-climbers," lightly structured large Zeppelins capable of raiding from altitudes up to 20,000 feet, with their crews using oxygen. These did confound the defenses, making interception almost impossible, but they introduced other problems, notably vulnerability at high altitudes to equipment failure, and to being blown far off course by high-altitude winds. Zeppelin reconnaissance flights over the North Sea ran afoul of Curtiss flying boats, and two were shot down. Forced to higher altitude, the Zeppelin flights lost their usefulness for mine and submarine spotting. Sopwith Pups and Camels launched from platforms on ships or from towed lighters scored successes against the maritime airships and in July 1918 a daring strike by six Sopwith Camels launched from the aircraft carrier H.M.S. *Furious* — an ominous portent of the striking power of naval aviation — blew up two German airships, the L 54 and L 60, in the sheds at Tondern, opposite the island of Sylt. Each Camel had carried two

50-pound bombs. Finally, on August 5, 1918, Strasser himself fell in the flame-wrapped L 70, shot down by an intercepting De Havilland D.H. 4 as he neared the British coast on a pathetic "death or glory" raid aimed at London. The German naval airship division, as historian Douglas Robinson stated, "was finished as a fighting service."[11]

The long-range bomber, which took over the mission of the airship, was a far more serious menace. Zeppelins could carry a very large bomb load, but they were frightfully vulnerable and presented a target virtually impossible to miss. Aircraft carried smaller bomb loads, but were faster, more agile, and much more difficult to intercept. On the Eastern Front, Igor Sikorsky's four-engine *Ilya Mourometz* proved the striking power and ruggedness of the heavily defended bomber. Eighty of the craft were built, only one of which was lost to intercepting fighters, after it had shot down four of its attackers. In 1915, German aeronautical pioneer Oskar Ursinus developed a twin-engine armor-plated "battle plane" (*Kampfflugzeug*), and from this start sprang the best-known of all German multiengine bombers, the Gotha family. As early as November 1914, the German air staff had proposed bombing England by airplane, and had even set up a bombwing comprised of six squadrons under the obscure cover name *Brieftauben Abteilung — Ostende* (Carrier Pigeon Detachment — Ostende). The limited range of early German aircraft prevented German aircrews from carrying through on this plan, and they contented themselves with raids on Allied targets in northern France and Belgium. By the end of 1916, however, new and more powerful twin-engine aircraft built by *Gothaer Waggonfabrik* had entered service with German forces, serving with distinction in the Balkan campaign. These new designs, notably the G II, III, and IV, were as fast as contemporary fighters, had a duration up to six hours, carried up to three defensive machine guns and up to 1,100 pounds of bombs. A design cut-out allowed the defensive tail gunner to fire his weapon downwards through the fuselage, surprising any fighter with the temerity or foolhardiness to attack from directly below.[12] Even larger aircraft, the so-called *Riesenflugzeug* (Giant airplanes), or R planes, were on the verge of entering service.

With the failure of the long-range Zeppelin, all hopes for a sustained bombing campaign against Great Britain rested with the Gotha and R plane bombers. The air staff laid plans for operation *Türkenkreuz* (Turk's Cross), the bombing of England.[13] Small airplanes attacked London sporadically from November 28, 1916 — a day, ironically, on which two of the now-vulnerable Zeppelins went up in flames under fighter attack — but it was not until after Bloody April 1917 that the Gothas flew into action across the Channel. On May 25, 1917, twenty-one Gothas left airfields near Ghent and raided the coastal city of Folkestone, killing 95 and injuring another 195 citizens. One Gotha fell to antiaircraft fire, and another crashed on its return (the Gotha had notoriously poor handling qualities when lightly loaded as a result of poor aerodynamic design). Another raid followed against Sheerness. Then, on June 13, came a raid that stunned all England. Seventeen Gothas raided London, killing 162 and injuring 432 others, causing nearly £130,000 worth of damages, and escaping without loss. "Where were Great Britain's airmen?" ran the outcry, and the RFC, much to Trenchard's and Haig's displeasure, had to strip vitally needed fighter squadrons from the Western Front and return them to England for home defense duties: the pilots, as might be expected, had few objections to returning to Blighty.[14]

The problems confronting the defense planners were not inconsiderable; they had to reorient their thinking from slow Zeppelins to faster airplanes, a task analogous, as historian Raymond Fredette has written, to "having to switch overnight from whale harpooning to mosquito swatting."[15] In July 1917, Great Britain established the London Air Defence Area, (LADA) under the command of Brigadier General Edward B. Ashmore. At first the LADA had nine air defense squadrons, six equipped with older machines that had been used against the Zeppelins, and three others armed with the newer Sopwith Pup and Sopwith Camel fighters. Compared to the docile single-gun Pup, the twin-gun Camel, the first British fighter armed with twin synchronized guns, was a vicious little airplane that fully lived up to the reputation of its namesake. Basically unstable and endowed with dervish-like qualities by its rotary engine, the Camel demanded excellent piloting and constant vigilance. The reward for competence was a highly agile aircraft capable of outturning virtually all German fighters; the penalty for inexperience or clumsy handling, however, could be fatal for, as Camel pilot Norman Macmillan recollected after the war, it was a "fierce little beast . . . utterly remorseless against brutal or ignorant treatment."[16] As could be expected, Ashmore placed his faith not only in new aircraft, but in an extensive gun ring surrounding London; an observer network linked by telephones to the air defense squadrons was set up, and Klaxon horns were installed around the men's quarters at the airfields. A raid warning from the horns sent aircrew scrambling to their fighters to fire up the engines; if a raid signal followed, the fighters could scramble aloft in less than a minute. Here the system broke down somewhat, for, unlike the radar-directed and radio-linked fighters that confronted Göring's *Luftwaffe* over England in 1940, the aircraft of 1917 did not possess air-to-ground and air-to-air radio communications; interception still depended on sighting the enemy and visually setting up an attack. Some air defense squadrons never did come to grips with the enemy; 46 Squadron, for one, flying from Sutton's Farm airfield in Essex, spent six weeks on air defense duties without firing its guns in anger.[17]

Ashmore's defense planning set the stage for ending the daylight Gotha raids. In May, the Gothas encountered few intercepting fighters. By mid-August, however, the Gothas were encountering serious air opposition as hundreds of fighters tried to intercept them, the majority of which were fourth-generation types — S.E. 5's, Bristol Fighters, and Camels. What saved the daytime Gothas from total destruction were the basic and inherent weaknesses of the command, control, and communications system. (Ironically, it seemed the bombers were their own worst enemies. On one mission, four cracked up on landing, leading to a mission loss rate of nearly fifty percent.) The lesson, however, was clear: German planners switched from risking the bombers in daylight assaults and relying on mutual gunfire support and speed for defense to operating them under the protective cloak of darkness. Like the Zeppelin before them, the Gotha and the R planes became creatures of the night. The fallacy of running unescorted daylight bombing raids in the face of stiff fighter opposition was a lesson that virtually all the warring powers in World War II — the Royal Air Force, the *Armee de l'Air*, the *Luftwaffe*, the Red Air Force, and the U.S. Army Air Forces, among others — would have to relearn at great cost.[18]

The night attacks caused major problems for the defense. Proper night-flying instrumentation did not exist before 1930, and pilots had difficulty reading what few instruments they had. Conventional ring and bead gunsights were practically invisible; muzzle flash and tracer bullets induced flash blindness for critical seconds during an attack. Few airfields had any sort of night landing and take-off aids. New equipment took care of some of these problems. Barrage balloons draped with aprons of steel wire hung ominously in the path of German aircraft, forcing the Gothas and R planes — the wingspans of the latter only marginally shorter than that of a Second World War Boeing B-29 Superfortress — to attack London and its surrounding environs from above 10,000 feet.[19] Camels and other "night-fighters" were given illuminated instruments; tracer bullets were either dispensed with altogether, or mixed much more infrequently in the machine-gun bullet belts. A new illuminated gunsight developed by Lieutenant H. B. Neame passed its trials and came into general service. It used a ring covered with luminous paint, coupled with a bead having an internal electric bulb that cast a small spot of light at the top of the post. The diameter of the ring corresponded to the wingspan of a Gotha raider at 100 yards in front of the fighter — ideal killing range. (However, against the larger R planes, with wingspans sometimes twice as broad, the Neame sight caused pilots to fire before they were within the proper range needed to down these elusive night-flyers.) S.E. 5's and Camels equipped with Neame sights started patrols in late 1917, and they proved their value on the evening of January 25, 1918, when two Camels shot down a Gotha over Kent. Flash suppressors prevented machine-gun fire from temporarily blinding interceptor pilots, and night lights along runways eased take-offs and landings. Finally, intensive night-flying practice by home defense squadrons made the all-too-frequent casualties of the Zeppelin days a thing of the past.[20]

The development of a genuine night-fighter capability within the Royal Flying Corps improved not only the home defense situation, but offensive operations over the Western Front as well. As early as September 1917, the RFC sent Camels and Bristol Fighters aloft at night to intercept German bombers operating against targets in northern France. In 1918, this strategy extended to using Camels as night intruders, patrolling at night in the vicinity of German bases in Belgium to shoot down the Gotha and R aircraft as they began their landing approach. In this fashion, the night-fighter pilots of 151 Squadron shot down four confirmed German bombers, and possibly six others. They also shot down sixteen on the British side of the front. This was a pattern of night attack emulated by the German *Nachtjagdgeschwadern* of the Second World War, and the Royal Air Force's Beaufighter and Mosquito night-fighters of that later conflict. One of the most successful of British night-fighters was 151 Squadron's A. B. Yuille, who forced down a Gotha over Etaples, causing the capture of its crew, and then on August 10, 1918, shot down the huge five-engine Staaken R 43 Giant near Talmas.[21] In fact, the decline of the German night bombers had come earlier. In May 1918, in the biggest German raid of the war, when twenty-eight Gothas, three Giants, and two smaller aircraft raided England at night, six Gothas were lost over England to night-fighers and flak, and another one crashed on the return home. The Gothas never returned to England again.[22]

Gotha and Giant bombers accounted for roughly sixty percent of all British casualties inflicted during the Zeppelin and bombers' raids. The major German accomplishment had not been the expected collapse in British morale and will to fight. Rather, the bombers had forced vitally needed fighters to be kept on home defense duties, fighters that could have rendered valuable service in France during the climactic battles of 1918. In November 1918 there were no less than eleven fighter squadrons assigned to the London Air Defence Area; a further five squadrons guarded the so-called Northern Air Defence Area. But the seeds of aerial fighting at night had been planted, and the first lessons were learned: the need for coordination between ground and air defenses, and for good communication between observers, command, and the squadrons on alert — in short, the whole Command, Control, Communications and Intelligence (C³I) network — would influence an intensive and far more important Battle of Britain over two decades later, altering forever the conduct of air defense operations. There were lessons for bomber advocates, but many of these were subsequently misread and lost. At first the Gothas relied on daylight raids in formation with mutual fire support from defending gunners. And against primitive defenses it worked—just as it would work during the Spanish Civil War, muddying thinking on bomber employment before World War II. Rising losses and a growing awareness of the vulnerability of unescorted bombers to fighter interception and attack forced a switch to night bombing—just as it would for the *Luftwaffe* and Bomber Command in 1940. But improved night-fighter technology worked to limit the effectiveness of night bombers as well. This technological and tactical tail-chase began in the skies over Great Britain and the Western Front in 1917-1918, and reached its peak in the massive night battles over Europe in the Second World War, where fighters and bombers, equipped with radar and electronic countermeasures and counter-countermeasures (ECM and ECCM) dueled to the death. Its logical extension is the sophisticated air defense environment of interceptors, surface-to-air missiles, antiaircraft artillery, ECM and ECCM, and C^{3}I that confronts attackers today.

Increasingly, after April 1917, the fighter was used as a light attack and ground-strafing machine. Though Britain toyed with the idea of developing specialized armored "trench fighters" (which eventually led to the Sopwith Salamander, two of which reached France for service by the beginning of November 1918), it was Imperial Germany who developed the most sophisticated ground-attack aircraft—the so-called *Schlachtflugzeug* organized in special *Schlachtstaffeln (Schlasta:* attack squadrons). It is ironic that while the *Jagdstaffeln* fought *defensively* throughout the war, Germany exploited as best she could the *offensive* striking power of aircraft as strategic bombers and close air support tactical assets operating over the battlefields. (Fittingly, the work "strafe," a common verb in the fighter and attack community, has its origins in the German verb *strafen*: to punish.) Nevertheless, there can be little doubt that German efforts were hastened along this path because of what can only be described as the Royal Flying Corps's enthusiastic, all-out, and intensive use of conventional fighters as ground-attack aircraft and interdictors from the spring of 1917 onwards.

During the battle of the Somme in the summer of 1916, German troops grumbled about the low-flying English aircraft that occasionally attacked their positions. These attacks, however, were initiated by British aircrews, and not as the result of any official ground-attack policy. Eventually, the Royal Flying Corps distinguished between two kinds of ground attack: trench-strafing, a self-explanatory term for close air support over the battlefield, and ground-strafing, which meant operations further behind the lines, in what would now be considered an interdiction role.[23]

It was in the battles of 1917 that the fighter emerged as an instrument of ground-attack warfare, and these battles were but a prologue to the truly violent and cataclysmic struggles of 1918. Early in the war, the French had developed primitive bombs that were little more than finned adaptations of existing artillery shells; by late 1914 and early 1915, in contrast, the Royal Laboratory at Woolwich Arsenal and the Royal Aircraft Factory were developing bombs ranging in size from 16 pounds to 585 pounds, and eventually, at war's end, special 1,600-, 1,800-, and even a 3,360-pound bomb had been developed for use on Britain's two strategic bombers, the Handley Page O/400 and V/1500, equivalents to the Gotha and R planes. Along with this wide-ranging group of bombs appeared two smaller ones ideally suited for use by fighters and other small aircraft: the 20-pound steel-cased Hale and 25-pound Cooper bombs, each of which could carry approximately 4 to 4.5 pounds of Amatol explosive. Eventually, the Cooper bomb superseded the Hale weapon as the standard fragmentation anti-personnel and anti-vehicle weapon, primarily because its nose fuse, in contrast to the Hale's tail fuse, gave it better bursting characteristics with little delay between impact and detonation. Germany likewise developed a variety of small 4.5-kilogram to 50-kilogram Carbonit high-explosive bombs, whose quaint Gothic appearance belied their deadly effect; as well as other carefully streamlined shapes, which anticipated the modern bomb; and a large number of magnesium and petroleum-based incendiary bombs.[24]

The first organized British ground-attack sorties began with attempts to destroy enemy balloons. In early 1917, Lieutenant Colonel Wilfred R. Freeman hit upon the idea of using artillery fire on German trenches to keep German troops pinned down while low-flying fighters streaked un-molested across the front, hit balloons, and then returned. On May 2, the plan was put into effect by Nieuport pilots of 40 Squadron who had prac-ticed flying low using terrain-masking offered by the contour of the ground as well as trees and houses—a form of flying later dubbed "hedge-hopping" and "contour-chasing." Six Nieuports flew low across the front, reached the German balloon line undetected, popped up to 2,000 feet, and shot down four of the vital observation platforms; all the Nieuports returned safely, but well-punctured by rifle and machine-gun fire. The next day, five Sopwith 1½ Strutters of 43 Squadron were sent out to break up German troop formations massing for a counterattack against a British position; they attacked the troops from altitudes of 50 to 100 feet. A major change, however, and one that anticipated future practice, came on the evening of May 11, when F.E. 2b's and Nieuports were used to sup-port advancing troops. A formation leader led two flights of F.E.'s and

Nieuports from 11 and 60 Squadrons in an attack on German infantry dug-in in front of the advancing troops; as the planes exhausted their ammunition, they returned to their airfields, replenished, and resumed the attack, the Nieuports with machine-gun fire, and the F.E.'s with both guns and two 20-pound bombs. The first steps towards a British ground-attack doctrine had been taken.[25]

There was still a large role for individual initiative, and in the Battle of Messines, in June, Canadian pilot Billy Bishop gave a classic example of what a low-level interdictor could accomplish given surprise—and luck. His motive was more to run up his score of German aircraft shot down than to open a new era in air combat, but he succeeded in doing both. On June 2 he crossed the lines and attacked a German airfield near Cambrai, strafing the hangers and ground crews with his machine gun; he then turned his Nieuport on three German fighters trying to take off, and shot down all of them, damaging a fourth as well. As might be expected, he received a Victoria Cross for his action—and again, one wonders at the lack of initiative that prevented the pilots from the *Jagdstaffeln* from exploiting the superiority of their Albatros a few short months before by making similar attacks against the overworked and harassed RFC.[26]

During the Messines attack, roving RFC pilots had a commission to attack German troops, gun emplacements, and logistics, Trenchard's advice being to "cross the line at Armentières very low and then shoot at everything. . . ."[27] Attacks were also made on German fighter fields by S.E. 5's, Spads, Pups, 1½ Strutters, and even a few outdated F.E. 8 pushers. Loss rates were high, but not excessively so in light of subsequent casualties: out of fourteen aircraft sent out on June 7, for example, two were shot down and two others damaged.[28] By now, German two-seater crews were taking advantage of the withdrawal of British fighter squadrons from the Western Front to confront the Gotha menace at home, and were attacking British trenches sporadically, and from June of 1917 onwards, organized British and German ground-attack sorties became an accepted (if detested) part of trench warfare. With increased ground-attack sorties came intense air fighting. One dogfight over Polygon Wood, for example, saw as many as ninety-four German and British fighters dueling it out in a dogfight ranging from 5,000 feet to above 17,000 feet.[29]

By the end of July a new twist had been added to ground-attack missions by British fighters: single-seaters were equipped with 25-pound Cooper bombs hurriedly fitted to racks beneath the wings. At first, S.E. 5's were hastily modified for this duty, but later the agile little Camel proved more useful in low-level attack (much as a modern A-10 would have greater agility over the battlefield than a "hot" F-4). Though the S.E. 5 appeared on ground-attack missions, especially in the desperate "anything goes" ef-

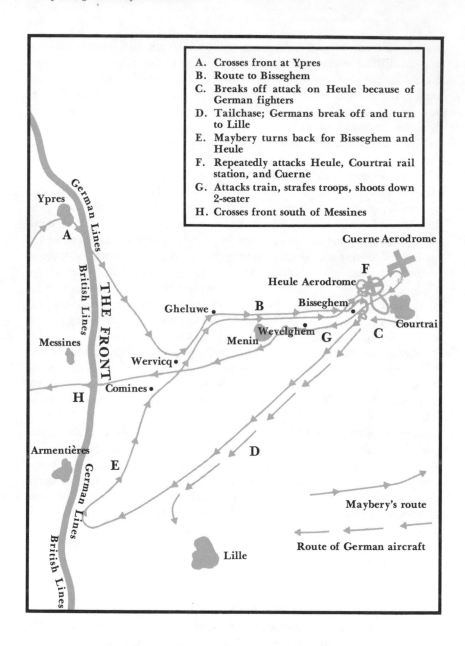

A. Crosses front at Ypres
B. Route to Bisseghem
C. Breaks off attack on Heule because of German fighters
D. Tailchase; Germans break off and turn to Lille
E. Maybery turns back for Bisseghem and Heule
F. Repeatedly attacks Heule, Courtrai rail station, and Cuerne
G. Attacks train, strafes troops, shoots down 2-seater
H. Crosses front south of Messines

Cuerne Aerodrome

Heule Aerodrome

Ypres

German Lines

British Lines

THE FRONT

Gheluwe

Menin

Wervicq

Comines

Messines

Armentières

Bisseghem

Wevelghem

Courtrai

German Lines

British Lines

Lille

Maybery's route

Route of German aircraft

Ground Attack on the Western Front: Lt. R.A. Maybery's S.E.5 sortie of 31 July 1917

forts of March and April 1918 as Britain sought to stem the tide of Luden-dorff's final offensives, the Camel served as the principal British ground-attack aircraft, together with the two-seat Bristol Fighter. Lieutenant R.A. Maybery's S.E. 5 sortie on July 31 offers a classic example of this kind of work by bomb-loaded fighters. He took off from Estree Blanche under "very thick clouds," crossed the front, dived to thirty feet to get under artillery smoke, flew from Wervicq to Gheluwe, on to Bisseghem, and on to Courtrai and the cluster of German airfields surrounding it. He turned to attack the airfield at Heule, but two intercepting Albatros attacked him; he outmaneuvered them adroitly, then turned for the front. Nearing Armentières he saw them turn away towards Lille, and he turned back to Comines, and onwards to Heule once again where he made multiple attacks, dropping three bombs. He flew over Courtrai rail station and dropped his last bomb, returned to Heule, strafed it again, then pressed on to Cuerne airfield and attacked it. He turned for home, spotted a goods train on its way from Courtrai to Menin, and strafed it as well as a column of German troops. Constantly checking the sky paid off, as he saw a two-seater above him, climbed after it, and after a brief dogfight, shot it down near Wevelghem. He then strafed more Germans on the ground and shot up yet another train, but his ammunition ran out, and he prudently flew home, crossing the front south of Messines. Unfortunately, this gallant pilot was later killed on a subsequent sortie. On another mission, a Spad pilot from 23 Squadron attacked Beveren airfield north of Roulers, dropping two Cooper bombs. He then returned and shot down a two-seater taking off, strafed a line of German artillery batteries, shot down an observation balloon, flew across the front, and returned home. His colleague attacked Ingelmunster airfield with bombs, strafed the field, shot up groups of troops near Menin, attacked an artillery battery, and strafed a train before returning to base. Close air support continued as well; as "zero hour" arrived, F.E. 2b's and the new (and disappointing) De Havilland D.H. 5 single-seaters, sometimes with S.E. 5's as well, would fly no higher than 500 feet over advancing troops, attacking German troop positions, mortar emplacements, and machine-gun positions ahead of the advancing line of infantry. Aircraft also flew artillery spotting missions and offensive fighter patrols to hinder enemy two-seaters and ground-attackers from undertaking similar missions. Accounts of these actions from the summer and fall of 1917 discredit the commonly accepted myth that air-ground cooperation, close air support, and interdiction were products of the Second World War, not the First.[30]

This new demonstration of the value of aircraft did not come without increasing losses. Some were caused simply by the dangers of low-flying in the mist and cloud of Northern Europe. On November 20, the opening of the see-saw Battle of Cambrai, three Camels attacked the base of *Jasta* 5 at Estourmel. The *Jasta* commander had already determined the weather to be too bad for flying, when out of the mist and damp roared three Camels. A waiting Albatros at once took off and managed to shoot down one of them. The other two bombed the landing ground and strafed the hangers, but as they pulled off target, they collided with trees barely visible in the thick weather, killing their pilots. Modern-day advocates, who speak blithely about operating interdiction and close air support sorties amid the weather, terrain, and threat environment of eastern Europe, despite sophisticated electro-optical aids would do well to bear in mind the experience of the RFC in the Great War.

Casualties during trench-strafing (close air support) were, again as might be expected, much heavier than casualties during interdiction missions behind the front. Thirty-five percent of the attack aircraft sent across the front during the opening of the Battle of Cambrai were lost, and, throughout the battle, casualties never dropped to less than thirty percent. The angular rotary-powered D.H. 5's, with their backward-staggered upper wing to improve the pilot's forward visibility, did yeoman service, but took very heavy losses; this aircraft, so reminiscent of the Bell P-39 of the Second World War, soon left the front, replaced by the S.E. 5. The thirty percent losses caused the destruction of a squadron in about four days, so that new replacements had to be brought in if the squadron were to continue fighting at the front. (Again, the loss rates were comparable to loss rates in the Yom Kippur War, the Falklands—Argentinian losses—and perhaps to the losses that might be expected of close air support aircraft in a Warsaw Pact-NATO war.) Pilots made three or four sorties per day. In 46 Squadron, Arthur Gould Lee was one of only three flight commanders left after a week of low-level attacks. Lee himself had been shot down on three of his first seven sorties, fortunately managing to crash-land on the Allied side of the lines in each case. Flying about 80 to 100 miles per hour, at about the altitude a modern-day crop-duster flies, the unarmored fighters of World War I flew through a literal hail of gunfire on trench-strafing sorties. Lee concluded that "with few exceptions," trench-strafing missions constituted "a wasteful employment of highly trained pilots and expensive aeroplanes," stating that "rather than face a single trench-strafing foray, I would much prefer to go through half a dozen dogfights with Albatroses."[31]

Still, the aircraft could inflict horrendous losses on targets, especially exposed artillery and marching troops. Particularly vulnerable were horse-drawn artillery, and nothing so exemplifies the First World War's blending of the old and new in military affairs than aircraft attacking horses. (Machine-gun emplacements, on the other hand, were difficult to find, and as a plane turned and banked trying to spot them, the gunners on the ground could often get it clearly in their sights.) The Battle of Cambrai introduced the tank to ground warfare, and even before the conclusion of this pioneering experiment in altering traditional ground tactics, the first episodes of cooperation between tanks and aircraft had occurred. On November 23, for example, D.H. 5's operated ahead of tanks, clearing out artillery positions threatening the advance of the tanks across the front at Bourlon Woods; post-battle analysis concluded that "the aeroplane pilots often made advance possible when the attacking troops would otherwise have been pinned to the ground."[32] This classic cooperation between air and ground forces advancing in assault presaged the close-knit cooperation evident in the *Wehrmacht's* drive across Poland, France, and the Low Countries in 1939-1940, and the Allied thrust across Northern Europe in 1944-1945, as well as more recent campaigns in Korea, Southeast Asia, and the Mideast.

Germany's approach to the ground-attack problem was significantly different from Great Britain's, and, in some ways, more perceptive. At the beginning of the war, Germany had a class of two-seat aircraft designated the C class machines, which were armed with an observer-operated machine gun. At the end of 1915, the air service established so-called "infantry" flying units, operating these C class aircraft (such as the Albatros C V and D.F.W. C V) as liaison aircraft flying low over the trenches; sometimes their duties included harassment strafing of Allied troops. Because of increasing losses from rifle and machine-gun fire, these C aircraft were modified to incorporate armor plating around the cockpit and engine. This trend reached its logical conclusion in 1917 with the introduction of a new aircraft of steel and aluminum construction, the Junkers J I. The J I was a truly revolutionary warplane: a heavily armored aircraft having the crew, fuel system, and engine encased in a 5-millimeter chrome-nickel steel bathtub shell that anticipated such later attack airplanes as the Ilyushin Il 2 *Sturmovik* and the more recent A-10. The J I was the result of Dr. Hugo Junkers' passionate belief in the future of all-metal aircraft, and it established the tradition of the all-metal military airplane. Naturally, the same qualities that made it virtually impervious to ground fire made it somewhat sluggish and difficult to handle, but the J I, an angular biplane characterized by Junker's corrugated external skinning, compensated for this by being reasonably fast (approximately 100 miles per hour), and having a heavy armament of twin forward-firing Spandaus plus a Parabellum machine gun for the observer-gunner, and a payload of small bombs and grenades. Complementing the introduction of this formidable attack airplane were two new so-called "Cl" types, lighter than the C class and closely approximating the Bristol Fighter in performance and capabilities:

the Halberstadt Cl II (which entered service on the Western Front in October 1917), and the Hannover Cl II which followed it into service in December 1917. Advanced models of both followed in 1918; both aircraft had fighter-like agility, close-placement of the crew for maximum efficiency, forward-firing guns, and an observer-operated Parabellum. These two had been intended for operation with so-called *Schutzstaffeln,* protection or escort flights that accompanied regular C class aircraft, but eventually they served, together with the J I, in the specialized *Schlasta* and *Schlachtgeschwader.* Creation of the *Schlachtgeschwader*, as with expansion of the number of *Jasta* and *Jagdgeschwader,* constituted a critical element of the so-called *"Amerikaprogramm"* intended to offset the expected arrival of large numbers of American troops and aircraft. As in the Second World War, German industry worked wonders in producing large numbers of aircraft; by the first of March 1918, shortly before the final offensives began, Germany had added thirty *Schlasta* to the *Luftstreitkräfte* representing a strength of 180 aircraft.[33]

The Germans were quick to learn from British low-flying attacks, and developed a doctrine of use that stressed the demoralizing effect that attack from the sky had upon troops: this was, after all, something quite new to warfare, literally changing the tradition of centuries. The doctrine, issued in February of 1918, emphasized massed formation attacks by not less than four machines with the intent of destroying the forward line of enemy resistance and attacking artillery emplacements. The doctrine also recognized the value of such aircraft in defensive operations, and stressed planning, good communication (via ground signals) with troops, and operational training.[34]

Germany made up for its previous lack of organized ground-attack formations with a vengeance on November 30, 1917, at the end of the Battle of Cambrai, when a number of Halberstadts accompanied German infantry in an assault that opened the German counterthrust. The Halberstadts flew at less than one hundred feet, harassing British infantry with their fire, forcing British machine gunners to exhaust most of their ammunition leaving them little with which to confront advancing German troops — and attacking targets behind the lines as well. These attacks achieved their purpose, and the Halberstadts made their appearance in subsequent assaults, helping turn Cambrai from success to a great disappointment for the British. The stage had been set for the employment of fighters in both counter-air and attack roles in the great battles of 1918.[35]

VIII.
The Final Cataclysm

The collapse of the Russian government and the settlement between Germany and the Bolsheviks freed large numbers of German troops and material for service on the Western Front. Ludendorff immediately moved to strengthen German forces in the west in preparation for a massive spring offensive that would, once and for all, determine the outcome of the war. On the eve of the offensive, code-named Operation Michael, he had six thousand artillery pieces arranged along a forty-mile front, as well as sixty-two divisions spearheaded by specially trained assault troops and supported by tanks. An impartial observer might have expected that, following the Nivelle debacle of the previous spring, Ludendorff would concentrate his forces against the French, hoping to destroy them. Instead, cannily, he aimed his thrust at the stronger of the two opponents, the British Expeditionary Force, directing it against the relatively weak Fifth Army, commanded by General Hubert Gough.[1] The disposition of German fighter forces followed the well-established tradition of regarding the RFC as its most dangerous foe: no less than fifty-one *Jasta* stood arrayed against Trenchard's airmen; only eighteen confronted French forces. Nine months before, the *Luftstreitkräfte* had combined the *Jasta* into special *Jagdgeschwader* (fighter wings), large formations that could move quickly from one sector of the front to another as the need arose. The premier of these wings was von Richthofen's own *JG I*, consisting of *Jasta 4, 6, 10,* and *11,* and shortly before the opening of the offensive on March 21, these units moved into advanced airfields along the front. On the morning of the 21st, a massive German artillery bombardment saturated British positions with gas shells. Prevailing cloud, fog, and mist hindered the defenders, as Ludendorff's troops advanced across the front in an assault that eerily presaged von Rundstedt's 1944 Ardennes offensive in the Second World War. Gough's forces fell back, disorganized but fighting as best they could. So rapid was the advance that eventually several British airfields were overrun, and planes had to be destroyed lest they fall into German hands.

Despite the weather, RFC counterattacks from the air began almost immediately, adding to the confusion of a front already under attack by German *Schlasta*. Captured German documents are filled with accounts of casualties caused by British trench-strafers; one recorded the loss of sixty horses of a German artillery unit to air attack—the unit was immobilized. In another case early in the offensive, S.E. 5a's flew continuous ground-attack sorties against German troops along the St. Quentin-Amiens road and the Transloy-Lesboeufs road. One German regiment reported an attack by twenty low-flying planes flying "within 2-3 metres" of the ground, one of which flew so low that its wheels literally ran over the back of the company commander.[2] Such attacks, by both sides, came to characterize the battles of 1918. Ernst Udet, one of Germany's outstanding fighter pilots, had joined the von Richthofen *Jagdgeschwader* shortly before the offensive. Even this elite counter-air unit found itself engaged in low-flying attacks (despite the total lack of suitability of its Fokker triplanes for this mission), and Udet followed von Richthofen in skimming low over the ground as *JG I* strafed troops and artillery.[3] Both British and German ground-attack planners recognized how unnerving such an experience could be to infantry in the trenches. Stuart Cloete, a young infantry officer with the Coldstream Guards, recollected an attack by German fighters that resembled "giant monsters . . . giant birds of prey" that "poured machine-gun fire into our trenches. . . . It was a very frightening experience. . . . One had a great desire to run away."[4]

The structure of the RFC attacks during the March offensive bespoke an already well-thought-out doctrine of using airplanes to strike at ground targets. The Somme had hinted at what could be done; Cambrai had confirmed it. In the urgent press of March 1918, the RFC threw every airplane it could muster against German forces both in the air and on the ground. The basic RFC ground-attack doctrine generally followed called for staggered fighter employment, with S.E. 5's and Sopwith Dolphins in a counter-air role high over the battlefield, Camels operating at medium altitudes below them to furnish protection for artillery spotting, ground attack, and reconnaissance aircraft, and, finally, the ground-attack fighters (such as the Bristol Fighter, or bomb-loaded Camels and, less frequently, S.E. 5's and Dolphins) "on the deck" with Cooper bombs and machine-gun fire. The "cab rank" tactics commonly associated with the Legion Kondor in Spain and the Royal Air Force over the Falaise Gap in the Second World War, appeared in 1918 as well. Ground-attack aircraft generally maintained a circling attack pattern over the troops, with one group attacking, another group rolling in on the target, and a third pulling off the target. In one case during the battles of the Lys in April 1918, no less than twenty-seven Camels and S.E. 5's from four different fighter squadrons maintained constant attacks against German troops in the Festubert region, and the postwar historian of one regiment attacked concluded that the unit had "suffered severely from the British low-flying aircraft which attacked them savagely with machine-gun fire and bombs."[5] Such successes did not come without losses and strain to aircrew; one S.E. 5a pilot wrote after one day's work, "Our low work today has been hellish. I never did like this ground strafing."[6]

Elaborate plans were developed for the working of fighters and bombers together, anticipating the strategies developed in later wars. Railyards, bridges, and airfields all came under attack. Bombers were used to bait German fighters, and high-flying fighters would wait until the *Jasta* had committed themselves before dropping from above onto the unsuspecting enemy interceptors. Bridges proved difficult to destroy; British attacks on the Somme River bridges failed to down them, for much the same reason that attacks on bridges in Korea and Vietnam proved so ineffective — the bomb blast did little damage to the heavy structure. Worse, standing German fighter patrols cost the British dearly in these bridge attacks, though the official history somewhat lamely concludes that German fighter losses during these missions must have included "the flower of the German air service." Why this particular lesson was missed during the collapse of France and the Low Countries is unknown; by a closer reading of the Somme bridge experience, British and French air leaders might have avoided the futile Royal Air Force and *Armee de l'Air* assault on the Maastricht River bridges that cost so many gallant aircrew their lives in 1940.[7] Bridge-bombing has never been easy — James Michener's novel *The Bridges at Toko-ri* describes one such campaign — and the American experience with the Thanh Hoa and Paul Doumier bridges in North Vietnam illustrated that, fifty years after World War I, bridges were still elusive targets but great flak traps for aircraft. Not until the development of the precision-guided "smart bomb" did the bridge lose its invulnerability to general pattern-bombing.[8] One lesson that emerged from the ground-attack experience in 1918 was that aircraft were safer operating at very low altitudes using terrain-masking than operating at medium altitudes. One British directive cautioned pilots that they should consider themselves "less vulnerable very low than at heights of 3, 4, or 500 feet. Thus, after picking their targets at about 1,000 feet and diving, they should remain very low until clear, and then climb again."[9]

Airfields came under particularly heavy assault, and, for the first time, German *Schlasta* formations attacked British airfields as well; in one notable attack, five German attack fighters raided Bertangles airfield, destroying five hangers and five Bristol Fighters, and damaging one hanger with two Bristols inside, as well as blowing up yet another Bristol and burning down another hanger with an S.E. 5a inside. For the most part, however, airfield-raiding remained a British specialty in which both fighter and bomber units partook. In one such raid against *Jasta 35, Jasta* commander Rudolf Stark witnessed an attack by no less than fifty British fighters and bombers on his airfield; their pilots, he recollected, "were most amazingly impertinent and hardly knew how to find outlets for their arrogance." No doubt some did, for when they left, *Jasta 35* had lost eleven new Fokker D VIIs, putting the *Jasta* out of business for several days.[10] Such raids met Trenchard's expectations that the best way to destroy an enemy air service was by destroying it on the ground. A dogfight in which eleven Fokkers had been shot down would have been news along the front for weeks. Complementing these attacks was the development of new attack strategies. William Brown, a pilot with 84 Squadron flying S.E. 5a's developed the first genuine dive-bombing techniques following a suggestion from a fellow pilot. Bombs had been released in diving attacks before — witness Marix's airship raid of 1914 — but Brown's attack was the first in which the pilot aimed the aircraft like a rifle at the target. The low cloud and fog that occasionally spread across the Western Front mitigated against a general adoption of Brown's technique by other fighter squadrons, but it certainly was a precursor to the deadly Stuka attacks of the Second World War.[11]

In April, Marshal Ferdinand Foch, the Supreme Allied Commander, issued instructions to the French and British air services stating that "the first duty of fighting aeroplanes is to assist the troops on the ground by incessant attacks, with bombs and machine-gun, on columns, concentrations, or bivouacs. Air fighting is not to be sought except so far as necessary for the fulfillment of this duty."[12] Thereafter, pilot accounts and squadron histories abound with instances of ground targets struck in force with the expenditure of dozens and sometimes hundreds of bombs, and literally tens of thousands of rounds of ammunition. Obviously, the ground-attack role was not limited to specially trained and equipped units, as was the case in the *Luftstreitkräfte*. The fighters, as might be expected, took heavy losses. In March and April, the RFC/RAF lost a total of 528 fighters, of which 130 were listed as missing.* By comparison, the actual British strength on the Western Front on the day the March offensive opened was 1,232. Next to fighters, the artillery spotters and reconnaissance aircraft faired worst, with 295 lost or missing. Next came day bombers (117 lost or missing), fighter-reconnaissance Bristol Fighters (69 lost or missing), and night bombers (23 lost or missing).[13]

---

*On April 1, 1918, the RFC and RNAS merged to form the Royal Air Force, the world's first independent air force.

Undeniably the intensive British ground-attack activities played a major role in blunting the Ludendorff thrust. The unexpected resilience and steadfastness of France's army—a tribute to Marshal Henri Petain—and the critical deployment and skill of arriving American troops—a tribute to John Pershing—bolstered the efforts of Britain's company grade officers and the average "Tommies" who made up the fighting force, and led to the collapse of this last great German offensive in August 1918. Thereafter, the Kaiser's Germany was on the skids. Overseas, in a bloody action that anticipated the Mitla Pass massacre of 1967, Germany's ally Turkey lost thousands of troops to a day of concentrated ground attacks by S.E. 5a's, D.H. 9's, and Bristol Fighters bombing and strafing the Wadi El Far'a. And on the Western Front two days before the armistice, the RAF made a ground attack that exemplified just how far military aviation, and especially the fighting scout, had come since the days of 1914. On the afternoon of November 9, a squadron of D.H. 9 bombers, accompanied by two squadrons of Camel and S.E. 5 fighter-bombers, and escorted by a squadron of Bristol Fighters and a squadron of the new Sopwith Snipe (essentially a tamer derivative of the Camel having greater visibility and safer handling qualities than its predecessor), took off for a low-level bombing strike on targets of opportunity near Enghien. The strike aircraft attacked two airfields, causing large fires, destroying several aircraft, and damaging others. Horse and vehicle transport were strafed, bombed, and thrown into confusion on the Ath-Enghien road near Bassilly. The bombers attacked the railroad station at Enghien, scoring twenty direct hits on trains, causing numerous fires and secondary explosions. Without opposition aloft, the Bristol Fighters came down to join in the attack, and thereafter, as strike leader R. S. Maxwell reported, "The ground targets were so obvious and numerous that every pilot and observer kept firing until stoppages or lack of ammunition compelled him to cease."[14] It was a long way from the Moranes and *Taube* of 1914 with their crews dropping an occasional homemade bomb or can of *fléchettes* overboard.

No less decisive were the actions of the fighters aloft as the Allies and Germany struggled for air superiority. The year 1918 was a year in which Germany introduced a number of first-class aircraft into air combat, typified by the excellent Fokker D VII. But there were others as well, notably the Siemens-Schuckert D III and D IV (whose tubby appearance belied a fine performance), the L.F.G. Roland D VIa and VIb (a highly agile fighter built as a hedge against failure of the Fokker D VII), and the Pfalz D XII (another excellent airplane that never quite succeeded in overcoming the German fighter pilots' love affair with Tony Fokker's angular D VII). The parasol-winged Fokker E V (D VIII) "Flying Razor" and the revolutionary all-metal Junkers D I fighter and Cl I ground-attack fighter were too late to have a meaningful impact on the conduct of the air war. Besides, they, too, had to overcome the intense attachment that most German fighter pilots developed for the D VII, for it was the magnificent D VII upon which the *Luftstreitkräfte* rested its hopes for regaining air supremacy in the spring of 1918. The 160-horsepower Mercedes engine endowed the basic D VII with a good performance, superior to its predecessors. But the 185-horsepower BMW engine turned it into quite another airplane entirely, one that had excellent performance at both high and low altitudes, with a reserve of power to pull the craft through the most punishing maneuvers.

As Boelcke had been present at the birth of the Halberstadt and Albatros biplanes that ushered in the third generation of fighter designs, so von Richthofen had presided over the gestation of the Fokker D VII. And as Boelcke had been fated to miss the resurgence of the *Luftstreitkräfte* into 1917, so von Richthofen was fated not to fly the D VII into combat, for he lost his life in aerial battle on April 21, 1918, a Sunday.

Von Richthofen's death has been recounted so often that it does not merit re-examination in detail here. It occurred in a dogfight that started in the fashion of so many others. A formation of four Fokker triplanes attacked two Australian R.E. 8's plodding along on reconnaissance duties. The R.E. 8's managed to avoid being shot down—no mean feat—and British antiaircraft fire directed against the attacking triplanes alerted Captain Roy Brown, leading a patrol of Sopwith Camels, to the dogfight. Brown and his formation dived down to help, and just then, another formation of triplanes led by von Richthofen stumbled across the combat, and the baron led his formation down on Brown. A wild dogfight erupted. Lieutenant Wilfred May, a close friend of Brown, was flying his first offensive patrol. He had been strictly cautioned by Brown not to engage in combat, and, to the best of his ability, he did not. At one point, however, he could not resist the impulse to fire at a triplane (apparently flown by von Richthofen's cousin Wolfram), and following it into the center of the "fur ball," he soon discovered enemy aircraft "coming at me from all sides." Following instructions, he dove away from the fight, following a northwesterly course along the Somme.* Just when he believed himself safe, he heard the rattle of twin Spandaus, and turned to see a Fokker on his tail. It was von Richthofen, who had spotted May diving away, and as was his fashion, had dived down for the kill. Now it was a tail chase, May jinking, and von Richthofen closing the gap. Brown saw the triplane (not recogniz-

---

*May did exactly what Brown wanted him to; this is not a necessarily important point, except that some recent writers, notably Stephen Longstreet, have unjustly accused May of having "lost his nerve." May's wartime record needs no defenders; he soon shot down thirteen confirmed and five probable German aircraft, winning the Distinguished Flying Cross.

ing the identity of its pilot), dived on it, and crept up without von Richthofen "checking six" and spotting him. All three aircraft were low over the Somme and its shoreline; von Richthofen's Fokker was under fire from the ground. Brown had a perfect sight picture, fired, and watched his bullets stitch the triplane from its tail surfaces along the fuselage towards the pilot. Von Richthofen, startled, turned and for an instant stared straight at Brown — one wonders what thought went through the great executioner's mind as he found himself in the position of so many of his victims — and then he slumped down. Brown saw the triplane going down, and banked away. The stricken plane landed in a gentle glide, the Red Baron dead at the controls.[15] A great controversy erupted after the war over who actually shot von Richthofen down; over the years the picture has become more muddled, not less, and a cult of professional von Richthofen buffs have analyzed bullet tracks, positions of guns and planes, etc., in exercises that, for their ghoulishness, morbidity, and ultimate pointlessness, are matched only by the cultists forever reexamining the assassination of John Kennedy.[16] At the end, it doesn't really matter.* What *does* matter is that von Richthofen's death illustrated several basic lessons of air combat: you only make one mistake; "check six" — someone is probably there, hosing you; don't get so entranced by your target that you forget your back. In any case, von Richthofen's accumulated errors placed him deep into enemy territory, flying through heavy ground fire, with a fighter at his six o'clock. His being shot down at that point was inevitable.

Von Richthofen's death shook the *Jagdflieger* of the *Luftstreitkräfte* to the core. Rudolf Stark's diary entry for April 23, 1918, expressed the feeling: "Richthofen dead! We whisper the dread tidings softly to one another. . . . A gloomy silence broods over all."[17] Allied reaction was relief tinged (in most quarters) with a grudging wish that he might have survived the war. Ira "Taffy" Jones, already one of the rising fighter pilots in 74 Squadron headed by the charismatic Edward "Mick" Mannock, penned his own diary entry: "The great Baron von Richthofen has been killed in our lines. Thank God for that. . . . he has destroyed his last British machine, which precludes any possible chance of my name being added to his bag."[18] His death symbolized the decline of the *Luftstreitkräfte* over the spring and summer and on down to inexorable defeat in November 1918. Despite the new warplanes, despite a generally good fighting spirit and a good team of leading fighter pilots, the failure to adopt an offensive air doctrine, the failure to pay more than lip service to the Boelcke *dicta*, the over-emphasis on running up huge individual scores in place of carefully

---

*I believe Roy Brown shot von Richthofen down, despite all revisionist claims to the contrary. Many critics of Brown seem less concerned with what actually happened than with defending a misguided belief in the infallibility of the Red Baron.

training a pool of thoroughly competent pilots, the failure to progress beyond the Albatros formula in the critical months of 1917, the failure of *Idflieg* to properly mobilize the German aircraft industry, the failure to overcome labor and materials shortages, and, finally, the swamping of German air defenses by hundreds and eventually thousands of Allied warplanes doomed the *Luftstreitkräfte* to defeat. Even in the elite *JG I* of von Richthofen, thirty-six fighter pilots were killed or captured, and another eleven were wounded, between the opening of the great offensive and the armistice. In many regular *Jasta*, the figures were worse. Two-seater pilot Oscar Bechtle compared his compatriots to "the cavalry of earlier days, ever charging into the fray." In fact, the charge was more Cardigan and the Light Brigade than Blücher at Waterloo. After the war, that great compiler Georg Neumann published an anthology on the *Luft-streitkräfte* entitled *In der Luft Unbesiegt*: Unconquered in the Air. In fact, the *Luftstreitkräfte had been* defeated in the air, as had the army on land, and the navy at sea. Myths like Neumann's, coupled with the "stab-in-the-back" propaganda of the 1920s and 1930s, prevented the real lessons from the First World War being taken to heart by the new Germany. (Such myths actually were essential if the Nazi state were to win popular acceptance.) Von Richthofen's shoes as *Geschwaderkommandeur* were briefly filled by Wilhelm Reinhard, until his death in the crash of an experimental fighter; then came the last wartime commander of *JG I*, Oberleutnant Hermann Göring, who later helped create the *"unbesiegt"* myth before eventually running his own air force into the ground in the 1940s.[19]

Trenchard did not miss the lessons, however, nor did his flight crews. From 1917 onwards, they stressed training and operational practice. Whereas in 1916 and 1917, pilots went to the front with minimal training, after the spring of 1917 all that changed: pilot accounts are replete not merely with stories of how much flying practice they had before entering combat in 1918, but with stories of how prospective pilots were carefully examined for their experience in specific aircraft (say, for example, the Sopwith Dolphin or S.E. 5a) before being posted to the front.[20]

In the fighting that broke the back of the *Jagdstaffeln*, the British, the Americans, and to a lesser extent the French, incorporated the benefit of tactical experience developed in 1916 and 1917. For the Americans, participating in the European air war involved getting familiar with the conflict, learning how to survive, and then learning how to win. Britain had developed a strong air tactician in Irish-born Edward "Mick" Mannock, a tempermental and emotional air leader capable of unswerving loyalty to his men, and fierce hatred for his foes. Mannock had begun his fighting career in 1917 and was very much in the mold of Albert Ball: a superb

WESTERN FRONT: Line of German Advance, June 1918

marksman who constantly flew on the offensive. Here the comparison ended, for unlike Ball, Mannock carefully thought out his strategy. And like the German Boelcke, Mannock imparted it to his pilots. His skill and understanding of air fighting helped him offset what would appear to be an insurmountable obstacle to his becoming a successful fighter pilot: his almost total lack of vision in his left eye. Mannock eventually went on to score seventy-three victories before dying in combat; like von Richthofen, he grew careless and ignored some of his own rules. But like his great friend and fellow Irishman James McCudden of 56 Squadron, Mannock made his own 74 "Tiger" Squadron one of the Royal Air Force's finest. He took particular interest in new pilots, cautioning them against over-confidence, and gradually initiating them into the mysteries of air combat. He had a very basic set of rules: "Always above, seldom on the same level, never underneath." There was another one, the one that killed him when he ignored it: "Never follow a machine down to the ground." Mannock constantly stressed teamwork, attacking in force, and never attacking at a disadvantage—particularly from beneath your opponent. As a result of his example and leadership, 74 Squadron ended the war with a total of 225 German aircraft destroyed for a loss of fifteen pilots killed or taken prisoner. The pilots added their own roster of rules, including keeping fit, learning to spot the enemy as soon as possible so as to gain an early initiative in a dogfight, practicing air to ground gunnery, closing to within one hundred yards before firing, firing in short bursts to conserve ammunition and avoid gun jams, making certain to allow the proper deflection while shooting, and three psychological ones: "Keep cool when the fight begins," "Be determined to get your man," and "Develop the offensive spirit."[21] Squadrons such as 74 and 56 were filled with truly exceptional airmen, but even in the less well-known fighting squadrons of the RFC the same careful approach to air fighting predominated. Mannock's death, like von Richthofen's and even McCudden's (in a stall-spin accident shortly after take-off when his engine quit and he tried to turn back to the field) stemmed not from a basically unsafe or "lone wolf" approach to air combat, but rather from errors of judgment brought about in great part by the strain of constant combat flying.

By 1918, the day of the "lone wolf" was definitely over, just as the day of the makeshift fighter plane had passed. Arguably there were three kinds of successful fighter pilots in the First World War. The first category may be termed "roving freebooters": men like Ball, Billy Bishop, Guynemer, Voss, and Garros. Bishop is the only survivor of those listed; he received reassignment from combat in 1917, and returned to the front in 1918, but he was canny and shrewd, and recognized that times and tactics had changed. All the rest, with the exception of Garros, perished in 1917 when cut down on lone sorties. Garros, who had started the whole business, escaped from German captivity in January 1918, returned to France and joined *Escadrille Spa 103*, one of the four Spad squadrons comprising *Les Cigognes*. According to René Fonck, who would become the Allies' highest-scoring pilot and survive the war to die of old age, Garros impressed his squadron mates by his self-imposed isolation. He did not adapt easily to the new air war. Fonck, ever the master of the careful stalk and the well-aimed burst, considered Garros to be "reckless without bounds." Fellow pilots such as Fonck and Xavier de Sévin tried to caution him, but to no avail. On October 5, 1918, the inevitable occurred, and he fell alone, in combat with over a dozen Fokkers.[22]

The second group were canny individuals, who concentrated on running up large scores of victories, but who were careful tacticians, and excellent marksmen. They knew the advantages of teamwork, but their emphasis on building up their own string of victories caused them, at best, to place secondary importance on instruction and tutelage of fellow pilots. Some of these would still undertake individual patrols, but only under carefully controlled conditions—such as McCudden's interception of high-flying Rumpler reconnaissance aircraft in 1917 and early 1918. Pilots like von Richthofen, Udet, McCudden, Fonck, and Nungesser—indeed, virtually all of the great French aces—fall into this category. Their philosophy is exemplified in McCudden's wartime memoirs, when he wrote, "I think that the correct way to wage war is to down as many as possible of the enemy at the least risk, expense and casualties to one's own side."[23] The third group were the true tacticians and masters of air fighting who spent at least as much time looking after their fellow pilots and instructing them as they did flying combat themselves, and here two names stand out above the others, Oswald Boelcke and Mick Mannock. Such individuals were very rare; Boelcke, the great defensive expert, shaped the German *Jagdflieger* in a way that influenced its outlook far beyond the Great War and into the formation of the Nazi *Luftwaffe* as well. Mannock, on the other hand, epitomized the offensive use of aircraft, likewise starting traditions that extended to the RAF in the Second World War.

The arrival of large numbers of Americans flying British and French-designed aircraft added a new twist to the air war. The American aircrews were very enthusiastic, but possessed little of the expertise that came from studying under instructors who had served in combat. It is perhaps a measure of the relative decline of German fighter pilot skills that so many German fighters were, in fact, shot down by these newcomers from across the Atlantic. In 1918, the American air service fulfilled the roles and missions of the other Allied forces, flying counter-air, interdiction, close air support, reconnaissance, and bombardment sorties over the front. There was a core of skilled American personnel who had flown with the French or British before American involvement in the war, men such as Charles Biddle, Harold Hartney, and Raoul Lufbery, and they proved invaluable in instructing new arrivals into the mysteries of the Western Front air war. Lufbery in particular acted as an American Boelcke or Mannock, imparting to pilots such as Douglas Campbell and Eddie Rickenbacker the basic lessons of survival.[24] American fighter pilots first flew patrols along the relatively tranquil Toul sector where, as one analyst wrote, "The enemy pursuit aviation was neither aggressive, numerous, nor equipped with the best types of machines."[25]

Still, a lot of learning came from trial and error, much of which was painful. Some pilots—such as balloon-buster Frank Luke—emulated the "lone wolf" tactics that had worked in 1915 and 1916 and met predictable ends. Bombing sorties in the face of fighter opposition proved particularly costly. In September, during the first four days of the St. Mihiel offensive, the First Day Bombardment Group lost thirty-one pilots and observers, sixteen from one squadron alone.[26] On September 14, an American bombing squadron attached to a French bomb group left for a raid on the city of Conflans, escorted by three three-seat Caudron R.11 escort fighters, a twin-engine design armed with no less than six machine guns. A group of Spads scheduled to protect the bombing formation failed to rendezvous, and the bomb group continued on its own. German fighters intercepted the formation and, in a running forty-minute fight, shot down two of the three-seat escorts and thirteen out of the eighteen bombers. In a subsequent raid, four Breguet Bre 14 bombers went after the same city and, in a confrontation with no less than twenty-five Fokkers, all were shot down; a few days later, five out of six American-flown D.H. 4 bombers disappeared in the same fashion. It is easy to see how the tradition of pressing on in the face of intense opposition that manifested itself in the skies over Schweinfurt, Regensburg, and Ploesti first originated.[27] One European example the American air service quickly abandoned was the notion of employing large unwieldy formations of fighters in massed patrols. Following combat experience in the Battle of Chateau Thierry, the American air service decided to utilize large formations, but spaced out in such a fashion that if German fighters attacked, they could attack only one small unit at a time, and the rest of the large formation would be in a better position for counterattack. This strategy demanded constant lookout lest smaller units be destroyed piecemeal, but the purpose was to reduce the confusion that resulted when a German formation burst upon a large tightly-flown gaggle of American aircraft.[28] Asked to talk about their own "lessons learned" from combat, the pilots and observers gave views that indicated not only how quickly they had learned the rules of the game, but how passionately they believed in their conclusions. The following are two examples from many:

There is an old saying that eternal vigilance is the price of peace. In air work it is the price of life. One's safety and one's usefulness alike demand absolutely that pilot and observer should both be everlastingly on the lookout for enemy planes. Half the planes brought down, one pilot ventures to suggest, are brought down in surprise attacks, and this is probably true. It is essential that pilot and observer practice "picking up" and reporting to each other any planes that appear, always remembering to keep an especially sharp watch under the tail of the machine and in the direction of the sun; for that, above all on hazy days, is the enemy's best friend.

Successful aerial attacks like all other military offensive maneuvers, depend to a large extent on position and surprise. Other things being equal, the aviator that can surprise his opponent or accelerate his speed by diving from a higher altitude will win the battle. The best possible position to have is to be in line between your adversary and the sun and to be at least a couple of hundred meters higher. An attack on equal numbers from such an opportunity should bring a victory every time.[29]

Confusion existed over the role of two-place fighters. Colonel Thomas De Witt Milling, chief of the Air Service for the U.S. First Army, stated after the war, "It is not believed that the so-called two-place fighter has yet demonstrated the fact that it can be considered to exist." But Milling was talking only of two-place aircraft relying on the gunner for offensive fire. While he correctly perceived the weaknesses of this approach, which von Richthofen had dramatically affirmed in his fight with Leefe Robinson and the unimaginatively flown Bristol Fighters, he ignored the subsequent use of the Bristol Fighter and its very successful use in counter-air operations. Perhaps Milling was simply unaware of how well the Bristol had done, though this would be strange, considering that the U.S. Air Service tried to develop its own Liberty-engined model of it. A Canadian Bristol crew, Andrew McKeever and his gunner L.F. Powell, flew with particular success; not counting his observer's numerous kills, McKeever downed thirty aircraft, mostly Albatros fighters, before returning to Canada. Another Bristol pilot, John Gurdon, shot down twenty-seven German planes. The Germans, too, were successful with the heavy two-seat fighters of the *Schlachtstaffeln*. Flying a Halberstadt Cl II, Vizefeldwebel Friedrich Huffzky and Gottfried Ehmann of *Schlasta 15* shot down nine enemy aircraft in June and July of 1918; earlier, in May, another two-seater crew, Leutnant Karl Eisenmenger and Vizefeldwebel Georg Gund, shot down four Allied fighters while on a single mission. (Such two-seat successes foreshadowed the exploits of pilots in the Second World War, such as the U.S. Navy's John Leppla and John Liska who flew their Douglas SBD Dauntless so aggressively during the Battle of the Coral Sea that they claimed three Japanese fighters and a Japanese two-seater in a single day.) Despite these examples, Milling's sentiments reflected popular thought concerning two-seat fighters; their development was almost ignored in favor of single-seat aircraft during the 1920s and 1930s, an unfortunate result of such thinking.[30]

Out of the Western Front experience came summary documents, which, unfortunately, seem to have had little influence upon postwar American thinking about the employment and use of fighters (as well as other forms of military aircraft). One classic report, prepared early in 1919, was Lieutenant Colonel William C. Sherman's "Tentative Manual for the Employment of Air Service," which included some valuable and interesting sections on the employment of fighters in both counter-air and ground-attack roles. By the end of the war, the air service had, at least for the time being, recognized the foolishness of operating bombers without adequate fighter escort. An operational diagram in the Sherman manual shows how a bombardment group should stage a raid. It shows three V formations of ten Breguets each, the Vs arranged in line-astern flight, escorted by six Caudron R.11 heavy fighters, and no less than fifty-eight Spads. (It makes an interesting comparison with a later drawing from a book on the air war in Southeast Asia showing a strike force of sixteen F-105D Thunderchiefs in staggered line-astern formation, escorted by two flights—four each—of F-105 "Wild Weasels" and a screen of F-4 Phantom II's. The similarities are striking.)[31]

Overall, American participation in the air war on the Western Front in 1918 is best exemplified by the massive St. Mihiel aerial offensive, in which 1,481 Allied aircraft participated, the greatest concentration of air power seen to that time. They were commanded by Colonel William "Billy" Mitchell, America's flamboyant equivalent to "Boom" Trenchard—but without the latter's often accommodating and astute touch. No less than 701 of the aircraft participating in this offensive were fighters, and they served in the roles and missions that the RFC had pioneered, fighting enemy aircraft, trench-strafing, and interdicting behind the front. This was an example of tactical aviation at its finest, Mitchell working to meet the needs of American force commander John Pershing and his troops. His fighter pilots quickly established ascendancy over the *Jasta* facing them, and despite frequent bitter dogfights, the outcome was never in doubt.[32]

The same was true in the closing weeks of the war up and down the Western Front. Everywhere the German air service was shot out of the sky, and on the ground the German army fell back as well. Only the rainy and foggy weather of fall prevented the orderly retreat towards the German frontier from being turned into a bloody rout; had Allied ground-attack fighters had clear skies in which to operate, scenes from the Turkish massacre at the Wadi El Far'a would have been commonplace on the roads

WESTERN FRONT: Armistice, 11 Nov 1918

and paths leading back to Germany. As it was, Allied fighters did fearful damage to unprotected troops and transport. Aloft, the Fokkers seemed powerless to intervene. Fokker's new E V (the D VIII parasol monoplane) experienced a disastrous series of structural failures that prevented its large-scale use. The Junkers D I and Cl I all-metal fighters had only just arrived at the front, and could not make a difference. New Allied aircraft, notably the Sopwith Snipe, coupled with the high level of Allied fighter experience, ensured the destruction of the *Luftstreitkräfte*. In four days, one Snipe squadron shot down thirty-six German aircraft, thirteen in one day. Ten Australian Snipes engaged six D VII's over Ath on October 28, shooting down all of them. On October 30, fighting reached its climax. In a series of prolonged and vicious engagements, sixty-seven German airplanes went down over the front in exchange for forty-one RAF aircraft; twenty-nine RAF pilots were killed or missing, and eight were wounded. In early November, the weather turned damp and rainy, curtailing flight operations. On November 11, the first air war ended.

IX.
Lessons

Speaking before the Eighth Military History Symposium at the U.S. Air Force Academy in 1978, Brigadier General Noel F. Parrish, USAF (Ret.), alluded to many of the myths that afflict military aviation history, including "the myth of ineffective air power in World War I."[1] And, indeed, in the view of most writers, the first war in the air was a sideshow of no consequence to the fighting on the ground. Yet assaults were planned on the basis of reconnaissance; attacks and preparations were foiled by artillery fire directed from the air; and roads, railroads, and gun and troop positions were bombed and strafed. Even so, the myth persists. One otherwise perceptive student of military airpower has written that "from World War II emerged the three basic missions of tactical airpower: counter air, interdiction, and close air support."[2] A recent interview with four noted American fighter leaders trained in the 1920s and 1930s produced a general consensus that air superiority as a doctrine arose only from the Second World War; indeed, one of the participants (reflecting on fighter aviation in the First World War) stated that "the fighter airplane in those days was basically an ego trip. The fighter airplane didn't do a hell of a lot of good . . . there was no great strategic effort that was being executed or fulfilled . . . the fighter business in those days was a bunch of guys going up and fighting another bunch of guys without a known objective."[3]

Such statements do not reflect on the speakers; rather, the statements reflect the fact that the lessons of the First World War have been lost. Doubtless, the same beliefs were held by most airmen who were trained in the late 1920s and 1930s, and who rose to prominence as air combat leaders in the Second World War or later. They were the ones who developed air superiority tactics used to such good effect in Europe,

Africa, the Southwest Pacific, and the fighter sweeps that so seriously disrupted transportation, communications, and production over the German and Japanese homelands. It is apparent from these statements, and from the memoirs of many pilots and airpower leaders of the Second World War that during the 1920s and 1930s in the United States very little transfer or teaching of the lessons on using fighters that emerged from World War I occurred. There were exceptions, individuals who drew upon their wartime experience, notably the dashing Frank O'Driscoll "Monk" Hunter, but it really remained for Claire Chennault (who had not learned to fly until after World War I) to open the eyes of the U.S. Army Air Corps to the potential of fighter aviation when he taught students at the Air Corps Tactical School. And, it is interesting to note, Chennault stressed defensive, not offensive, "pursuit."[4] It was not until visits by British fighter leaders to the United States in 1941 (by which time the Royal Air Force had moved from the defensive posture of the Battle of Britain to an offensive one of using fighters for raids across the Channel) that, as General James Ferguson has recalled, "we gained some very helpful ideas on the modern use of fighters."[5]

The United States was not alone in losing sight of the value of fighters for air superiority, interdiction, and close air support. Britain, under the lasting influence of the Gotha raids, placed most of its emphasis on fighters as bomber interceptors. Even the great Supermarine Spitfire, as well as its less attractive brother-in-arms, the Hawker Hurricane, were designed as bomber interceptors, and their potential as interdictors remained totally unexplored until wartime necessity forced their development as fighter-bombers. As Britain's leading fighter ace of the Second World War, Group Captain James E. Johnson, has written, for the Royal Air Force of the 1930s, "dogfighting was a thing of the past, and rigid air-fighting tactics were introduced which, by a series of complicated and time-wasting manoeuvres, aimed at bringing the greatest number of guns to bear against the bombers."[6] All this went out the window in the summer of 1940, but not, unfortunately, before a number of Fighter Command pilots had died attempting to carry out the tight vic (V) and section formation attacks of prewar training ritual.

Consider the following statement:

The contest for air superiority is the most important contest of all, for no other operations can be sustained if this battle is lost. To win it, we must have the best equipment, the best tactics, the freedom to use them, and the best pilots. We had the best pilots. Our experiences suggest that superiority in equipment and superiority in tactics must be viewed as two elusive goals to be constantly pursued, not as assumed conditions. We are not apt to have marked superiority in both equipment and tactics for an extended period; neither side is likely to corner the market on ingenuity for long. Because so much depends on this battle, because it is so fiercely contested, and because it is so readily affected by technology, tactics, and rules of engagement, this is the battle in which our airpower can most easily be crippled by external restraints.[7]

Trenchard? Von Hoeppner? Mitchell? No—this is General William W. Momyer, former commander of the U.S. Air Force's Tactical Air Command, reflecting on the air war against North Vietnam. But it could just as easily have been any of the others talking about the First World War. *Plus ça change, plus ça la même chose.* Lessons learned from air combat in the First World War were many and varied. Many would now seem commonsense, but the fact that they were first learned in the Great War serves to demonstrate yet again how complex and organized that struggle was, in contrast to the myth that air operations were casual and irrelevant. Most of the lessons fall into two areas, fighter *development* and air combat *operations*.

FIGHTER DEVELOPMENT

1. Sophistication should not be sacrificed to numbers. It seems strange to speak of 1914-1918 aircraft in terms of sophistication vs. simplicity—often termed the question of "high" technology vs. "low" technology. Yet it is valid to consider this familiar argument with regard to the First World War. On the whole it is difficult to avoid the conclusion that sophisticated aircraft constantly outperformed or contributed more than unsophisticated ones. They had longer service lives—the fourth-generation Bristol Fighter, for example, lasted into the 1930s—and they could do more. Because of the pace of wartime technological development, yesterday's sophisticated machine, such as the Nieuport 11 or the Albatros D III, quickly became today's and tomorrow's unsophisticated and obsolescent type. Without question, the air combat of 1917-1918 illustrated the value of the high-low mix, but demonstrated that the "high" side of the mix cannot afford to be much smaller than the "low" side. By the armistice in 1918, for example, Great Britain had built nearly 5,500 of the relatively unsophisticated Sopwith Camel, 3,100 Bristol Fighters (a further 1,300 were built after the war), and 5,200 S.E.5/S.E. 5a's. Taking just the single-seaters, and not including the two-seat Bristol Fighter, this works out to a high-low mix of 1:1.05. Including the Bristol Fighter, the high-low mix rises to 1.5:1 in favor of the "high" side. Figures for Albatros production are less certain. At the end of April 1918, the German fighter force on the Western Front was essentially an obsolescent unsophisticated one, over 63% of its fighters being Albatros D III, V, and Va aircraft. A further 22% were the equally outdated Pfalz D IIIa, and the obsolescent Dr I triplane comprised nearly 9% of the total. The state-of-the-art Fokker D VII (which was just entering the inventory) was included in the nearly 6%

of German fighters that composed a miscellaneous D class serving at the front. Eventually over 410 Fokkers were delivered for service to the *Luftstreitkräfte*. In August 1918, there were still some 470-odd Albatros and Pfalz fighters at the front; at best the ratio at this time of Albatros/Pfalz to Fokker D VII cannot have given a high-low mix of better than 1:2 — virtually the reverse of the RAF's. All through the climactic battles of 1918, Germany fought at a qualitative as well as a quantitative disadvantage.

At first glance, there does not seem to be much to choose in singling out fighter aircraft performance after late 1916; fighters had performances of about 110 miles per hour, ceilings of about 16,000 feet, and endurances of about two hours. Yet one must be careful in generalizing about the state of fighter development. The value of the fourth-generation aircraft was in their capability for a variety of uses, and their ability to withstand prolonged and difficult service. Within each generation there were sophisticated and unsophisticated designs; the fourth-generation Bristol Fighter, for example, was sophisticated as compared to the Sopwith Camel. But an unsophisticated fourth-generation fighter like the Camel was certainly superior to the third-generation Albatros D III, which was a sophisticated aircraft when compared to the Sopwith Pup and similar aircraft of its day. Aside from its abilities in air-to-air combat, the Camel had true multimission capabilities — as exemplified by its fighter-bomber role late in the war.

In short, World War I teaches us that *large numbers of good fighters are better than a few great ones plus a lot of mediocre ones*. Germany in 1918 found itself with the latter situation, as did Great Britain in the fall of 1916. But whereas Great Britain had time to turn this around, Germany lacked the resources, support infrastructure, and time to do so. Germany's problem lay in overstandardization; the *Idflieg* stressed doubling the size of the fighter force in response to expected U.S. intervention, and neglected the development of a quality force. In 1918, the *Luftstreitkräfte* possessed the finest single-seat fighter produced during the war: the Fokker D VII, but not in the numbers needed to make it an effective force on the Western Front. Interestingly, in the Second World War, the *Luftwaffe* made similar errors, stressing production of the Bf 109 and the Fw 190 long after these aircraft should have passed from the inventory. In 1945 Germany again possessed the finest air-to-air fighter of the war, the Messerschmitt Me 262, but it was again a case of too little, too late.

One should not have to choose *either* quality *or* quantity; if such a choice appears to be the only one open, something is wrong with the selection process. As a rule, the First World War experience (and subsequent ones as well) indicates that a high-low balance is desirable, but that quality is overall more significant than quantity. Quantities of Albatros and Pfalz did not save the *Jagdflieger* in 1918. But quality cannot do it alone. Quality enables the fighter commander to engage and disengage at will in combat; it furnishes, in General Momyer's words, "the option of the initiative."[8] However, if not balanced with a quantity *of only marginally less sophisticated aircraft,* one's quality force will rapidly disappear through attrition. Great Britain's 1.5:1 high-low mix of Bristol Fighters and S.E. 5's to Camels seems ideal.

2. *There is no substitute for good design.* This is, of course, a truism. The experience of World War I, however, illustrates just how important this is. The fighter aircraft of the First World War, including even the third generation of those aircraft, were generally weak machines. Pilot memoirs and squadron histories abound with examples of pilots inadvertently overstressing their aircraft and breaking them up. Aircraft lost in this way included D.H. 2's, Nieuports, and even Sopwith Pups, as well as German types. The fourth-generation fighters—such as the S.E. 5a, Snipe, and Fokker D VII, proved generally trouble-free in this regard, thanks to thorough stress analysis during their design, and a pilot could operate the aircraft in abrupt maneuvers with relative abandon. The D VII, with its steel-tube fuselage structure, typified the trend towards metal in aircraft design. However, one must note that it wasn't until the work of the U.S. Army and the National Advisory Committee for Aeronautics in the late 1920s that a clear idea was formed of the magnitude of flight loads experienced by a maneuvering fighter.[9]

Handling qualities constitute an important area of study in relation to First World War aircraft. Generally speaking, if one translated their idiosyncracies into the framework of the Cooper-Harper flight testing pilot opinion rating system, most of the fighter aircraft produced in the First World War would have satisfactory characteristics (i.e., ranging from optimum to mildly unpleasant). Some, such as the Dr I triplane and even the Sopwith Camel, had pronounced unsatisfactory characteristics that did not affect the accomplishment of their mission (in fact, the instability of these two enhanced their combat maneuverability) but certainly made more work for the pilots and resulted in a reluctance to exploit the "edge of the envelope" of the aircraft in all but the best pilots, and caused heavy training and operational losses.

Some fighters simply suffered from bad design. An example was the lower wingspar-fuselage interface on the Nieuport, which made an otherwise good airplane a potential killer, and limited its combat effectiveness by inspiring mistrust in the pilots flying it. When the Germans copied the Nieuport sesquiplane formula in an attempt to improve the Albatros D II, they unknowingly built this fault into the D III "V-strutter" Albatros, and later into the D V Albatros as well. By mid-1918, with the Albatros already outdated, the last thing German fighter pilots should have had to worry about was the wings falling off their aircraft, but they had to and were reluctant as a result to exploit the maximum performance of the machine. This story illustrates another essential of aircraft design: thoroughly understand the design problem; don't copy without realizing *why* something is significant. Germany's efforts to copy the Nieuport and the Sopwith Triplane, and the British B.E. 12 story, are good examples. Some problems stemmed less from ignorance than from carelessness in the design, manufacturing, and quality control process. Fokker's wooden-wing triplane and the E V (D VIII) "Flying Razor" all were delayed from entering service because they broke up in flight. The delays prevented these aircraft from serving in significant numbers until after their moment of relative excellence had passed.

3. Understand the operational needs. By 1918, both Great Britain and Germany, as well as France, understood what the desirable attributes of a fighter airplane should be. But it had taken a long time for this realization to come. In late 1916 and into 1917, British fighter pilots often complained vehemently about the lack of armament on the Sopwith Pup. They recognized that a single forward-firing machine gun, while acceptable for 1915, was totally out of place in the air war of 1917. Yet, it was not until the summer of 1917 and the introduction of the two-gun Camel that British pilots received a fighter that was equivalent in firepower to the Albatros, which had entered service the previous September. Likewise the Spad was hamstrung because of its single-gun armament until the introduction of the later Spad 13. In brief, fighters, to be effective, must have a good armament system. All the agility and handling qualities in the world—which the Pup had—may keep the pilot alive but will accomplish little more if he lacks the ability to destroy his opponent as quickly and expeditiously as possible. That is certainly as true for the present as it has been in the past.

Related to this is the question of speed and agility. "Speed is life" runs an old fighter pilot saying, and so is agility—but agility should not be purchased at the expense of speed. Speed enables one to accelerate rapidly and to undertake attacks in climbing and turning. The Fokker Dr I triplane was an excellent interceptor of such reconnaissance aircraft as the B.E. 2 and R.E. 8. In an out-and-out dogfight, it could more than hold its own. But by May of 1918, the last month it was in production, the nature of the air war had changed. The Camel could defeat it in straight dogfighting, and the S.E. 5a—which had excellent maneuverability, though it was not in either the Camel's or Dr I's class—simply used proper energy management techniques for attack: diving from high altitude,

154

singling out an opponent, going for a gun pass, diving away, zooming back up, and then repeating the performance. All the agile Dr I could do was stay in a relatively small area of sky and point at the opponent. The death of German ace Werner Voss, confronted by McCudden and a flight of pilots from 56 Squadron was an illustration of this. Voss was not in top form, was flying alone, and was almost out of fuel. Though he managed to put bullets through every one of the S.E. 5's that attacked him, he could not break off — just as Lanoe Hawker, in his D.H. 2, had been unable to break away from von Richthofen's Albatros. It is most likely that the S.E. 5's ran him out of fuel; otherwise, the last moments of his flight before he was blown out of the sky make little sense. The fourth-generation fighters, and the two fifth-generation German Junkers D I and CL I lacked the agility of several earlier third-generation and even second-generation machines, but their speed and power more than compensated. The greater power available to fourth-generation aircraft enabled them to undertake attacks in climbing and turning maneuvers to a much greater degree than previous fighters. As with the high-low mix, designers and pilots preferred neither straight speed, nor just agility. There was a desirable blend. Such aircraft as the Spad represent the "excellent speed — good agility" end of the equation, and the Fokker D VII the "good speed — excellent agility" side. The S.E. 5a is about in the middle, as is the Sopwith Snipe.

The fighter pilot needs the proper environment to do his job. For example, at war's end, the Sopwith Snipe offered its pilot excellent visibility from a raised cockpit, and provisions for an electrically heated flying suit and oxygen, for greater comfort and efficiency on high altitude patrols. Modern designs with head-up displays and flight and fire controls consolidated on the control stick illustrate this trend towards an efficient environment for the pilot. But it began in the First World War. British scout pilots often went to great lengths to modify their fighters so that the trigger mechanism controlling the machine guns was located on the control stick. Cecil Montgomery-Moore, for example, recalls modifying Sopwith Dolphin fighters in the field so that pilots would not have to remove their hands from the stick to fire the guns. In 1918, the Fokker D VII and Junkers D I control sticks combined not only the plane's two gun triggers, but its throttle as well, giving the pilot his flight, engine, and armament controls all on a single stick.[10]

FIGHTER OPERATIONS

1. Fly when fit. Again, this is a truism today, but no conflict illustrates better the wastage of skilled aircrew who were unfit for service than the First World War. On the day von Richthofen died, neither he nor Brown should have been flying; von Richthofen was obviously not fully recovered from the head wound he suffered months previously, and Brown had severe stomach ulcers and, in fact, left combat after his victory over von Richthofen. The great psychological strain of constant combat flying caused numerous medical problems. There was no magic number of missions to look forward to, to complete a tour of duty, as in later wars. Being shot down usually meant at best being wounded, and at worst going down in flames without a parachute. The constant strain led skilled pilots to make elementary mistakes—like von Richthofen's failure to "check six" on his last flight. The strain shows in photographs of pilots; Boelcke, von Richthofen, Mannock, Ball, and especially Guynemer all have Tom Lea's "thousand-yard stare," the look of men who have seen too much combat.

The physical environment of scout-flying in the First World War imposed medical strains: flying unheated open-cockpit fighters at altitudes above 12,000 feet without benefit of oxygen led to hypoxia and hypothermia, and doubtless contributed to loss rates. In 1917, dogfights at altitudes of 16,000 to 18,000 feet were commonplace, and some encounters took place even higher.* Again, war memoirs are filled with accounts of pilots who passed out in the air, were taken by surprise (reflecting the mental confusion that often accompanies hypothermia and hypoxia), or who developed chronic medical problems. Naturally, the physical strains weakened the pilots' resistance to more conventional ailments. In the fall of 1918, when influenza swept the Western Front and British Isles, aviation units seem to have been particularly hard hit. One German fighter squadron, *Jasta 56*, was grounded from October through the armistice because of sick aircrew, some of whom died.[11]

There are, of course, elements of physical health that pilots can control themselves: exercise, partying, and the like. Then as now, "Those who hoot with the owls by night should not fly with the eagles by day." The death of Werner Voss illustrates this point. In combat after combat, Voss had demonstrated his absolute skill and excellence as a fighter pilot. There is little question that, had he survived, Voss would have rivaled von Richthofen for the title of Germany's leading fighter ace. Voss had gone to Berlin with many of his fellow pilots to help Bruno Loerzer, a popular fighter leader, celebrate the award of his *Pour le Mérite* in a huge party thrown by Tony Fokker at the Bristol Hotel. Voss and fellow pilots Hermann Göring, Loerzer, and "the Black Knight," Eduard von Schleich, stood around a piano, singing and drinking copious amounts of champagne; the von Richthofen brothers were there, as was Ernst Udet, sketch-

---

*A log of a Royal Naval Air Service Camel pilot flying with 9 Squadron is filled with entries for high altitude patrols of 1 to 1½ hours duration at altitudes above 15,000 feet during the fall and early winter of 1917. (This log is in the archives of the American Aviation Historical Society, Santa Ana, California.)

ing his colleagues. Well-hung-over, Voss returned in the early hours of the morning. Incredibly, he almost immediately took off on a combat sortie, shooting down a D.H. 4 that crossed the front. He returned to base, and late in the afternoon took off on his final sortie that ended in his being trapped and shot down by 56 Squadron; at the time of his last dogfight he was alone, low on fuel, obviously tired, and without question still suffering the effects of Loerzer's party the night before. It is a real tribute to Voss that he survived against McCudden, Rhys-Davids, and the rest as long as he did; he was aided by the timely arrival of a red-nosed Albatros (also shot down), which caused his attackers to divide their attention, and there is little question that the S.E. 5's got in each others' way as they strove to shoot down the frantically gyrating triplane.

2. *You only make one error.* Voss's death illustrates the merciless nature of fighter combat. Complacency, overconfidence, and forgetfulness spell death. It is truly amazing how many skilled pilots perished before the end of the war because of elementary mistakes. Many errors stemmed from the constant strain of combat flying: the pilots had simply been at the front too long, and their fatigue showed up in accidents, mid-air collisions, and inexplicable failures to take adequate measures of protection in combat. The death of Roderick Dallas, an Australian fighter ace of note, demonstrated that there was "no margin for error" in air fighting in the First World War—no more than now. Dallas always had lone-wolf tendencies, but had managed, through great skill, to get away with solo attacks. In June 1918, he took off for a solitary patrol over the front, intending to hide up-sun and then swoop down on some unsuspecting German reconnaissance airplane. Instead, he saw a solitary Fokker triplane. He dived on it, falling for the old trap; two other Fokkers were lurking about, using their comrade for bait, and they dove on Dallas, shooting him down before he realized that they were even there.

Other errors were perhaps more understandable but equally foolish. Many fighter pilots developed target fixation, concentrating on shooting down the plane in front of them to the exclusion of all else, and in turn being shot down. When the fangs are out, the temptation to press on for those vital few seconds is virtually overwhelming, but prudence dictates remembering that you are not the only plane in the sky. A similar mistake was made by ground-attack pilots cruising over the front, looking for machine-gun nests and the like; the nests, because of the debris and churned-up nature of the battlefield, were almost invisible against the earth; not so the plane, which clearly stood out. Multiple passes at the same ground target, then as well as now, were a virtual guarantee of being shot down.

3. *Avoid the furball.* Then as now, keeping track of multiple threats proved difficult. Dogfights evolved from solitary engagements between two airplanes in 1914 and 1915, to formations of several dozen, and, rarely, as many as eighty to one hundred aircraft, maneuvering at various altitudes over the front. The most successful aces, and the ones who survived longest, were the ones who did not stay around and mix it up; they dove in, got a kill or two, and kept on going, keeping to the edge of the battle, and constantly checking for opponents. Those who did join in the swirl at the center of the "furball" often perished, shot down by opponents who closed in from the rear before the victims had a chance to recognize the threat. Almost every memoir recounts examples running along the lines of "there I was, just about to fire at a Fokker (Spad, etc.), when the flash of tracer alerted me to someone on my tail." One gains the impression that had marksmanship been better, and had pilots used less tracer in their ammunition loads, the number of postwar memoirs would be significantly smaller. And it must be remembered that the pilots who survived to write memoirs were often the *best* pilots. It is commonly held that in sixty percent—and some sources state eighty percent—of all kills in all wars, the victims were unaware of being attacked until they were shot down. Certainly this appears true for the First World War. In a dogfight with several opponents, keeping track of three, let alone eight, or ten, or twenty, was difficult. It soon became impossible with the larger numbers. Prudent pilots recognized that they had the best chance of scoring and surviving by staying to the outside; besides, the risk of mid-air collision was much less.

Successful pilots also developed threat awareness. It took a while for new pilots simply to learn how to spot a threat. There is a fascinating section in Rickenbacker's memoir, *Fighting the Flying Circus*, where he relates the story of his first patrol over the front with Doug Campbell and Raoul Lufbery. Rickenbacker and Campbell returned smug with overconfidence; they had flown right over the front and the Germans hadn't dared send any planes up against them. Lufbery asked what they had seen; both replied that there hadn't been an enemy airplane in the sky. Lufbery gave a knowing chuckle, and then narrated the facts. Two formations of five Spads each had passed at less than five hundred yards at fifteen-minute intervals, a formation of four Albatros had been waiting two miles ahead of the three fighters when Lufbery turned back, and a German two-seater had been even closer, 5,000 feet above the front. "You must learn to look about a bit when you get in enemy lines," he cautioned.[12] Thus was America's future ace-of-aces initiated into air combat.

The most common error was forgetting to "check six." Many neophytes—and sometimes experienced pros as well—simply forgot to check behind. Every fighter pilot who believes himself beyond the peril of making this error should remember that even the Rittmeister himself did, paying with his life. Again, it is astounding the number of times that the tracer flashing by was the first clue that many a pilot had of being attacked. True, this happened most frequently in maneuvering dogfights with more than one opponent, but there were also the surprising cases of pilots flying over enemy territory, complacent and overconfident, who suddenly noticed tracer zipping by the wing or, even worse, heard the sudden nasty rattle of Spandaus or Vickers close behind. Equally amazing is the number of times the same situation recurs in some memoirs, when the pilot-author refers, within ten or twenty pages, to a *similar* episode. Again, remembering that memoirs are written by the untypical pilot, one has to conclude that there were a lot of slow learners on the Western Front who were possessed of an abundance of luck. Less fortunate airmen perished by the score. For this reason, one should be suspicious of the claim that a pilot could fly an operational tour in fighters without once seeing enemy aircraft. Given the localized nature of the Western Front air war, with the dense concentrations of fighters near battle areas, a pilot who didn't see a "bogie" on at least one out of every four flights probably wasn't looking too hard. True, the enemy aircraft might be too far away to engage, but they were certainly there.

Being seen first, of course, is one of the great disadvantages in air combat. One practical defense measure is camouflage and deceptive markings schemes. By mid-1916 onwards, the typical prewar aircraft finish of plain doped fabric had given way to somber-toned camouflage shades of green, brown, and tan. Some standardized patterns eventually emerged, such as Germany's initial use of green, mauve, and brown, and later a complicated "lozenge" pattern, and Great Britain's olive drab. The bright individual markings of many pilots (especially German) oftentimes defeated the purpose of camouflage, but the majority of aircraft flew in overall matte or semi-matte earth-toned finish that enhanced their security as they flew above the torn mud of the Western Front. Undersides generally remained in plain doped finish, giving them a light sky-blending hue, or were doped in light blues or greys. There were even experimental attempts to develop deceptive schemes, for example, replacing the colorful cockades of Allied aircraft with elliptical insignia shapes, painting converging "wing ribs" to distort perspective, or locating wing markings in asymmetric patterns that could cause an enemy airman to misjudge his aiming point if he relied on them for reference. Both sides experimented unsuccessfully with "see-through" coverings to give an airplane an "invisible" appearance—an odd precursor of subsequent low observable "stealth" technology! It is remarkable how similar the variety of camouflage schemes incorporated on the tactical aircraft of the NATO and Warsaw Pact today are to those that first appeared in 1916-1918, including deceptive paint schemes, light grey or blue dapples for air superiority dogfighting, and darker greens, earths, and greys for aircraft operating at medium and low altitudes. (It is significant that the brightly-colored German "flying circus" of 1917-1918 did not reappear in 1939-45. Nazi airmen favored more realistic markings with smaller individual badges of recognition than, for example, an all-white or all-red airplane. They realized, perhaps, that the bright hues of their forebears, while conductive to cameraderie and sense of pride, attracted Allied fighters as a light draws moths. Likewise, the brightly banded bare-metal fighters which the USAF's Tactical Air Command fielded in the late 1950s and early 1960s gave way to the more subdued finish applied for Southeast Asia and the "lizard" tones and air superiority greys of today.) Camouflage cannot compensate for failure to maintain an adequate watch for enemy aircraft. All other factors being equal, however, camouflage in the First World War proved itself as a valuable aid for the fighter pilot as he went about his duties.

4. Training is everything. Lack of good training programs, coupled with the inferiority of contemporary fighters, almost doomed the RFC in the fall of 1916 and early 1917. In contrast to the RFC whose aircrews were hastily shoveled into the furnace of the Western Front, the *Luft-streitkräfte*, at that time, sent its newly minted pilots to a fighter weapons school at Valenciennes that functioned much like the lead-in fighter program does for the U.S. Air Force today. As a result, the German Albatros and Halberstadt pilots were much more comfortable with their machines than were their Allied counterparts. All this changed, however, largely as a result of the RFC's recognition that flight instruction required competent, dedicated instructors who could teach — not rejects from the front badly in need of a rest and hastily assigned to training establishments. At the end of 1916, Robert Smith-Barry received official RFC support to create a "School of Special Flying" at Gosport that would turn out instructors. Believing communication to be critical, Smith-Barry developed the one-way Gosport — a mouthpiece for the instructor connected by a tube to earpieces for the student, enabling the instructor to explain every characteristic and quirk of an airplane as it flew. Smith-Barry emphasized training instructors who could explain to pupils the intricacies of controlling an airplane, and then demonstrate them, letting the pupil develop confidence and skill. By the end of 1917, however, the School of Special Flying had become much more, and was teaching combat flying techniques such as "contour-chasing" and the like to instructors who later imparted this information to students before they arrived at the front. At the front, squadrons took greater care with new arrivals, letting them get their feet wet on local patrols and hops, and making certain that newcomers flew with air-wise old-timers until they were ready for their first crossings of the front. The result was that by 1918 the RFC had a large pool of competent airmen, backed up by a strong training establishment; flying new and improved fighter aircraft, the well-trained pilots ensured the ability of the service to fight efficiently and effectively during the bitter battles of 1918. Conversely, pressed and harassed by the Allied fourth-generation fighters, many of the most experienced *Jasta* pilots went to their death in late 1917 and early 1918. The large number of inexperienced replacements, coupled with curtailments of training because of shortages of material and petroleum, oil, and lubricants, resulted in a decline in the relative abilities of German pilots at the front. British training methods carried over to the Americans when the United States entered the war, and, in the words of the postwar analysis of U.S. Air Service training, the assistance of the British instructors proved "invaluable."[13] The stages of training that an American fighter pilot went through reflected the growing care with which aircrew were treated towards the end of the war. First the pilot went to Issoudun, France, for advanced flight training in aerobatics, formation flying, and aerial combat, using aircraft equipped with camera guns; training sometimes included night-flying for interceptor pilots. After successfully completing these courses, he went on to either Cazaux or St. Jean-de-Monts, or a shooting range near Issoudun, for advanced gunnery including air-to-ground firing. Only then was the fledgling "pursuit pilot" passed along to an operational squadron. A total of 766 American pilots graduated from this program before going to the front, explaining in large measure why America's air service performed so well over the front in 1918. While there was nothing that, in comprehensiveness, approached the American fighter weapons schools and Top Gun and Red Flag efforts of the present day, the state of training was remarkably thorough for the time.

5. No guts, no glory. It is historically interesting to compare the fighter tactics and strategy developed during the First World War by Boelcke, Mannock, et al., to a major and influential document of the 1950s: then-Major Frederick C. "Boots" Blesse's "No Guts No Glory," a summary of this double jet ace's "lessons learned" from Korea. Because of the major changes in technology, much of what Blesse wrote—about matters such as Mach number, radio communication, dropping external fuel tanks, and the like—bears little relationship to the air war over the Western Front. But there are major sections that could have been written by the fighter leaders of the First World War about lessons from their war. They were lessons applicable thirty-five years later in the skies over "MiG Alley," and many are still applicable. The following are Blesse's basic principles of fighter offense and defense:

Offense

1. The element of two aircraft is your most effective basic fighting team. When the fight is over, you will be coming home in two's about 90% of the time.

2. Two elements represent your most effective fighting unit—the flight.

3. If enemy aircraft are anywhere in the area, get rid of external tanks as soon as empty.

4. When in doubt in a dogfight, trade airspeed for altitude.

5. Two good aerial training fights a week are minimum necessary to stay in practice. If you aren't fighting the enemy, practice among yourselves.

6. Never continue turning with another aircraft after you are unable to track him with your sight. Pull up immediately and keep your nose behind his tail. If he pulls up, you'll always end up on top because of your attacking airspeed.

7. If, by using speed brakes, you can drift into the radius of turn of the aircraft you are attacking, do it in preference to the YO YO maneuver. It takes less time to get your kill and you don't run the risk of being out-maneuvered by the aircraft you are attacking. What you are leery about is slowing down and thus subjecting yourself to attack. You are at your opponent's airspeed either way and for less time if you use your speed brakes properly. Obviously, the combat area is no place to experiment with this theory. Don't waste your flying time—practice!

8. Cruise at a high Mach.

9. Look around; you can't shoot anything until you see it.

10. Keep the aircraft you are attacking in sight. One glance away is enough to make you kick yourself for ten years.

11. Generally speaking, have an element high and fast when you slow down to maneuver. If you are trying to snip one up in the traffic pattern, you'll find it difficult at best with all the flak. Don't make the job harder by leaving yourself open for a bounce by the always present enemy CAP flights.

12. Attack from low and behind whenever possible. That's a fighter's poorest visibility area.

13. If you have an enemy aircraft in front, assume there is one behind; there usually is.

14. Know the performance data on all aircraft you are apt to be fighting.

15. Know your "Big Three." Be familiar with glide characteristics, air-start procedures and fuel consumption at altitude at idle RPM. If you are attacked on the way home, you may need all three to make it back safely.

16. Assume every pilot you meet is the world's best (you can swallow your pride that long) and maneuver your aircraft accordingly until he shows you he is not.

17. Don't shoot unless you're positive it's an enemy aircraft. When it's time to fire, you'll know if it's an enemy aircraft or not. If you can't tell, you are out of range.

18. There are three distinct phases in destroying another aircraft in the air:
    a. Maneuvering = 85%
    b. Positioning the pipper = 10%
    c. Firing and sighting the burst = 5%

75% of all the lost kills are the result of attempting phase (b) and (c) before (a) has been adequately solved.

19. Guts will do for skill but not consistently. Know your job in combat or someone else will be flying in your place.

20. Shut up on the radio; if it doesn't concern everyone, get on another channel.

21. Play on the team—no individualists. The quickest way to be an element leader is to be the best wingman in the Squadron.

22. When in doubt—attack!

23. Learn the value and the proper procedure for harmonization.

24. Divide the enemy and conquer. It is very difficult even for the best pilots to work mutual support tactics in high-speed jet aircraft. If you can split the tactical formation of the enemy, more often than not his mutual support efforts against you will be ineffective.

25. One last word before you set out to be the next jet ace—*no guts, no glory*. If you are going to shoot him down, you have to get in there and mix it up with him.

Defense

1. If you slow down, have an element high and fast for support.

2. Except at extreme ranges, always turn into the attack.

3. If there are enemy aircraft anywhere in the area, get rid of external tanks and get your Mach up. It's too late after you spot him.

4. Keep your attacker at a high angle off.

5. Keep airspeeds up when patrolling.

6. Don't ever reverse a turn unless you have your attacker sliding to the outside of the radius of your turn.

7. If you have a "hung" external tank, leave the combat area.

8. If you lose your wingman, both of you should leave the combat area.

9. Know the low speed characteristics of your aircraft. If you are fighting aggressive pilots you'll need all the know-how you can lay your hands on.

10. Have a "last ditch" maneuver and practice it.

11. Keep a close check on your fuel.

12. "Best defense is a good offense" is good most of the time—but know your defensive tactics.

13. Don't play Russian Roulette! When you're told to break—DO IT!

14. Avoid staring at contrails or the only aircraft in sight. There are a dozen around for every one you can see.

15. Watch the sun—a well-planned attack will come out of the sun when possible.

16. The object of any mutual support maneuver is to sandwich the attacker in between the defending aircraft.

17. In any dogfight, the objective for the defender should be lateral separation. When this is achieved, a reverse and a series of scissors will, if properly executed, put your attacker out in front. The rest is up to you.

18. Place yourself in your attacker's shoes. How would you like to find an enemy flight positioned? Be smart and avoid this formation for your flight.

19. Don't panic—panic is your most formidable enemy![14]

The continuum of fighter experience running from the skies over the Western Front to the Second World War, and on into Korea is obvious. And readers familiar with subsequent air warfare experience will see that it remains unbroken to this day.

The first air war cost nearly 9,400 British casualties and over 11,100 German ones. The United States lost less than 250 while French losses cannot be accurately determined.[15] Several schools of thought exist with regard to the pilots of that war. They are often called the "Knights of the Air," in part a reference to an address by Lloyd George before Parliament as well as to the romantic school of journalism that emphasized the noble aspects of aerial dueling. The other extreme views them as nothing more nor less than prototypical 20th-century techno-soldiers, doing their job efficiently and usually mercilessly. Actually, in the range of their emotions and feelings, the fighter pilots seem as varied a lot as the soldiers in the trenches. They were realists; they were horrified at the daily slaughter that they saw from the air, and recognized the stupidity of those who had brought the armies of Europe to the morass of horror that constituted the Western Front. They recognized, too, their own small chance of survival if they were shot down. There is no doubt, however, about the conclusion reached by one of their own number, Sir Robert Saundby, over a half-century after the armistice: "They were," he wrote, "a gallant band of warriors."[16] Because of them, the fighter aircraft emerged as a combat weapon in all its roles as we presently know them. The legacy of the fighter over the Western Front can be found today in the fighter forces of the Western alliance.

Appendix A

Specifications and Performance Characteristics of Selected British, French, and German Fighters

BRITISH

Vickers F. B. "Gunbus"

General configuration: pusher biplane
Wingspan: 36 ft 6 in
Length: 27 ft 2 in
Height: 11 ft 6 in
Weight (loaded): 2,050 lbs
Crew: two
Armament: one free-firing Lewis machine gun
Maximum speed: 70 mph
Engine: 100-hp Gnôme Monosoupape rotary

Bristol Scout D

General configuration: tractor biplane
Wingspan: 24 ft 7 in
Length: 20 ft 8 in
Height: 8 ft 6 in
Weight (loaded): 1,440 lbs
Crew: one
Armament: varied; some had one fixed, forward-firing Vickers machine gun
Maximum speed: 100 mph
Engine: 110-hp Clerget rotary

de Havilland D.H. 2

General configuration: pusher biplane
Wingspan: 28 ft 3 in
Length: 25 ft 2½ in
Height: 9 ft 6½ in
Weight (loaded): 1,441 lbs
Crew: one
Armament: one forward-firing Lewis machine gun

Maximum speed: 93 mph
Engine: 100-hp Gnôme Monosoupape rotary

Royal Aircraft Factory F.E. 2b

General configuration: pusher biplane
Wingspan: 47 ft 9 in
Length: 32 ft 3 in
Height: 12 ft 7½ in
Weight (loaded): 3,073 lbs
Crew: two
Armament: two free-firing Lewis machine guns
Maximum speed: 91 mph
Engine: 160-hp Beardmore inline

Sopwith Pup

General configuration: tractor biplane
Wingspan: 26 ft 6 in
Length: 19 ft 3¾ in
Height: 9 ft 5 in
Weight (loaded): 1,225 lbs
Crew: one
Armament: one fixed forward-firing Lewis or Vickers machine gun and/or eight Le Prieur rockets
Maximum speed: 111 mph
Engine: 80-hp Le Rhône rotary

Sopwith Triplane

General configuration: tractor triplane
Wingspan: 26 ft 6 in
Length: 18 ft 10 in
Height: 10 ft 6 in
Weight (loaded): 1,541 lbs
Crew: one
Armament: one (sometimes two) fixed, forward-firing Vickers machine gun
Maximum Speed: 113
Engine: 130-hp Clerget rotary

Royal Aircraft Factory S.E. 5a

General configuration: tractor biplane
Wingspan: 26 ft 7⅞ in
Length: 20 ft 11 in
Height: 9 ft 6 in
Weight (loaded): 1,953 lbs
Crew: one
Armament: one Vickers and one Lewis fixed, forward-firing machine gun and four 25-lb Cooper bombs
Maximum speed: 121 mph
Engine: 200-hp Hispano Suiza inline

Sopwith F.1 Camel

General configuration: tractor biplane

Wingspan: 28 ft
Length: 18 ft 9 in
Height: 8 ft 6 in
Weight (loaded): 1,482 lbs
Crew: one
Armament: twin fixed, forward-firing Vickers machine guns and four 25-lb Cooper bombs
Maximim speed: 104.5 mph
Engine: 130-hp Clerget rotary

Bristol F.2B Fighter

General configuration: tractor biplane
Wingspan: 39 ft 3 in
Length: 25 ft 10 in
Height: 9 ft 9 in
Weight (loaded): 2,848 lbs
Crew: two
Armament: one fixed, forward-firing Vickers machine gun and one or two gunner-operated Lewis free-firing machine guns plus up to twelve 25-lb Cooper bombs
Maximum speed: 123 mph
Engine: 275-hp Rolls Royce Falcon III inline

de Havilland D.H. 5

General configuration: tractor biplane
Wingspan: 25 ft 8 in
Length: 22 ft
Height: 9 ft 1½ in
Weight (loaded): 1,492 lbs
Crew: one
Armament: one fixed, forward-firing Vickers machine gun plus four 25-lb Cooper bombs
Maximum speed: 104 mph
Engine: 110-hp Le Rhône rotary

Sopwith 5F.1 Dolphin

General configuration: tractor biplane
Wingspan: 32 ft 6 in
Length: 22 ft 3 in
Height: 8 ft 6 in
Weight (loaded): 1,970 lbs
Crew: one
Armament: twin fixed, forward-firing Vickers machine guns plus four 25-lb Cooper bombs
Maximum speed: 119.5 mph
Engine: 200-hp Hispano Suiza inline

Sopwith 7F.1 Snipe

General configuration: tractor biplane
Wingspan: 30 ft
Length: 19 ft 2 in
Height: 9 ft 6 in
Weight (loaded): 2,015 lbs
Crew: one
Armament: twin fixed, forward-firing Vickers machine guns plus four 25-lb Cooper bombs

Maximum speed: 119 mph
Engine: 230-hp Bentley B.R.2 rotary

FRENCH

Morane-Saulnier Type L

General configuration: tractor parasol monoplane
Wingspan: 33 ft 9½ in
Length: 20 ft 9 in
Height: 10 ft 4 in
Weight (loaded): 1,499 lbs
Crew: one or two
Armament: varied; some equipped with forward-firing Lewis or Hotchkiss machine gun
Maximum speed: 72 mph
Engine: 80-hp Gnôme or Le Rhône rotary

Morane-Saulnier Type N

General configuration: tractor monoplane
Wingspan: 27 ft 2¾ in
Length: 21 ft 11¾ in
Height: 8 ft 2½ in
Weight (loaded): 981 lbs
Crew: one
Armament: one fixed, forward-firing Hotchkiss or Vickers machine gun
Maximum speed: 102 mph
Engine: 80-hp Gnôme or Le Rhône rotary

Nieuport 11

General configuration: tractor biplane
Wingspan: 24 ft 9 in
Length: 19 ft ½ in
Height: 8 ft ½ in
Weight (loaded): 1,058 lbs
Crew: one
Armament: one fixed, forward-firing Lewis machine gun
Maximum speed: 97 mph
Engine: 80-hp Le Rhône rotary

Nieuport 17

General configuration: tractor biplane
Wingspan: 26 ft 11⅝ in
Length: 18 ft 10 in
Height: 7 ft 7¾ in
Weight (loaded): 1,246 lbs
Crew: one
Armament: one fixed, forward-firing Vickers or Lewis machine gun
Maximum speed: 110 mph
Engine: 110-hp Le Rhône rotary

Spad VII

General configuration: tractor biplane
Wingspan: 25 ft 6 in
Length: 20 ft 1 in
Height: 7 ft 8½ in
Weight (loaded); 1,550 lbs
Crew: one
Armament: one fixed, forward-firing Vickers machine gun
Maximum speed: 119.5 mph
Engine: 180-hp Hispano Suiza inline engine

Spad XIII

General configuration: tractor biplane
Wingspan: 26 ft 11 in
Length: 20 ft 8 in
Height: 7 ft 11½ in
Weight (loaded): 1,815 lbs
Crew: one
Armament: twin fixed, forward-firing Vickers machine guns
Maximum speed: 130 mph
Engine: 200-hp Hispano Suiza inline engine

Nieuport 28

General configuration: tractor biplane
Wingspan: 26 ft 9 in
Length: 21 ft
Height: 8 ft 1¾ in
Weight (loaded): 1,540 lbs
Crew: one
Armament: twin fixed, forward-firing Vickers machine guns
Maximum speed: 128 mph
Engine: 160-hp Gnôme Monosoupape rotary

GERMAN

Fokker E III

General configuration: tractor monoplane
Wingspan: 32 ft 2¾ in
Length: 23 ft 11⅓ in
Height: 9 ft 1¾ in
Weight (loaded): 1,342 lbs
Crew: one
Armament: one (sometimes two) fixed forward-firing Spandau or Parabellum machine guns
Maximum speed: 87.5 mph
Engine: 100-hp Oberursel U I rotary

Fokker D II

General configuration: tractor biplane
Wingspan: 28 ft 8 in

Length: 20 ft 11 in
Height: 8 ft 3½ in
Weight (loaded): 1,267 lbs
Crew: one
Armament: one fixed, forward-firing Spandau machine gun
Maximum speed: 93 mph
Engine: 100-hp Oberursel U I rotary

Halberstadt D II

General configuration: tractor biplane
Wingspan: 28 ft 11 in
Length: 23 ft 11 in
Height: 8 ft 9 in
Weight (loaded): 1,606 lbs
Crew: one
Armament: twin fixed, forward-firing Spandau machine guns
Maximum speed: approximately 95 mph
Engine: 120-hp Mercedes inline

Albatros D II

General configuration: tractor biplane
Wingspan: 27 ft 10¾ in
Length: 24 ft 3⅛ in
Height: 8 ft 8 in
Weight (loaded): 1,976 lbs
Crew: one
Armament: twin fixed, forward-firing Spandau machine guns
Maximum speed: 109.4 mph
Engine: 160-hp Mercedes inline

Albatros D III

General configuration: tractor biplane
Wingspan: 29 ft 8¼ in
Length: 24 ft ⅝ in
Height: 9 ft 9⅓ in
Weight (loaded): 1,949 lbs
Crew: one
Armament: twin fixed, forward-firing Spandau machine guns
Maximum speed: 103 mph
Engine: 160-hp Mercedes inline

Albatros D Va

General configuration: tractor biplane
Wingspan: 29 ft 8¼ in
Length: 24 ft ⅝ in
Height: 9 ft 4 in
Weight (loaded): 2,013 lbs
Crew: one
Armament: twin fixed, forward-firing Spandau machine guns
Maximum speed: 106.9 mph
Engine: 185-hp Mercedes inline

Fokker Dr I

General configuration: tractor triplane
Wingspan: 23 ft 7 in
Length: 18 ft 11⅛ in
Weight (loaded): 1,290 lbs
Crew: one
Armament: twin fixed, forward-firing Spandau machine guns
Maximum speed: 97 mph
Engine: 110-hp Le Rhône rotary

Pfalz D III

General configuration: tractor biplane
Wingspan: 30 ft 10⅛ in
Length: 27 ft 9¾ in
Height: 8 ft 9⅛ in
Weight (loaded): 1,903 lbs
Crew: one
Armanent: twin fixed, forward-firing Spandau machine guns
Maximum speed: 103.1 mph
Engine: 160-hp Mercedes inline

Junkers J I

General configuration: tractor biplane
Wingspan: 52 ft 5⅞ in
Length: 29 ft 10¼ in
Height: 11 ft 1⅞ in
Weight (loaded): 4,795 lbs
Crew: two
Armament: twin fixed, forward-firing Spandau machine guns and one gunner-operated, free-firing Parabellum machine gun plus small bombs and grenades
Maximum speed: 96 mph
Engine: 200-hp Benz Bz IV inline

Halberstadt Cl II

General configuration: tractor biplane
Wingspan: 35 ft 4 in
Length: 23 ft 11⅜ in
Height: 9 ft ¼ in
Weight (loaded): 2,498 lbs
Crew: two
Armament: one or two fixed, forward-firing Spandau machine guns, and one gunner-operated, free-firing Parabellum machine gun plus small bombs and grenades
Maximum speed: 109 mph
Engine: 160-hp Mercedes inline

Hannover Cl IIIa

General configuration: tractor biplane
Wingspan: 38 ft 4⅔ in
Length: 24 ft 10⅝ in
Height: 9 ft 2¼ in
Weight (loaded): 2,381 lbs

Crew: two
Armament: one fixed, forward-firing Spandau machine gun, and one gunner-operated free-firing Sparbellum machine gun plus small bombs and grenades
Maximum speed: 103 mph
Engine: 180-hp Argus As III inline

Siemens-Schuckert D III

General configuration: tractor biplane
Wingspan: 27 ft 7⅞ in
Length: 18 ft 8½ in
Height: 9 ft 2¼ in
Weight (loaded): 1,595 lbs
Crew: one
Armament: twin fixed, forward-firing Spandau machine guns
Maximum speed: 112.5 mph
Engine: 160-hp Siemens Halske Sh III rotary

Fokker D VIIf

General configuration: tractor biplane
Wingspan: 29 ft 3½ in
Length: 22 ft 11½ in
Height: 9 ft 2¼ in
Weight (loaded): 2,112 lbs
Crew: one
Armament: twin fixed, forward-firing Spandau machine guns
Maximum speed: 125 mph
Engine: 185-hp BMW IIIa inline

Fokker E V (D VIII)

General configuration: tractor parasol monoplane
Wingspan: 27 ft 3 in
Length: 19 ft 5 in
Height: 9 ft 4 in
Weight (loaded): 1,331 lbs
Crew: one
Armament: twin fixed, forward-firing Spandau machine guns
Maximum speed: 125 mph
Engine: 110-hp Le Rhône rotary

Pfalz D XII

General configuration: tractor biplane
Wingspan: 29 ft 6 in
Length: 20 ft 11 in
Height: 8 ft 10½ in
Weight (loaded): 1,962 lbs
Crew: one
Armament: twin fixed, forward-firing Spandau machine guns
Maximum speed: 120 mph
Engine: 180-hp Mercedes inline

Junkers D I

General configuration: tractor monoplane
Wingspan: 29 ft 2 in
Length: 22 ft
Height: 8 ft 8½ in
Weight (loaded): 1,841 lbs
Crew: one
Armament: twin fixed, forward-firing Spandau machine guns
Maximum speed: 115.5 mph
Engine: 180-hp Mercedes inline

Appendix B

German Combat Aircraft Designations

Germany designated military aircraft by a letter code that corresponded to their function. Numbers after the letter referred to specific aircraft types.

A Unarmed two-seat monoplanes, especially Tauben, used for reconnaissance duties.

B Unarmed two-seat biplanes used for reconnaissance or flight training.

C Armed two-seat biplanes for reconnaissance or army liaison duties; later applied to some monoplanes as well.

Cl Light armed two-seat biplanes originally intended as escorts for heavier C types, but later applied to ground-attack aircraft, including monoplanes. First appeared in 1917.

D Armed single-seat single-engine fighter biplanes (*Doppeldecker*), but applied at end of war to fighter monoplanes as well.

Dr Armed single-seat single-engine fighter triplanes (*Dreidecker*).

E Armed single-seat fighter monoplanes (*Eindecker*).

G   Armed twin-engine multi-place biplanes for bombardment and attack duties.

J   Two-seat single-engine armed attack aircraft.

R   Armed multi-engine multi-place long-range bombers, commonly referred to as *Riesenflugzeug* (giant aircraft).

Appendix C

Luftstreitkräfte and Royal Flying Corps Aircrew Rank Structure

Luftstreitkrafte	Royal Flying Corps
Flieger	(No RFC equivalent: corresponds to Enlisted pilot)
Unteroffizier	Corporal
Gefreiter	Lance-Corporal
Feldwebel	Sergeant
Vizefeldwebel	Sergeant-Major
Feldwebel Leutnant	Warrant Officer
Offizier Stellvertreter	(No RFC equivalent: corresponds to Acting Officer)
Leutnant	Second Lieutenant
Oberleutnant	First Lieutenant
Hauptmann	Captain
Rittmeister	(No RFC equivalent: corresponds to Cavalry Captain)
Major	Major
Oberstleutnant	Lieutenant Colonel
Oberst	Colonel

Notes

PREFACE

1. W. E. de B. Whittaker, "Aircraft in the War," in C. G. Grey, ed., *Jane's All the World's Aircraft, 1919*, p. 5a.

CHAPTER I

[1]F.E. Humphreys, "The Wright Flyer and Its Possible Uses in War," *Journal of the United States Artillery*, XXXIII (March-April 1910), pp. 145-146.

[2]John R. Cuneo, *The German Air Weapon, 1870-1914*, p. 264.

[3]Anthony Robinson, *Aerial Warfare*, p. 127.

[4]Ezra Bowen, *Knights of the Air*, p. 26.

[5]For a thorough survey of European work in this time period, see Charles H. Gibbs-Smith, *The Rebirth of European Aviation, 1896-1908—A Study of the Wright Brothers' Influence*.

[6]See Charles H. Gibbs-Smith, *Aviation: An Historical Survey from its Origins to the End of World War II*. Early European scientific research is discussed in Paul A. Hanle's *Bringing Aerodynamics to America*.

[7]John Howard Morrow, *Building German Airpower, 1909-1914*, p. 87; *Reichsarchiv, Die Operationen des Jahres 1915: Die Ereignisse im Westen und auf dem Balkan vom Sommer bis zum Jahresschluss*, IX of *Der Weltkrieg 1914-1918*, pp. 403, 404; Cuneo, *The German Air Weapon 1870-1914*, p. 173; Bowen, *Knights of the Air*, p. 28; Walter Raleigh, *The War in the Air*, I, pp. 282-287. (Sadly, Raleigh died upon the completion of this first volume. Subsequent volumes were written to the same high standard by H.A. Jones.)

[8]Raleigh, *The War in the Air*, I, p. 329.

[9]Louis A. Strange, *Recollections of an Airman*, p. 42.

[10]Bowen, *Knights of the Air*, p. 39.

[11]John R. Cuneo, *The Air Weapon 1914-1916*, pp. 151-152. He established thirty artillery spotting *escadrilles* with Caudrons and sixteen bombing *escadrilles* with Voisin aircraft. Farman pushers were preferred for reconnaissance.

[12]H.A. Jones, *The War in the Air*, II, pp. 139-140.

[13]John M. Bruce, *British Aeroplanes, 1914-18*, p. 663; see also Bruce, "Vickers' First Fighters," *Air Enthusiast Twelve* (April-July 1980), pp. 54-70.

[14]Arch Whitehouse, *Heroes of the Sunlit Sky*, pp. 274-276.

[15]Bruce, "The Bullets and the Guns," *Air Enthusiast Nine* (February-May 1979), pp. 63-65; Bruce, *Fighters*, vol. V of *Warplanes of the First World War*, pp. 50-58.

[16]Bruce, *Fighters*, V, p. 58; Whitehouse, *Heroes*, p. 278. The account that appeared in the *Kriegszeitung* of the German Fourth Army is reprinted in Stephen Longstreet's *The Canvas Falcons*. Readers are cautioned to use Longstreet with great care, however.

[17]Anthony H.G. Fokker and Bruce Gould, *Flying Dutchman: The Life of Anthony Fokker*, *passim*. While good for personal details of Fokker's life, this is another book that must be used with caution, for it is not based on any documentary sources, and unfortunately contains many Fokker-inspired embellishments. A more reliable source for Fokker's technical work is A.R. Weyl's more scholarly *Fokker: The Creative Years*.

[18]Bruce, *Fighters*, V, pp. 47, 49, 59; Bruce, *AE 9*, pp. 65-66.

[19]Fokker and Gould, *Flying Dutchman*, pp. 129-143.

[20]*Ibid.*, pp. 143-144. A quaint story, and one hopes a true one; but his neutrality certainly did not prevent his manufacture of warplanes.

[21]Immelmann, letter, Aug. 3, 1915, in Franz Immelmann's *Der Adler von Lille*, pp. 102-105.

CHAPTER II

[1]Andrew Boyle, *Trenchard*, pp. 15-18, 36, 96-105, 140-144.

[2]Maurice Baring, *R.F.C. H.Q. 1914-1918*, p. 114.

[3]Ira Jones, *Tiger Squadron*, p. 41; John M. Bruce, "Vickers' First Fighters," pp. 62-63, 64, 66, 68.

[4]H.A. Jones, *The War in the Air*, II, pp. 144, 151.

[5]Bruce, "The Bullets and the Guns," pp. 67-72; Hawker's combat report is reproduced in Tyrrel M. Hawker's *Hawker, V.C.*, pp. 102-104.

[6]Louis A. Strange, *Recollections of an Airman*, pp. 112-114.

[7]William Sholto Douglas, *Combat and Command: The Story of an Airman in Two World Wars*, pp., 86-87.

[8]Frank T. Courtney, *The Eighth Sea*, pp. 67, 82-83; see also H.A. Jones, *The War in the Air*, II, p. 150; and Ira Jones, *Tiger Squadron*, p. 41.

[9]See, for example, James T.B. McCudden, *Flying Fury: Five Years in the Royal Flying Corps*, pp. 98-99, 107-109.

[10]Peter Supf, *Das Buch der deutschen Fluggeschichte*, II, pp. 328-332.

[11]Douglas, *Combat and Command*, p. 87; H.A. Jones, *The War in the Air*, II, p. 152.

[12]Ira Jones, *Tiger Squadron*, pp. 40-41. See also Duncan Grinnell-Milne, *Wind in the Wires*, p. 83.

[13]René Fonck, *Ace of Aces*, p.38.

[14]Boyle, *Trenchard*, p. 162.

[15]*Ibid.*

[16]Douglas, *Combat and Command*, p. 97.

[17]Oswald Boelcke, *Hauptmann Bölckes Feldberichte*, p. 101.

[18]Douglas, *Combat and Command*, pp. 93, 95, 97.

[19]Supf, *Deutschen Fluggeschichte*, II, p. 331.

[20]H.A. Jones, *The War in the Air*, II, pp. 156-157.

[21]*Ibid.*, p. 157.

[22]*Ibid.*, p. 158.

[23]James E. Johnson, *Full Circle*, pp. 28-30.

[24]*Ibid.*, pp. 24-25.

CHAPTER III

[1]Alistair Horne, *The Price of Glory*, p. 331.

[2]*Ibid.*, pp. 203, 205-206; John R. Cuneo, *The Air Weapon, 1914-1916*, pp. 225-226.

[3]Andrew Boyle, *Trenchard*, pp. 165, 168-169.

[4]Cuneo, *The Air Weapon, 1914-1916*, pp. 226-227.

[5]John M. Bruce, "Those Classic Nieuports," *Air Enthusiast Quarterly*, 2, (n.d.), pp. 137-138; Kenneth Munson, *Aircraft of World War I*, p. 84; C.F. Andrews, *The Nieuport 17*, Profile Publication 49, pp. 3-4.

[6]Ernst von Hoeppner, *Deutschlands Krieg in der Luft*, p. 52.

[7]Peter Supf, *Das Buch der deutschen Fluggeschichte*, II, p. 284.

[8]George Hocutt, " 'Les Cigognes': Groupe de Combat 12" *Cross & Cockade Journal*, I, no. 2 (Autumn 1960), pp. 41-54. Horne, *The Price of Glory*, p. 207; Peter M. Grosz and A.E. Ferko, "Biplanes for the *Fliegertruppe*," *Air Enthusiast Fourteen* (Dec. 1980-March 1981), pp. 63-64; Frank H. Winter, *Prelude to the Space Age*, p. 38; Rudolf Nebel, *Die Narren von Tegel*, pp. 36-42, 44. Nebel erroneously claims that the *Nebelwerfer* (a German bombardment rocket of the Second World War) owed its name to a pun bestowed upon his World War One rockets by a fellow fighter pilot who himself went on to bigger things: Hermann Göring. Despite the deceptive logic of this claim, there is no connection between Nebel's rockets of the

Great War and the *Nebelwerfer* of the Second, according to Frank Winter of the National Air and Space Museum, who has researched this claim.

[9]Boyle, *Trenchard*, pp. 169-170.

[10]*Ibid.*

[11]*Ibid.*

[12]*Ibid.*

[13]Supf, *Deutschen Fluggeschichte*, II, pp. 285, 623; Hoeppner, *Deutchlands Krieg in der Luft*, p. 85; Cuneo, *The Air Weapon, 1914-1916*, p. 212; Heinz J. Nowarra and Kimbrough S. Brown, *Von Richthofen and the "Flying Circus,"* p. 24.

[14]Cecil Lewis, *Sagittarius Rising*, p. 28.

[15]William A. Bishop, *Winged Peace*, p. 37.

[16]Harald Penrose, *British Aviation*, pp. 501-503, 536, 540-541; Bruce, *Fighters*, I, pp. 139-140; Bruce, *Fighters*, II, pp. 33-39; Bruce, *The De Havilland D.H. 2*, Profile Publication 91, pp. 3-5.

[17]Bruce, *The Sopwith 1½ Strutter*, Profile Publication 121, pp. 3-5, 16.

[18]H.A. Jones, *The War in the Air*, II, p. 159; Tyrrel M. Hawker, *Hawker, V.C.*, p. 165.

[19]Jones, *The War in the Air*, II, p. 160.

[20]Lewis, *Sagittarius Rising*, p. 53.

[21]*Ibid.*, p. 54; Maurice Baring, *R.F.C. H.Q., 1914-1918*, pp. 141-142.

[22]Harold E. Hartney, *Up & At 'Em*, p. 47.

[23]*Ibid.*, pp. 47-54.

[24]Jones, *The War in the Air*, II, pp. 201-202.

[25]Franz Immelmann, *Der Adler von Lille*, pp. 181-182.

[26]Anthony H.G. Fokker and Bruce Gould, *Flying Dutchman*, p. 206.

[27]Oswald Boelcke, *Hauptman Bölckes Feldberichte*, pp. 153-154.

[28]Supf, *Deutschen Fluggeschichte*, II, pp. 331-332.

CHAPTER IV

[1]Peter Supf, *Das Buch der deutschen Fluggeschichte*, II, pp. 316-318.

[2]Oswald Boelcke, *Hauptman Bölckes Feldberichte*, pp. 70-77.

[3]*Ibid.*, pp. 83-85; Erwin Böhme, *Briefe eines deutschen Kampffliegers an ein junges Mädchen*, p. 52.

[4]Boelcke, *Feldberichte*, pp. 157-158, 159-162; Carl Bolle, *"Jagdstaffel Boelcke,"* in Walter von Eberhardt, ed., *Unsere Luftstreitkräfte, 1914-1918*, p. 130.

[5]Alistair Horne, *The Price of Glory*, pp. 29-40; Martin Middlebrook, *The First Day on the Somme*, pp. 29, 34-38, 48-54, 66; S.L.A. Marshall, *World War I*, pp. 229-231, 248-252; Lyn Macdonald, *Somme*, pp. 12-20.

[6]Middlebrook, *First Day on the Somme*, pp. 243-247, 256; Macdonald, *Somme*, pp. 55-77.

[7]In report of Oberstleutnant Wilhelm Siegert, quoted in Georg Paul Neumann, ed., *Die Deutschen Luftstreitkräfte im Weltkriege*, pp. 473-475.

[8]Maurice Baring, *R.F.C. H.Q., 1914-1918*, p. 156.

[9]*Ibid.*

[10]Middlebrook, *First Day on the Somme*, p. 82.

[11]John H. Morrow, Jr., *German Air Power in World War I*, pp. 46-50, 55, 60-61.

[12]Peter M. Grosz and A.E. Ferko, "Biplanes for the *Fliegertruppe*," pp. 58-61.

[13]Peter L. Gray, *The Albatros D I-D III*, Profile Publication 127, pp. 3-8.

[14]W.M. Lamberton, *Fighter Aircraft of the 1914-1918 War*, p. 30; Raymond Vann and Colin Waugh, "The B.E. 12 in Combat," *Cross & Cockade Journal*, XX, no. 4 (Winter 1979), pp. 316-334.

[15]Lamberton, *Fighter Aircraft*, p. 166; Grosz and Ferko, "The Fokker Dr I: A Reappraisal," *Air Enthusiast Eight*, (October 1978-January 1979), pp. 9-26.

[16]Tyrrel M. Hawker, *Hawker, V.C.*, pp. 195-197.

[17]Joseph A. Phelan, *Heroes & Aeroplanes of the Great War, 1914-1918*, p. 64.

[18]R.H. Kiernan, *Captain Albert Ball, V.C., D.S.O.*, pp. 76-77, 93, 112.

[19]Colin Waugh, "A Short History of 70 Squadron, RFC/RAF, 1916-1919," *Cross & Cockade Journal*, XX, no. 4 (Winter 1979), pp. 289-315.

[20]Heinz J. Nowarra and Kimbrough S. Brown, *Von Richthofen and the "Flying Circus"*, p. 28; James E. Johnson, *Full Circle*, pp. 36-37.

[21]Boelcke, *Feldberichte*, p. 193; Böhme, *Briefe*, pp. 43-44.

[22]Ernst Schäffer, quoted in Supf, *Deutschen Fluggeschichte*, II, p. 400.

[23]Manfred von Richthofen, *Der Rote Kampfflieger*, pp. 78-79.

[24]*Ibid.*, p. 80.

[25]Böhme, *Briefe*, p. 44.

[26]von Richthofen, *Der Rote Kampfflieger*, p. 102.

[27]*Ibid.*, pp. 102-103; see also Alex Imrie, *Pictorial History of the German Army Air Service, 1914-1918*, p. 41.

[28]Boelcke, *Feldberichte*, p. 199.

[29]"Advice from an ace: Captain Oswald Boelcke, German Air Force, ca 1916," in Richard M. Suter's "Janus: Concept for a Multipurpose Fighter," *Air University Review*, XXXII, no. 4 (May-June 1981), p. 38; Johnson, *Full Circle*, pp. 43-45; Waugh, "A Short History of 70 Squadron," p. 295.

[30]H.A. Jones, *The War in the Air*, II, p. 282; Boelcke, *Feldberichte*, pp. 199-201; von Richthofen, *Der Rote Kampfflieger*, pp. 105-107.

[31]Hawker, *Hawker V.C.*, pp. 212-215.

[32]Memo reprinted in Andrew Boyle, *Trenchard*, pp. 196-197.

[33]Cecil Lewis, *Sagittarius Rising*, p. 154.

[34]John M. Bruce, "Those Classic Nieuports," *Air Enthusiast Quarterly*, 2(n.d.), pp. 141-143; Bruce, "The First Fighting Spads," *Air Enthusiast Fifteen* (April-July 1981), pp. 58-60, 65-66; Bruce, *British Aeroplanes, 1914-1918*, pp. 552-554.

[35]Hilary St. George Saunders, *Per Ardua*, p. 112.

[36]Boyle, *Trenchard*, pp. 195-196; Jones, *The War in the Air*, II, pp. 447-448, III, p. 285; G.R. Bromet, "Formation and Early Days in France," in E.G. Johnstone, ed., *Naval Eight: A History of No. 8 Squadron R.N.A.S.—Afterwards No. 208 Squadron R.A.F.—From its Formation in 1916 Until the Armistice in 1918*, pp. 10-14.

[37]See, for example, Morrow, *German Air Power in World War I*, pp. 63-66, 70-71, 75-94.

[38]Erich Ludendorff, *Meine Kriegserinnerungen 1914-1918*, p. 305; Supf, *Deutschen Fluggeschichte*, II, p. 282.

[39]Ernst von Hoeppner, *Deutschlands Krieg in der Luft*, pp. 82-83; Supf, *Deutschen Fluggeschichte*, II, pp. 290-293; Morrow, *German Air Power in World War I*, pp. 70-71; John R. Cuneo, *The Air Weapon, 1914-1916*, p. 277.

[40]Hoeppner, *Deutschlands Krieg in der Luft*, p. 85; Heinz J. Nowarra, *50 Jahre Deutsche Luftwaffe, 1910-1960*, II, *1916-1917*, pp. 12-13.

CHAPTER V

[1]Erwin Böhme, *Briefe eines deutschen Kampffliegers an ein junges Mädchen*, p. 69-71; Manfred von Richthofen, *Der Rote Kampfflieger*, pp. 110-111; H.A. Jones, *The War in the Air*, II, p. 312; Tyrrel M. Hawker, *Hawker, V.C.*, pp. 221-222, has the official RFC report submitted to RFC HQ by Hawker.

²Böhme, *Briefe*, p. 72; Heinz J. Nowarra and Kimbrough S. Brown, *Von Richthofen and the "Flying Circus,"* p. 31; Jones, *The War in the Air*, II, p. 312; Peter Supf, *Das Buch der Deutschen Fluggeschichte*, II, p. 337.

³Floyd Gibbons, *The Red Knight of Germany*, p. 3.

⁴Richthofen, *Der Rote Kampfflieger*, pp. 114-116; Hawker, *Hawker, V.C.*, pp. 230-236.

⁵Gwilym H. Lewis, *Wings Over the Somme, 1916-1918*, p. 98.

⁶James T. B. McCudden, *Flying Fury*, p. 149.

⁷Jones, *The War in the Air*, III, p. 320, and Appendix XXXVII.

⁸Denis Winter, *The First of the Few*, p. 153. This is an excellent study of the day-to-day existence of fighter pilots on the Western Front, including training and combat operations.

⁹Andrew Boyle, *Trenchard*, p. 209.

¹⁰Correlli Barnett, *The Swordbearers*, p. 201.

¹¹Jones, *The War in the Air*, III, p. 284.

¹²Details on deployment from Peter L. Gray, *The Albatros D I-III*, Profile Publication 127, p. 12; Peter M. Grosz and A.E. Ferko, "Biplanes for the *Fliegertruppe*," *Air Enthusiast Fourteen* (Dec. 1980-March 1981), p. 66.

¹³Richthofen, *Der Rote Kampfflieger*, pp. 118-119.

¹⁴Jones, *The War in the Air*, III, p. 322.

¹⁵S.L.A. Marshall, *World War I*, pp. 280-283.

¹⁶Jones, *The War in the Air*, Appendix XXXVII.

¹⁷Gordon Taylor, *Sopwith Scout 7309*, p. 75.

¹⁸Colin Waugh, "A Short History of 70 Squadron," *Cross & Cockade Journal*, XX, no. 4 (Winter 1979), pp. 298-299.

¹⁹Frank T. Courtney, *The Eighth Sea*, pp. 102-103.

²⁰Jones, *The War in the Air*, III, p. 334.

²¹John M. Bruce, "Those Classic Nieuports," *Air Enthusiast Quarterly*, 2 (n.d.), p. 146; Bruce, "The First Fighting Spads," *Air Enthusiast Fifteen* (April-July 1981), pp. 67-68, 74.

²²John W.R. Taylor, *C.F.S.: Birthplace of Air Power*, pp. 73-80; Jones, *The War in the Air*, III, p. 339; Winter, *First of the Few*, pp. 36-37; Courtney, *The Eighth Sea*, p. 102; Alan Morris, *Bloody April*, pp. 136, 138-141; for classic examples of the haphazard nature of flying instruction, see Taylor's *Sopwith Scout 7309*, pp. 17-23, and Ralph Barker, *Aviator Extraordinary*, pp. 13-16.

²³Gordon Taylor, *The Sky Beyond*, pp. 11-12.

²⁴Richthofen, *Der Rote Kampfflieger*, pp. 135-138; Heinz J. Nowarra and Kimbrough S. Brown, *Von Richthofen and the "Flying Circus,"* p. 156.

²⁵Jones, *The War in the Air*, III, pp. 335-337; Bruce, *British Aeroplanes 1914-1918*, pp. 126-127; Morris, *Bloody April*, pp. 49-50; Rudolf Stark, *Wings of War*, p. 53.

²⁶Taylor, *Sopwith Scout 7309*, p. 117.

²⁷*Ibid.*, pp. 35, 86-88; Arthur Gould Lee, *No Parachute*, pp. 7-8, 45-46.

²⁸There is an excellent account of the tribulations of 60 Squadron in William Arthur Bishop's *The Courage of the Early Morning*, pp. 55-82; see also Jones, *The War in the Air*, III, p. 337; Bruce, "Those Classic Nieuports," p. 146.

²⁹Jones, *The War in the Air*, III, p. 338.

³⁰Norman Macmillan, *Into the Blue*, pp. 100-101.

³¹Bruce, *The Sopwith Triplane*, Profile Publication 73, pp. 3-7; Morris, *Bloody April*, p. 153.

³²Macmillan, *Into the Blue*, p. 70; Jones, *The War in the Air*, III, pp. 341-342; Morris, *Bloody April*, pp. 60-61.

³³William Sholto Douglas, *Combat and Command*, p. 139.

³⁴Bishop, *The Courage of the Early Morning*, pp. 1-8, 67.

³⁵Jones, *The War in the Air*, III, pp. 350-351; Richthofen, *Der Rote Kampfflieger*, p. 139.

³⁶Boyle, *Trenchard*, pp. 214-215.

³⁷Ernst von Hoeppner, *Deutschlands Krieg in der Luft*, p. 104.

³⁸Jones, *The War in the Air*, Appendix XXXVII.

³⁹Alexander McKee's *The Battle of Vimy Ridge* is a useful and reliable account of the great Canadian offensive against the ridge.

⁴⁰Barnett, *The Swordbearers*, pp. 193-202, 211-232.

⁴¹Gibbons, *The Red Knight of Germany*, pp. 125-128; Maurice Baring, *R.F.C. H.Q., 1914-1918*, pp. 221-222.

⁴²Jones, *The War in the Air*, III, pp. 368-370; Morris, *Bloody April*, pp. 187-188.

CHAPTER VII

¹H.A. Jones, *The War in the Air*, Appendix XXXVII; Alan Morris, *Bloody April*, pp. 191-192.

²For a good discussion of the Fokker triplane and the subsequent Fokker E V/D VIII, see Peter M. Grosz and A.E. Ferko, "The Fokker Dr I: A Reappraisal," *Air Enthusiast Eight*, (October 1978-January 1979), pp. 9-26; and Grosz, "Fokker's D VIII . . . the Reluctant Razor," *Air Enthusiast Seventeen* (December 1981-March 1982), pp. 61-73. See Grosz, "The Agile & Aggressive Albatros," *Air Enthusiast Quarterly One (n.d.)*, pp. 36-51.

³John Howard Morrow, *German Airpower in World War I*, p. 115.

⁴Peter L. Gray, *The Fokker D VII*, Profile Publication 25, p. 10.

⁵Morrow, *Building German Airpower*, p. 87; John M. Bruce, "Vickers' First Fighters," *Air Enthusiast Twelve* (April-July 1980), p. 54.

⁶The definitive account of German airship operations in World War I is Douglas H. Robinson's *The Zeppelin in Combat;* Robinson's chapter "The Zeppelin as a War-Winning Weapon" in his *Giants in the Sky: A History of the Rigid Airship* is an excellent summary. Two popular and generally reliable accounts are Kenneth Poolman's *Zeppelins Against London* and Arch Whitehouse's *The Zeppelin Fighters*.

⁷Robinson, *Giants in the Sky*, pp. 84-86.

⁸*Ibid.*, pp. 87, 93, 103; Poolman, *Zeppelins Against London*, pp. 33-34, 37, 58-60, 63-65.

⁹John Slessor, *The Central Blue*, pp. 11-14.

¹⁰Jones, *The War in the Air*, III, p. 238.

¹¹Robinson, *Giants in the Sky*, p. 140; see also pp. 125-138. See also Hilary St. George Saunders, *Per Ardua*, pp. 129, 194-203, and Anthony Robinson, *Aerial Warfare*, pp. 307-308.

¹²Grosz, *The Gotha G I-G V*, Profile Publication 115, pp. 3-16.

¹³The definitive account of this "first Battle of Britain" is Raymond H. Fredette's *The Sky on Fire*.

¹⁴Fredette, *Sky on Fire*, pp. 17-61; for individual pilot opinions, see Cecil Lewis, *Sagittarius Rising*, pp. 183-187; Arthur Gould Lee, *No Parachute*, p. 87.

¹⁵Fredette, *Sky on Fire*, p. 63.

¹⁶Norman Macmillan, *Into the Blue*, p. 131.

¹⁷Fredette, *Sky on Fire*, pp. 89-92; Lee, *No Parachute*, p. 101.

¹⁸Fredette, *Sky on Fire*, pp. 96-112.

¹⁹Saunders, *Per Ardua*, pp. 208-209.

²⁰R. Wallace Clarke, "Drawing a Bead," *Aeroplane Monthly* (Feb. 1983), pp. 98-99; Saunders, *Per Ardua*, pp. 209-210.

²¹Jones, *The War in the Air*, IV, pp. 196-197, and VI, pp. 428-429; the definitive account of

R plane development is G.W. Haddow and Peter M. Grosz, *The German Giants*. See pp. 44 and 248 concerning the loss of R 43.

[22]Fredette, *Sky on Fire*, pp. 208-212.

[23]Lee, *Open Cockpit*, p. 138.

[24]Bryan Cooper and John Batchelor, *The Story of the Bomber, 1914-1945*, pp. 30-32.

[25]Jones, *The War in the Air*, III, pp. 371-373, 378-379.

[26]William A. Bishop, *Winged Warfare*, pp. 129-137; Jones, *The War in the Air*, IV, p. 129.

[27]Jones, *The War in the Air*, IV, p. 129.

[28]*Ibid.*, pp. 129-130.

[29]*Ibid.*, p. 157. An interesting account of this large dogfight—one of the largest ever fought on the Western Front—is to be found in Raymond Collishaw's *Air Command*, pp. 127-128, and Gordon Taylor, *Sopwith Scout 7309*, pp. 127-129.

[30]Jones, *The War in the Air*, IV, pp. 163-166, 175-180; Maurice Baring, *R.F.C. H.Q., 1914-1918*, pp. 244-250.

[31]Lee, *Open Cockpit*, pp. 139, 141; see also pp. 132-138. For further details, see Lee, *No Parachute*, pp. 161-194; Jones, *The War in the Air*, IV, pp. 233-239, 243, and 257.

[32] Jones, *The War in the Air*, IV, pp. 245-246.

[33]Georg Paul Neumann, ed., *Die Deutschen Luftstreitkräfte im Weltkriege*, pp. 74, 90-93; Peter Gray and Owen Thetford, *German Aircraft of the First World War*, pp. xii-xv, 154-157; W.M. Lamberton, *Fighter Aircraft of the 1914-1918 War*, pp. 132, 136; Paul Nami, trans., "Two-Seaters in Battle: The Recollections of Oscar Bechtle," *Cross & Cockade Journal*, XX, no. 2 (Summer 1979), pp. 155-172.

[34]A translation of a captured example of this document, entitled "Employment of Battle Flights," is reprinted in Jones, *The War in the Air*, Appendix XII.

[35]Jones, *The War in the Air*, IV, pp. 251-259.

CHAPTER VIII

[1]A good summary can be found in S.L.A. Marshall, *World War I*, pp. 341-347; the best overall account is John Toland's *No Man's Land: 1918, the Last Year of the Great War*, though Barrie Pitt's *1918: The Last Act* is still the most readable.

[2]H.A. Jones, *The War in the Air*, IV, pp. 299-301, 311, 315-317, 342-343, 376.

[3]Ernst Udet, *Ace of the Iron Cross*, pp. 56-59; Paul Nami, trans., "Two-Seaters in Battle," *Cross and Cockade Journal*, XX, no. 2, (Summer 1979), pp. 159-172; see also Johannes Hohmann, *"Wir Schlachtflieger,"* in Walter von Eberhardt, ed., *Unsere Luftstreitkräfte, 1914-1918*, pp. 249, 253-258.

[4]Stuart Cloete, *A Victorian Son*, p. 288.

[5]Jones, *The War in the Air*, IV, p. 376. See also pp. 290-291, and Jones, *The War in the Air*, VI, p. 507.

[6]Bill Lambert, *Combat Report*, p. 157. Lambert narrowly escaped death on a subsequent sortie.

[7]Jones, *The War in the Air*, VI, pp. 454-458; Alistair Horne, *To Lose a Battle*, pp. 246-249.

[8]See, for example, A.J.C. Lavalle's *The Tale of Two Bridges and The Battle for the Skies Over North Vietnam*, I and II of the USAF Air War College Airpower Research Institute's *USAF Southeast Asia Monograph Series* (Washington, D.C.: U.S. Government Printing Office, 1976).

[9]Jones, *The War in the Air*, VI, p. 464.

[10]*Ibid.*, p. 480; see, for example, Arch Whitehouse, *The Fledgling*, pp. 196-198; Rudolph Stark, *Wings of War*, pp. 96-99.

[11]Peter C. Smith, *The History of Dive Bombing*, pp. 16-19.

[12]Translated and reprinted in Jones, *The War in the Air*, VI, p. 348.

[13]*Ibid.*, IV, pp. 348, 402.

[14]*Ibid.*, VI, pp. 551; see also Hilary St. George Saunders, *Per Ardua*, p. 244.

[15]The best historical analysis of the dogfight is Heinz J. Nowarra and Kimbrough S. Brown's *Von Richthofen and the "Flying Circus,"* pp. 111-121; I do not find D.A. Russell's argument for ground fire (pp. 122-125) persuasive, though it is possible. Floyd Gibbons, *Red Knight of Germany*, pp. 191-205, is a good popular account.

[16]For a good summary of the various sides, see Frank R. McGuire's "Who Killed von Richthofen?" *Cross & Cockade Journal*, IV, no. 2 (Spring 1963), pp. 159-167.

[17]Stark, *Wings of War*, p. 47.

[18]Ira Jones, *Tiger Squadron*, p. 93.

[19]See, for example, Hermann Goring, *"Luftkämpfe,"* in Eberhardt, ed., *Unsere Luftstreitkräfte*, pp. 287-292.

[20]See, for example, Cecil Montgomery-Moore and Peter Kilduff, *"That's My Bloody Plane,"* pp. 20-34, 75-77.

[21]Jones, *Tiger Squadron*, pp. 170, 190-191; Jones, *King of Air Fighters*, pp. 248-249, 282-285; James E. Johnson, *Full Circle*, pp. 81-83.

[22]Renè Fonck, *Ace of Aces*, p. 98, 111; Aaron Norman, *The Great Air War*, p. 78; Herbert Molloy Mason, Jr., *High Flew the Falcons*, p. 51.

[23]James T.B. McCudden, *Flying Fury*, p. 264.

[24]See, for example. Eddie V. Rickenbacker, *Fighting the Flying Circus*, pp. 21-26.

[25]Maurer Maurer, ed., *The U.S. Air Service in World War I*, I: *The Final Report and a Tactical History*, p. 284.

[26]*Ibid.*, p. 369.

[27]*Ibid.*, p. 368; see William Mitchell, "The Great Attack on St. Mihiel," in Gene Gurney, ed., *Great Air Battles*, pp. 38-40.

[28]Maurer, ed., *USAS in WW I*, IV: *Postwar Review*, "Report of Col. Thomas De Witt Milling," p. 9.

[29]*Ibid.*, "Lessons Learned: 147th Aero Squadron, and 91st Aero Squadron," pp. 61 and 129.

[30]*Ibid.*, Milling report, p. 13; Nami, "Two-Seaters in Battle," p. 163; Alex Imrie, *Pictorial History of the German Army Air Service*, pp. 156, 164-165; Bruce Robertson, ed., *Air Aces of the 1914-1918 War*, pp. 36-37; Ronald Dodds, *The Brave Young Wings*, pp. 96-98; William A. Flanagan, "The Fighter Force: How Many Seats?" *Air University Review* XXXII, no. 4 (May-June 1981), p. 4.

[31]Maurer, ed., *USAS in WW I*, II: *Early Concepts of Military Aviation*, "Sherman: Tentative Manual for the Employment of Air Service," pp. 313-408; William W. Momyer, *Air Power in Three Wars* (Washington, D.C.: USAF, 1 January 1978), p. 128.

[32]Alfred F. Hurley, *Billy Mitchell*, pp. 35-36; James J. Hudson, *Hostile Skies*, pp. 138-193. Hudson's book is the definitive study of American air combat experience in the First World War.

CHAPTER IX

[1]Noel F. Parrish, "The Influence of Air Power upon Historians," in Alfred F. Hurley and Robert C. Ehrhart, eds., *Air Power and Warfare: The Proceedings of the 8th Military History Symposium United States Air Force Academy, 18-20 October 1978*, p. 10.

[2]William W. Momyer, *Air Power in Three Wars*, p. 163.

[3]Statement of Elwood R. Quesada in Richard H. Kohn and Joseph P. Harahan, eds., *Air Superiority in World War II and Korea*, p. 18. The other participants, besides General Quesada, were Generals James Ferguson, Robert M. Lee, and William Momyer.

[4]See, for example, Capt. Claire L. Chennault, USAAC, *The Role of Defensive Pursuit*. This became the standard fighter "bible" for many years; Chennault, of course, later formed the very successful American Volunteer Group, which began as a defensive fighter force.

[5]Statement of James Ferguson in Kohn and Harahan, eds., *Air Superiority in World War II and Korea*, p. 23.

[6]James E. Johnson, *Full Circle*, p. 103.

[7]Momyer, *Air Power in Three Wars*, p. 337.

[8]Quoted in Kohn and Harahan, *Air Superiority in World War II and Korea*, p. 84.

[9]Richard V. Rhode, *The Pressure Distribution over the Horizontal and Vertical Tail Surfaces of the F6C-4 Pursuit Airplane in Violent Maneuvers*, NACA Report No. 307 (1928). Earlier studies had been done by U.S. Army Corps test pilot James H. "Jimmy" Doolittle at McCook Field. See Richard P. Hallion, *Test Pilots: The Frontiersmen of Flight*, pp. 81-85.

[10]See C.R. Mackenzie, "Remarks on Future Design of Scouts and Suitable Armament for Them," in E.G. Johnstone, ed., *Naval Eight*, p. 197; Cecil Montgomery-Moore and Peter Kilduff, *"That's My Bloody Plane,"* p. 108; L.F.E. Coombs, "Front Office Evolution," *Air Enthusiast*, II, no. 2 (February 1972), p. 65.

[11]See, for example, Heinz Nowarra and William Puglisi, "War Diary of Royal Prussian *Jagdstaffel 56*," *Cross & Cockade Journal*, I, no. 4 (Winter 1960), p. 72.

[12]Edward V. Rickenbacker, *Fighting the Flying Circus*, p. 26.

[13]Major General Mason M. Patrick, "Final Report of the Chief of Air Service, A.E.F.," reprinted in Maurer, ed., *USAS in WW I: The Final Report and a Tactical History*, p. 103.

[14]Frederick C. Blesse, "No Guts No Glory" (March 1955), reprinted by the HQ 57th Tactical Training Wing, Tactical Air Command, *USAF Fighter Weapons Review*, 1977, pp. 26-30, 55.

[15]Statement of Oberstlt. Haehnelt, in Appendix *"Verlustliste der deutschen Luftstreitkräfte im Weltkrieg,"* in von Eberhardt, ed., *Unserer Luftstreitkräfte;* Ezra Bowen, *Knights of the Air*, p. 175; H.A. Jones, *The War in the Air*, Appendix XXXVI.

[16]Robert Saundby, *Early Aviation*, p. 76.

Selected Bibliography

Anderegg, Dick. "Meeting the Threat: Sophistication vs. Simplicity," *USAF Fighter Weapons Review* (Fall 1982).

Baring, Maurice. *R.F.C. H.Q. 1914-1918*. London: G. Bell and Sons, 1920.

Barker, Ralph. *Aviator Extraordinary: The Sidney Cotton Story*. London: Chatto & Windus, 1969.

Barnett, Corelli, *The Swordbearers: Supreme Command in the First World War*. New York: William Morrow & Co., 1964.

Biddle, Charles J. *Fighting Airman*. Garden City, N.Y.: Doubleday, 1968.

Bishop, William A. *Winged Warfare*. Garden City, N.Y.: Doubleday, 1967.

—————. *Winged Peace*. New York: Viking Press, 1944.

Bishop, William Arthur. *The Courage of the Early Morning: A Frank Biography of Billy Bishop*. New York: David McKay Company, Inc. 1965.

Blesse, Frederick C. "No Guts, No Glory" (March 1955), reprinted by the HQ 57th Tactical Training Wing, Tactical Air Command, *USAF Fighter Weapons Review*, 1977.

Boelcke, Oswald. *Hauptmann Bölckes Feldberichte*. New York: Deutschland Library Company, 1917.

Böhme, Erwin, *Briefe eines deutschen Kampffliegers an ein junges Mädchen*. Leipzig: K. F. Koehler, 1930.

Bordeaux, Henry. *Georges Guynemer: Knight of the Air*. New Haven: Yale University Press, 1918.

Bowen, Ezra. *Knights of the Air*. Alexandria, Va.: Time-Life Books, 1980.

Boyle, Andrew. *Trenchard: Man of Vision*. New York: W. W. Norton & Company, Inc., 1962.

Boyne, Walter J. "Technological Progress in World War One Aviation," in Pinson, J. D., ed., *Diamond Jubilee of Powered Flight: The Evolution of Aircraft Design*. Dayton, Ohio: American Institute of Aeronautics and Astronautics, in association with the U.S. Air Force Museum, 1979.

Bruce, John M. *British Aeroplanes, 1914-1918*. New York: Funk & Wagnalls, 1969.

—————. *Fighters*, I-V of *War Planes of the First World War*. Garden City, N.Y.: Doubleday, 1970-72.

—————. "Those Classic Nieuports," *Air Enthusiast Quarterly*, 2 (n.d.).

—————. "The Bullets and the Guns," *Air Enthusiast Nine*, (Feb.-May 1979).

—————. "Vickers' First Fighters," *Air Enthusiast Twelve*, (April-July 1980).

—————. "The First Fighting Spads," *Air Enthusiast Fifteen*, (April-July 1981).

Buckley, Harold. *Squadron 95*. Paris: The Obelisk Press, 1933.

Chennault, Claire. *The Role of Defensive Pursuit*. Maxwell Field, Alabama: Air Corps Tactical School, 1933.

Clarke, R. Wallace. "Drawing a Bead," *Aeroplane Monthly* (February 1983).

Cloete, Stuart. *A Victorian Son: An Autobiography, 1897-1922*. New York: The John Day

Company, 1973.

Collishaw, Raymond. *Air Command: A Fighter Pilot's Story.* London: William Kimber, 1973.

Coombs, L.F.E. "Cockpits of the RAF," *Aeroplane Monthly* (November 1983).

_____. "Front Office Evolution," *Air Enthusiast*, II, no. 2 (February 1972).

Cooper, Bryan, and **Batchelor, John.** *The Story of the Bomber.* London: Phoebus Publishing Co., 1974.

Copp, DeWitt S. *A Few Great Captains: The Men and Events That Shaped the Development of U.S. Air Power.* Garden City, N.Y.: Doubleday, 1980.

Coppens, Willy. *Flying in Flanders.* New York: Ace, 1971.

Courtney, Frank T. *The Eighth Sea.* Garden City, N.Y.: Doubleday, 1972.

Crundell, E. D. *Fighter Pilot on the Western Front.* London: William Kimber, 1975.

Cuneo, John R. *Winged Mars.* I: *The German Air Weapon, 1870-1914,* and II: *The Air Weapon, 1914-1916.* Harrisburg, Pennsylvania: The Military Service Publishing Co., 1942-1947.

Dodds, Ronald. *The Brave Young Wings.* Stittsville, Ontario: Canada's Wings, Inc., 1980.

Douglas, William Sholto. *Combat and Command: The Story of an Airman in Two World Wars.* New York: Simon and Schuster, 1966.

Driggs, Laurence LaTourette. *Heroes of Aviation.* Boston: Little, Brown, and Company, 1918.

Eberhardt, Walter von, ed. *Unsere Luftstreitkräfte, 1914-18.* Berlin: Vaterlandischer Verlag C. A. Weller, 1930.

Elliott, Stuart E. *Wooden Crates & Gallant Pilots.* Philadelphia: Dorrance & Company, 1972.

Flammer, Philip M. *The Vivid Air: The Lafayette Escadrille.* Athens, Georgia: The University of Georgia Press, 1981.

Flanagan, William A. "The Fighter Force: How Many Seats?" *Air University Review,* XXXII, n. 4 (May-June 1981).

Fokker, Anthony H. G. and **Gould, Bruce.** *Flying Dutchman: The Life of Anthony Fokker.* London: George Routledge & Sons, Ltd., 1931.

Fonck, René. *Ace of Aces.* Garden City, N.Y.: Doubleday, 1967.

Fredette, Raymond H. *The Sky on Fire: The First Battle of Britain, 1917-1918.* New York: Harcourt Brace Jovanovich, 1976.

Fussell, Paul. *The Great War and Modern Memory.* London: Oxford University Press, 1975.

Gibbons, Floyd. *The Red Knight of Germany: The Story of Baron von Richthofen, Germany's Great War Bird.* New York: Bantam Books, 1964.

Gibbs-Smith, Charles H. *The Rebirth of European Aviation, 1896-1908—A Study of the Wright Brothers' Influence.* London: Her Majesty's Stationary Office, 1974.

_____. *Aviation: An Historical Survey from Its Origins to the End of World War II.* London: Her Majesty's Stationary Office, 1970.

Gray, Peter L., and **Thetford, Owen.** *German Aircraft of the First World War.* London: Putnam, 1962.

Grey, C. G., ed. *Jane's All the World's Aircraft, 1919.* London: Sampson Low Marston, 1919.

Grinnell-Milne, Duncan. *Wind in the Wires.* Garden City, N.Y.: Doubleday, 1968.

Grosz, Peter M. "The Agile and Aggressive Albatros," *Air Enthusiast Quarterly,* 1 (n.d.).

_____. "Fokker's D VIII . . . the Reluctant Razor," *Air Enthusiast Seventeen* (Dec. 1981-Mar. 1982).

_____, and **Ferko, A. E.** "Biplanes for the *Fliegertruppe,*" *Air Enthusiast Fourteen* (Dec. 1980-March 1981).

_____. "The Fokker Dr I: A Reappraisal," *Air Enthusiast Eight* (Oct. 1978-Jan. 1979).

_____, and **Kruger, Egon.** *Pfalz.* West Roxbury, Massachusetts: WW I Aero Publishers, Inc., 1964.

Gurney, Gene, ed. *Great Air Battles.* New York: Franklin Watts, Inc., 1963.

Haddow, G. W., and **Grosz, Peter M.** *The German Giants: The Story of the R Planes, 1914-1918.* London: Putnam, 1962.

Hallion, Richard P. *Test Pilots: The Frontiersmen of Flight.* Garden City, N.Y.: Doubleday, 1981.

_____. "Wooden Aircraft and the Great War," *Journal of Forest History,* XXII, no. 4 (October 1978).

Hanle, Paul A. *Bringing Aerodynamics to America.* Cambridge, Massachusetts: MIT Press, 1982.

Hartney, Harold E. *Up & At 'Em.* New York: Ace Books, 1971.

Hawker, Tyrrel M. *Hawker, V.C.* London: The Mitre Press, 1965.

Higham, Robin D. S. *Air Power: A Concise History.* New York: St. Martin's Press, 1973.

Hocutt, George. " *'Les Cigognes': Groupe de Combat 12,*" *Cross & Cockade Journal,* I, no. 2 (Autumn 1960).

Hoeppner, Ernst von. *Deutschlands Krieg in der Luft.* Leipzig: K. F. Koehler, 1921.

Holley, Irving B. *Ideas and Weapons: Exploitation of the Aerial Weapon by the United States During World War I.* New Haven: Yale University Press, 1953.

_____. "Of Saber Charges, Escort Fighters, and Spacecraft: The Search for Doctrine." *Air University Review,* XXXIV, no. 6 (Sept.-Oct. 1983).

Horne, Alistair. *The Price of Glory: Verdun, 1916.* New York: Harper and Row, Publishers, 1967.

_____. *To Lose a Battle: France, 1940.* Boston: Little, Brown and Company, 1969.

Hudson, James J. *Hostile Skies: A Combat History of the American Air Service in World War I.* Syracuse, N.Y.: Syracuse University Press, 1968.

Humphreys, F. E. "The Wright Flyer and Its Possible Uses in War." *Journal of the United States Artillery,* XXXIII (March-April 1910).

Hurley, Alfred F. *Billy Mitchell: Crusader for Air Power.* Bloomington, Indiana: Indiana University Press, 1975.

_____. and **Ehrhard, Robert C.,** eds. *Air Power and Warfare: The Proceedings* *of the 8th Military History Symposium United States Air Force Academy, 18-20 October 1978.* Washington, D.C.: Office of Air Force History, 1979.

Immelmann, Franz. *Der Adler von Lille.* Leipzig: K. F. Koehler, 1934.

Imrie, Alex. *Pictorial History of the German Army Air Service, 1914-1918.* Chicago: Henry Regnery Company, 1973.

Jablonski, Edward. *The Knighted Skies.* New York: G. P. Putnam's Sons, 1964.

——————. *Warriors With Wings.* New York: Bobbs-Merrill Co., Inc., 1966.

Jackson, Robert. *Fighter Pilots of World War I.* New York: St. Martin's Press, 1977.

Johnson, Herbert W. "Air Force Fighters: Simple or Complex?" *Air University Review,* XXXIV, n. 4 (May-June 1983).

Johnson, James E. *Full Circle: The Tactics of Air Fighting, 1914-1964.* New York: Ballantine Books, 1964.

Johnstone, E. G., ed. *Naval Eight: A History of No. 8 Squadron R.N.A.S.—Afterwards No. 208 Squadron R.A.F.—From Its Formation in 1916 Until the Armistice in 1918.* London: Arms and Armour Press, 1972.

Jones, H.A. *The War in the Air,* II-VI. Oxford: The Clarendon Press, 1922-1937.

Jones, Ira. *King of Air Fighters.* London: Ivor Micholson & Watson, Ltd., 1934.

——————. *Tiger Squadron.* New York: Award Books, 1966.

Kiernan, R. H. *Captain Albert Ball, V.C., D.S.O.* London: The Aviation Book Club, 1939.

Killen, John. *A History of the Luftwaffe.* New York: Berkley Publishing Corporation, 1967.

Kohn, Richard H., and Harahan, Joseph P., eds. *Air Superiority in World War II and Korea.* Washington, D.C.: Office of Air Force History, 1983.

Lambert, Bill. *Combat Report.* London: Corgi Books, 1975.

Lamberton, W. M. *Fighter Aircraft of the 1914-1918 War.* Fallbrook, Calif.: Aero Publishers, Inc., 1964.

Lee, Arthur Gould. *No Parachute: A Fighter Pilot in World War I.* New York: Pocket Books, 1971.

——————. *Open Cockpit: A Pilot of the Royal Flying Corps.* London: Jarrolds, 1969.

Lewis, Cecil. *Sagittarius Rising.* New York: Collier Books, 1970.

Lewis, Gwilym H. *Wings Over the Somme, 1916-1918.* London: William Kimber, 1976.

Longstreet, Stephen. *The Canvas Falcons.* New York: Ballantine Books, 1983.

Ludendorff, Erich. *Meine Kriegserinnerungen, 1914-1918.* Berlin: E. S. Mittler & Sohn, 1921.

Mcdonald, Lyn, *Somme.* London: Michael Joseph, 1983.

Macmillan, Norman. *Into the Blue.* London: Jarrolds, 1969.

Marshall, S. L. A. *World War I.* New York: American Heritage Press, 1971.

Mason, Francis K. *Battle Over Britain: A History of the German Air Assaults on Great Britain, 1917-18 and July-December 1940, and of the Development of Britain's Air Defences Between the World Wars*. Garden City, New York. Doubleday, 1969.

Mason, Herbert Molloy, Jr. *High Flew the Falcons: The French Aces of World War I*. Philadelphia: J. B. Lippincott Co., 1965.

Maurer, Maurer, ed. *The U.S. Air Service in World War I*, I-IV. Washington, D.C.: Office of Air Force History, 1979.

McCudden, James T. B. *Flying Fury: Five Years in the Royal Flying Corps*. Garden City, N.Y.: Doubleday, 1969.

McGuire, Frank R. "Who Killed von Richthofen?" *Cross & Cockade Journal*, IV, n. 2 (Spring 1963).

McKee, Alexander. *The Battle of Vimy Ridge*. New York: Stein and Day, 1967.

_____. *The Friendless Sky: The Story of Air Combat in World War I*. New York: William Morrow, 1964.

Mersky, Peter B. *U.S. Marine Corps Aviation: 1912 to the Present*. Annapolis: The Nautical and Aviation Publishing Company of America, 1983.

Middlebrook, Martin. *The First Day on the Somme: 1 July 1916*. New York: W. W. Norton & Co., Inc., 1972.

Mikesh, Robert C. *Albatros D Va: German Fighter of World War I*, v. IV of *Famous Aircraft of the National Air and Space Museum*. Washington, D.C.: Smithsonian Institution Press, 1980.

Momyer, William W. *Air Power in Three Wars*. Washington, D.C.: United States Air Force, 1 January 1978.

Montgomery-Moore, Cecil, and Kilduff, Peter. *"That's My Bloody Plane": The World War I Experiences of Major Cecil Montgomery-Moore*. Chester, Connecticut: The Pequot Press, 1975.

Morris, Alan. *Bloody April*. London: Arrow Books, Ltd., 1968.

Morrow, John Howard. *Building German Airpower, 1909-1914*. Knoxsville, Tennessee: The University of Tennessee Press, 1976.

_____. *German Air Power in World War I*. Lincoln, Nebraska: University of Nebraska Press, 1982.

Mortane, Jacques, ed. *La Guerre Aérienne*. nos. 1-130 (Nov. 16, 1916 to May 8, 1919, weekly; no. 110, Dec. 19, 1918 is a summary volume on the air war).

Munson, Kenneth. *Aircraft of World War I*. Garden City, N.Y.: Doubleday, 1968.

_____. *Fighters, Attack, and Training Aircraft, 1914-1919*. New York: The Macmillan Company, 1968.

_____. *Bombers, Patrol, and Reconnaissance Aircraft, 1914-1919*. New York: The Macmillan Company, 1968.

_____. *Pioneer Aircraft, 1903-1914*. New York: The Macmillan Company, 1969.

Nami, Paul, trans. "Two-Seaters in Battle: The Recollections of Oscar Bechtle," *Cross & Cockade Journal*, XX, no. 2 (Summer 1979).

Nebel, Rudolf. *Die Narren von Tegel*. Dusseldorf: Droste Verlag, 1972.

Neumann, Georg Paul, ed. *Die Deutschen Luftstreitkräfte im Weltkrieg.* Berlin: E.S. Mittler und Sohn, 1920.

Norman, Aaron. *The Great Air War.* New York: The Macmillan Company, 1968.

Nowarra, Heinz J. *50 Jahre Deutsche Luftwaffe, 1910-1960.* I: *1910-1915;* II: *1916-1817.* Fallbrook, Calif.: Aero Publishers Inc., 1964.

_____, and **Brown, Kimbrough S.** *Von Richthofen and the "Flying Circus."* Letchworth, Eng.: Harleyford Publications Ltd., 1964.

_____, and **Puglisi,** "War Diary of Royal Prussian *Jagdstaffel 56,*" *Cross & Cockade Journal,* I, n. 4 (Winter 1960).

Penrose, Harald. *British Aviation: The Pioneering Years, 1903-1914.* London: Putnam, 1967.

Phelan, Joseph A. *Heroes & Aeroplanes of the Great War, 1914-1918.* New York: Grosset & Dunlap, 1968.

Pitt, Barrie. *1918: The Last Act.* New York: W. W. Norton, 1962.

Poolman, Kenneth. *Zeppelins Against London.* New York: The John Day Company, 1961.

Raleigh, Walter. *The War in the Air,* I. Oxford: The Clarendon Press, 1922.

Reichsarchiv. *Die Operationen des Jahres 1915: Die Ereignisse im Westen und auf dem Balkan von Sommer bis zum Jahresschluss,* IX of *Der Weltkrieg, 1914-1918.* Berlin: E. S. Mittler & Sohn, 1933.

Reynolds, Quentin. *They Fought for the Sky.* New York: Rinehart & Company, Inc., 1957.

Richthofen, Manfred von. *Der Rote Kampfflieger.* Berlin: Ullstein A. G., 1933.

Rickenbacker, Edward V. *Fighting the Flying Circus.* New York: Avon Books, 1969.

_____. *Rickenbacker: His Own Story.* Greenwich, Connecticut: Fawcett, 1969.

Robertson, Bruce, ed. *Air Aces of the 1914-1918 War.* Fallbrook, Calif. Aero Publishers Inc., 1964.

Robinson, Anthony. *Aerial Warfare.* New York: Galahad Books, 1982.

Robinson, Douglas H. *The Zeppelin in Combat.* London: G. T. Foulis & Co., Ltd., 1961.

_____. *Giants in the Sky: A History of the Rigid Airship.* Seattle: University of Washington Press, 1973.

_____. *The Dangerous Sky: A History of Aviation Medicine.* Seattle: University of Washington Press, 1973.

Saundby, Robert. *Early Aviation: Man Conquers the Air.* London: Macdonald, 1971.

Saunders, Hilary St. George. *Per Ardua: The Rise of British Air Power, 1911-1939.* London: Oxford University Press, 1945.

Schroder, Hans. *An Airman Remembers.* London: John Hamilton, Ltd., n.d.

Sims, Edward H. *Fighter Tactics and Strategy, 1914-1970.* New York: Harper and Row, Publishers, 1972.

Slessor, John. *The Central Blue: The Autobiography of Sir John Slessor, Marshal of the RAF.* New York: Frederick A. Praeger, 1957.

Smith, Myron J. *World War I in the Air: A Bibliography and Chronology.*

Metuchen, N.J.: The Scarecrow Press, 1977.

Smith, Peter C. *The History of Dive Bombing.* Annapolis: Nautical & Aviation Publishing Company of America, 1981.

Snowden-Gamble, C. F. *The Story of a North Sea Air Station.* London: Neville Spearman, 1967.

Stark, Rudolf. *Wings of War: An Airman's Diary of the Last Year of World War One.* London: Arms and Armour Press, 1973.

Strange, Louis A. *Recollections of an Airman.* London: John Hamilton, Ltd., 1933.

Supf, Peter. *Das Buch der deutschen Fluggeschichte,* II. Berlin: Grunewald Verlaganstalt Hermann Klemm A. G., 1935.

Suter, Richard M. "Janus: Concept for a Multipurpose Fighter," *Air University Review,* XXXII, no. 4 (May-June 1981).

Taylor, Gordon. *Sopwith Scout 7309.* London: Cassell & Co., Ltd., 1968.

——————. *The Sky Beyond.* New York: Ballantine Books, 1970.

Taylor, John W. R. *C.F.S.: Birthplace of Air Power.* London: Putnam, 1958.

Toland, John. *No Man's Land: 1918, the Last Year of the Great War.* New York: Random House, Inc., 1980.

Udet, Ernst. *Ace of the Iron Cross.* Garden City, N.Y.: Doubleday, 1970.

United States War Department. General Headquarters, American Expeditionary Forces, 2nd Section, General Staff. *American Air Service Intelligence Bulletins and Summaries.* (March 29, 1918 to November 16, 1918; privately compiled by Professor Howard G. Fisher of the University of California at San Diego, and copies deposited in the files of the National Air and Space Museum, Smithsonian Institution, and the San Diego Aero-Space Museum).

Vann, Raymond, and Waugh, Colin. "The B.E. 12 in Combat," *Cross & Cockade Journal,* XX, no. 4 (Winter 1979).

Walker, Dale. *Only the Clouds Remain: Ted Parsons of the Lafayette Escadrille.* Amsterdam, N.Y.: Alandale Press, 1980.

Waugh, Colin. "A Short History of 70 Squadron, RFC/RAF, 1916-1919," *Cross & Cockade Journal,* XX, no. 4 (Winter 1979).

Weyl, A. R. *Fokker: The Creative Years.* London: Putnam, 1965.

Whitehouse, Arch. *The Fledgling: An Aerial Gunner in World War I.* New York: Duell, Sloan and Pearce, 1964.

——————. *The Zeppelin Fighters.* Garden City, N.Y.: Doubleday, 1966.

——————. *The Years of the Sky Kings.* New York: Curtis, 1964.

——————. *Heroes of the Sunlit Sky.* Garden City, N.Y.: Doubleday, 1967.

Winter, Denis. *The First of the Few: Fighter Pilots of the First World War.* London: Allen Lane, 1982.

Winter, Frank H. *Prelude to the Space Age: The Rocket Societies, 1924-1940.* Washington, D.C.: Smithsonian Institution Press, 1983.

Wolff, Leon, *In Flanders Fields: The 1917 Campaign.* New York: Time Incorporated, 1958.

A note should be made concerning two generally useful sources for information on the First World War in the air: the *Cross & Cockade Journal* of the Society of World War I Aero Historians, which contains a wealth of articles and correspondence from aero historians around the world on technical, operational, and administrative aspects of World War I military aviation; and the Profile Publications reference series. I have used volumes I-XXIII (1960-1982) of the *Cross & Cockade Journal*, as well as the following Profiles, which were published individually by Profile Publications Ltd., Leatherhead, England, and bound in hardback volumes by Doubleday and Company, Garden City, N.Y.

Profile Number and Author	Title	Year
1 J. M. Bruce	The S.E. 5a	1965
9 Peter L. Gray	Albatros D V	1965
13 J. M. Bruce	Sopwith Pup	1965
17 C. F. Andrews	SPAD XIII C.I	1965
21 J. M. Bruce	Bristol Fighter	1965
25 Peter L. Gray	Fokker D VII	1965
26 J. M. Bruce	De Havilland D.H. 4	1965
38 J. M. Bruce	Fokker Monoplanes	1965
43 Peter L. Gray	The Pfalz D III	1965
49 C. F. Andrews	Nieuport 17	1965
50 J. M. Bruce	Sopwith 7F.1 Snipe	1965
55 J. M. Bruce	Fokker Dr I	1965
73 J. M. Bruce	Sopwith Triplane	1966
79 Peter M. Bowers	Nieuport N.28C-1	1966
85 J. M. Bruce	R.E. 8	1966
86 Peter L. Gray	Siemens Schuckert D III and IV	1966
91 J. M. Bruce	De Havilland D.H. 2	1966
103 J. M. Bruce	S.E. 5	1966
115 Peter M. Grosz	Gotha G I-G V	1966
121 J. M. Bruce	Sopwith 1½ Strutter	1966
127 Peter L. Gray	Albatros D I-III	1966
133 J. M. Bruce	B.E. 2, 2a, and 2b	1966
139 J. M. Bruce	Bristol Scouts C & D	1967
157 J. M. Bruce and Jean Noel	The Breguet 14	1967
163 Peter M. Grosz	Roland C II	1967
169 J. M. Bruce	The Sopwith Dolphin	1967
181 J. M. Bruce	De Havilland D.H. 5	1967
187 Hugh Cowin	The Junkers Monoplanes	1967
199 Peter M. Grosz	Pfalz D XII	1967
200 J. M. Bruce	Martinsyde Elephant	1967

Index

Hoeppner, Generalleutnant Ernst von: 61-62, 80, 114, 120, 151
Horne, Alistair: 27
Hue, Jules: 9
Huffzky, Vizefeldwebel Friedrich: 105, 145
Humphreys, Lt. Fred: 1-2
Hunter, Frank O'Driscoll "Monk": 150

I

Idflieg (*Inspektion der Fliegertruppen*: The Inspectorate of German Military Aviation): 44, 48, 50, 60-61, 78, 102, 112, 114, 117, 140, 152
Immelmann, Leutnant Max ("The Eagle of Lille"): 14, 16, 18-23, 39-40, 42, 48, 64, 69, 93
"Immelmann Turn": 18-19, 39
In der Luft Unbesiegt (Neumann anthology): 140
Ingelmunster: 11, 129
Interdiction: *see* Ground attack and Ground strafing
Iseghem: 11
Issoudon: 161

J

Jagdflieger (the German fighter community): 41, 139, 143, 152
Johannisthal: 12-13, 86
Johnson, Group Captain James E. "Johnny": 150
Jones, H.A.: 120
Jones, Ira "Taffy": 21, 98, 139
Joyce Green aerodrome: 119
Junkers, Dr. Hugo: 103, 131

K

Kaiser Wilhelm II: 39-40, 42, 61, 64, 118, 137
Kampfeinsitzer (single-seat fighter): 32
Kampfflugzeug (lit. "battleplane": warplane, esp. heavy attack or light bomber aircraft): 121
Kármán, Theodore von: 3
Kennedy, President John: 139
Kent: 124
Klaxon horns: 122
"Knights of the Air" (stmt. of David Lloyd George): 164
Kogenluft (*Kommandierender General der Luftstreitkräfte*: Commander of the Imperial German Air Service): 61, 80
Kovel: 52, 54
Kriegsministerium (German War Ministry): 60, 62
Kreutzer, Martin: 12

L

Lagnicourt: 54-56, 63-64
Lanchester, Frederick W.: 26
"Lanchester's law": 26
Langley Field: 107
Lea, Tom: 156
Lecluse: 81
Lee, Arthur Gould: 130
Leefe Robinson, Capt. W.: 74, 76, 120, 145
Legion Kondor (Spanish Civil War): 134
Le Hameau: 66
Leith-Thomsen, Oberstleutnant (later Oberst) Hermann von der: 12, 46, 61, 120
Leppla, John: 145
Le Prieur air-to-air rockets: 30, 52, 91
Le Prieur, Y.P.G.: 30
Le Quesnoy: 6
Lesboeufs: 134
Lewis, Cecil: 33, 36
Lilienthal, Otto: 2, 20
Lille: 37, 71, 129
Liska, John: 145
Lloyd George, David: 164
Loerzer, Bruno: 156-157
London: 119, 122-125
London Air Defence Area (LADA): 122, 124
Longstreet, Stephen: 138
Ludendorff, General Erich: 60-61, 64, 129, 133, 137
Luebbe, Heinrich: 11-12
Lufbery, Raoul: 144, 158
Luft-Verkehr Gesellschaft (*L.V.G.*): 9
Luftsperre ("Air blockade"): 28-29, 31-32
Luke, Frank: 144

M

McCubbin, Lt. G.R.: 38-39
McCudden, James T.B.: 66, 98, 142-143, 155, 157
McKeever, Andrew: 145
Maastricht river: 135
MACHINE GUNS:
  Early use on aircraft: 4, 6-13
  Synchronizer mechanisms:
    Alkan: 17
    Constantinesco-Colley (C.C.): 17
    Heber-Luebbe (Fokker): 12-13, 39
    Scarff-Dibovsky: 17, 35
  Types:
    Hotchkiss: 7, 9, 11-12
    Lewis: 8, 17, 20, 28, 34, 52, 66, 74, 76, 91, 98
    Parabellum: 12, 104, 131-132
    Spandau: 48, 66, 76, 131, 159

V

Valenciennes: 70, 73, 160
Verdun (*see also* Battles: Verdun): 13
Vert Galand: 60, 73, 81
Very flares: 37
Victoria Cross (V.C.): 17, 36, 74, 89, 119, 127
Vimy Ridge: 80

W

Wadi El Far'a: 137, 146
Waller, Corporal J.H.: 38-39
Warneford, Reginald A.J.: 74, 88, 119
War Office (Great Britain): 67, 78
Warsaw Pact: 130, 159
Wervicq: 129
Wevelghem: 129
Whittaker, Major W.E. de B.: iii
"Wild Weasels": 146
Wilhelm, Crown Prince: 13, 27
Wilson, Capt. Robert: 55, 64
Wintgens, Leutnant Kurt: 13
Wolff, Kurt: 69, 81
Wright brothers (Orville and Wilbur): 2, 84-85

X-Y-Z

Yom Kippur War: 77, 130
Ypres: 64
Yuille, A.B.: 124
Zälbach: 11
Zillebecker Teich: 64
Zouaves: 31

Design: Aïda Milbergs
Production: Amy Grimm
Typesetting: Meg Kerr
Printing: John D. Lucas
Bindery: Delmar